LEGENDARY
SAFARI
GUIDES

ISBN: 978-1-920434-94-6
e-ISBN: 978-1-920434-95-3

First edition, first impression 2014

Published on behalf of Susie Cazenove by
Bookstorm (Pty) Ltd
PO Box 4532
Northcliff 2115
Johannesburg
South Africa
www.bookstorm.co.za

Distributed by On the Dot
www.onthedot.co.za

Parts of this book were first published in *Licensed to Guide*, Jacana Media, Johannesburg 2005
Proofread by John Henderson
Photographs by Susie Cazenove except photo of Grant Cumings by Francois d'Elbee
and photo of Howard Saunders by Stephanie Dloniak
Illustrations by Jessica Hoffman
Cover photo by Michael Lorentz, Passage To Africa
Cover design by publicide
Book design and typesetting by René de Wet
Printed by Interpak Books, Pietermaritzburg

FSC
www.fsc.org
MIX
Paper from
responsible sources
FSC® C105735

LEGENDARY SAFARI GUIDES

SUSIE CAZENOVE

BOOKSTORM

To my husband Dick
and my children Heather, Jessica, Dominic
and Olivia

CONTENTS

Preface   VI

1.   The world of safari travel   1
2.   The origins of game viewing in South Africa   21
    Lex Hes   36
    Mike Myers   43
    Map Ives   51
3.   Botswana's fragile beauty and harmony   61
    Ralph Bousfield   64
    Super Sande   80
    John Barclay   86
    Michael Lorentz   92
    Mothupi Morutha   107
    Onkgaotse Manga   114
4.   The wildlife diversity of Zimbabwe and Zambia   121
    Garth Thompson   124
    Benson Siyawareva   143
    Ivan Carter   158
    Anthony Kaschula   169
5.   North and South Luangwa and the Zambezi Valley   183
    Robin Pope   185
    Rod Tether   201
    Grant Cumings   211
6.   The enduring imagery of East Africa   215
    Nigel Perks   224
    Ron Beaton   245
    Jackson Saigilu Ole Looseyia   260
    Betty Nayiandi Maitai   274
    Calvin Cottar   276
    Howard Saunders   290
7.   Namibia's primeval landscapes and radiant light   297
    Bertus & André Schoeman   300
8.   Into the future   315

Acknowledgements   335
Websites & contact details   337
References   338
Glossary   339
Index   340

PREFACE

When I left Cazenove and Loyd Safaris, a travel company that my business partner, Henrietta Loyd, and I had set up to specialise in providing African holidays, I realised there was one crucial ingredient in any trip I have ever sent anyone on – the guide. It is the guide who makes both the safari and its African backdrop an unforgettable experience. This book is about those people.

I have travelled extensively throughout southern and eastern Africa during my career as a tour operator, and in this book I draw on my own deep passion for the continent and on my personal observations. There are many excellent professional guides with impeccable reputations. I have not had the opportunity to travel on safari with all of the guides I have met, but the criterion for the guides I have selected to profile here is that I have been on safari with all of them. I have enjoyed their humour and their stories, and this is the reason for writing this book: I would like to share some of their best experiences and stories with you, the guides' own tales of adventure and hardship (and sometimes of love). This is a book about the lives they've led; it tells of their concerns, hopes and plans for the future. They have helped me understand why they made the choices they did. Wherever possible, I have authenticated their family legends. I cannot tell their stories though without including some of my own too, because they are so closely linked to the guides I have travelled with.

The book also provides some background information about the places where the guides have worked or perhaps where their spiritual selves reside. For the reader who may never have experienced the terrain these people work in – the intense heat, the luxuriance or sheer magnitude of the landscape – a small description of each area is included.

My daughter, the artist Jessica Hoffman, has drawn magnificent charcoal portraits of the guides profiled, in each case capturing their personalities in her sketches.

So much has happened in the intervening years since my previous book about the guides that I decided to provide an update on the guides I wrote about and to include four more guides, one of whom is a Maasai woman. A few of them have now retired from guiding, but all are still deeply involved one way or another in the protection of wildlife and the continuation of tourism at its best – in other words, exciting, inspiring and thought-provoking tourism.

In 2004, around the time I was doing most of the first interviews with the guides, we thought that poaching in Africa was under control. But, unfortunately, that is not the case. Increasing affluence in the Far East has given rise to the most gruesome and hideous trade in animal body parts. Thousands of elephants and rhinoceroses are being slaughtered in many horrific ways, not only with guns and machetes but also with poison, which has now become a favoured weapon. Poison laid on the ground kills any creature that eats it, and the animals die in agony, and it's a trade not just in the animals that we are aware of as the usual victims. Clive Stockil, a Zimbabwean conservationist, told the audience at a lecture he gave at the Royal Geographical Society in London in 2013 about how an elephant had its carcass poisoned after the tusks had been removed so that hundreds of vultures could be killed for their beaks. What next?

Charitable foundations, such as Tusk, do an incredible job to raise awareness and to help with projects in the field. It is enormously expensive to create sound security systems to provide protection, but the battle goes on even though very few can afford the equipment.

Tourism is also helpful in mitigating the trade and the guides realise this evil can only end through public pressure. They do their very best to educate and create awareness not only in Africa but worldwide, wherever they are.

THE WORLD
OF SAFARI TRAVEL

Journeys through Africa with specialist guides can have a significant impact on those who make them. Life is never quite the same again - you have joined an exclusive club whose members alone truly understand how intense and moving the African experience can be.

I t is surprising how many safari guides there are, given the range of attributes they must possess. The guide must have detailed knowledge of all the animals and birds, and their habitats. He must also be an excellent host, organiser and mechanic; he must be good with the gun, and an intelligent conversationalist, a paramedic and a mind reader. Above all, he must remain enthusiastic and alert all day long.

I say 'he' because, in reality, most safari guides are men. There are some women who take to it, but, by and large, it is a male-dominated profession. Politically incorrect that may be, the fact is most people take comfort from the masculine strength of their guides. This is partly because the guide's guests are completely dependent on him, and this is not always an easy situation for people who are normally used to being in control. Some people become terrified in the bush and find that not being in control is difficult to deal with. Someone may be used to managing people at work, for example, and giving the orders, but finds that he or she cannot be in control when walking in lion-infested terrain and has to acknowledge the guide as the superior.

Women often find the guides irresistible, which is not really surprising. When people are catapulted out of their familiar lives into an unexpectedly stimulating setting, where the earthy smells, endless vistas, glittering stars and, most of all, the underlying edge of fear create a frisson of excitement that many may not have felt for years, a strong, confident, attentive man with a sense of humour can be very appealing! This phenomenon is known as 'khaki fever', and the guide usually handles it with great discretion and tact.

When I became involved in the safari business and travelled more extensively, I soon began to realise the impact the safari guides had on visitors. Good guides make the experience exceptional, not just because they open your eyes to the wildlife around you, but because they have come to terms with their own strengths and weaknesses. A mediocre guide may not ruin the experience, because no one can take away the beauty of the surroundings and the excitement of seeing the animals close up in their own environment, but a good one raises the experience to another level.

A BASEMENT IN MAYFAIR

Although I now live in England, I have the good fortune to have been born and raised in Africa, where my life was filled with sunshine, space and freedom. My father had a farm in the Magaliesberg, 80 kilometres from Johannesburg, where he bred trout and pedigree Ayrshire cattle. The Hartley family, who ran a rose farm nearby, were friends of my father and I got to know David, the eldest son. Our ways parted, but David and I met up again years later through mutual friends. I then discovered that he and his wife, Tessa, owned Xugana Lodge (now known as Xugana Island Lodge) in the Okavango Delta, and a travel company, Okavango Explorations. In 1987, they invited me to spend a few days with them in Botswana at a time when they were contemplating taking over Tsaro, a land-based lodge that perfectly complemented the water-based Xugana Island property.

That visit was a catalyst for me. I found the beauty and excitement of this watery paradise completely captivating. On our last evening, while we were sitting under the trees at Tsaro Lodge, with the full moon's silvery light shining on a hippo grazing nearby, my thoughts suddenly crystallised and, turning to David, I said, 'I can sell this for you in England – I know I can. I really want other people to come and experience this for themselves.'

Six months later, Okavango Explorations (UK) opened in a basement just off Berkeley Square, in central London.

Although I was a complete greenhorn in the travel industry, I knew that the most important thing was to ensure that every client we sent to Africa would experience the magic and love it, as I did. But, first, I had to learn more about the safari environment in Botswana, so I revisited the two camps I had already stayed at – Tsaro, on the Khwai River, which is in a dry area of the Moremi Game Reserve, where game drives are available, and Xugana, which is in a lagoon in the heart of the delta and offers water-based activities. Map Ives, then the resident guide at Tsaro, was my first experience of a top guide. His knowledge and enthusiasm were spellbinding, and he set a very high standard for me to bear in mind when planning safaris and choosing guides for our clients.

Our trip ended in the northern part of the Chobe National Park, at the Chobe Chilwero Camp, which was then owned by Brian and Jan Graham. There I met Henrietta Loyd, whom I had spoken to in England before she left to spend six months working at Chilwero. She had spent much of her early youth running camps and lodges in Botswana and South Africa, and wanted to get into the travel business in the United Kingdom. Brian and Jan were close friends of Henrietta, and they were on hand with generous help and support when she and I later started our own company. We were very fortunate to have her join us at Okavango Explorations in London before the end of our first year. We both enjoyed the travel business, and had great fun learning how it all worked, making friends and exploring new places.

After four years with Okavango Explorations (renamed Hartley's Safaris) and craving independence, we started our own company, Cazenove and Loyd Safaris, which launched in January 1993.

One of the most important aspects of a tour operator's life is to research the destinations to which we send our clients and familiarise oneself with them. Known as 'fam trips' or 'educationals', these visits can be demanding undertakings: spending every night in a different bed, writing copious notes and making sure photos are labelled correctly (it can be easy to confuse one bedroom with another). Our trips were arranged to allow us plenty of time to understand and appreciate the various destinations. They were great fun and opened many doors to interesting experiences and people.

On one such trip, Henrietta and I went to Namibia, and spent 19 days covering about half the country. (On arrival, we found that our local operator had grossly inflated our importance to the car-hire company, which upgraded us to a Mercedes! In this most unsuitable low-slung saloon car, we skidded and bumped our way along the country's gravel roads, miraculously without getting a cracked sump or punctured tyre.) We learnt a great deal about travel in Namibia, which included visiting the Skeleton Coast with the Schoeman family and their safari company. I would later do many more fly-in safaris with the Schoemans. Our final stop was a small guest farm called Okonjima. We arrived at a most auspicious time – it was the day Nelson Mandela was released from prison. The generator was turned on so there could be television coverage of this great event, and Hen and I will never forget sitting with the family in their darkened living room watching those historic moments alongside two cheetahs and Elvis, a large male baboon.

Okonjima is now an award-winning lodge, known for its cheetah- and leopard-rescue programme called Africat, which is run by the Hanssen family. But back then it was still a cattle ranch and the animal-rescue operation was just in its infancy. The family, clearly naturals when it came to rescuing animals, had cheetahs, warthogs and a baboon as pets. Elvis, who ate porridge with us at breakfast – admittedly, on the floor rather than at the table – and was part of the family, enchanted us. In the afternoon, we took a walk along a winding path up the koppie near the house, and learnt about the medicinal plants the Bushmen used and how they made their snares and traps. Elvis came along too. He walked directly behind Wayne Hanssen, his alpha male, and would sit quietly when Wayne stopped to talk to us. As inferior females, we were not allowed to pass Elvis or look him in the eye. Wayne had brought drinks in his backpack and we sat at the top of the koppie, sipping our sundowners and gazing over a thousand square miles of Africa bathed in the evening light. Elvis drank his Coca-Cola sitting on a rock nearby and nonchalantly tossed the empty can back to Wayne!

As the years went by and I travelled more extensively, the impact the safari guides had on the visitors became very clear. Good guides make the experience exceptional, not just because they open your eyes to the wildlife around you, but because of all the little things they think of to make your safari that extra bit special.

A graphic example of this was an experience we witnessed in the Ngorongoro Crater, in Tanzania, where our guide had spotted a wildebeest giving birth. We spent 25 minutes watching entranced as she kept standing up, then lying down to push again and again, until finally the little creature dropped to the ground. The newborn calf was up in a moment, wet and wobbling, and seven minutes later it was running with its mother. No wonder it is the most successful antelope in Africa. They all give birth at the same time of year, assuring the survival of the majority in spite of the attendant predators, which gorge themselves during the calving. While we had our binoculars trained on this little miracle with our guide, Nigel Perks, no fewer than six vehicles had stopped to see what we were looking at before immediately moving on. Perhaps the guides were looking only for lions and rhinos, or racing to be on time for lunch, but whatever it was, their guests would have had no idea what they had missed.

It wasn't until the late 1970s and early 1980s that guides were trained specifically to look after photographic safari visitors. Up until then, they had been professional hunters, for the most part working as guides when the hunting season was closed. The guides may have been excellent shots, but few of them knew much about the bush, and they relied mostly on their local trackers to find the animals.

Gradually, realisation dawned that the guides had to know more about the environment around them. Norman Carr, a legendary safari guide and ex professional hunter in Zambia, started making all his trainee guides in the 1970s learn the names of the birds. Up until then, according to Robin Pope, the best-known guide in Zambia today, visitors were generally told that all the birds were either turkey buzzards or blue jays.

In 1969, when John and David Varty inherited Londolozi, their father's farm, which borders on the Kruger National Park, and now a game reserve, the general public was not deeply interested in conservation and most had never heard of ecology. The Varty brothers were already passionate about conserving their land and they soon realised that they needed to train guides to inform and entertain their guests at their budding safari lodge. This was the first formal training course in this field and it did not take long for their vision to be emulated and further developed around Africa. Marvellous wildlife films and books began to create a demand for interesting, well-informed safari guides and stimulated the travelling public's thirst for knowledge.

ANIMAL INTELLIGENCE

On my first 'educational' through Botswana, I visited Lloyd's Camp, in Savuti. The owner, Lloyd Wilmot, was a safari operator and guide in the days when Botswana was becoming very popular. He had a reputation for being fearless – he was even known to have plucked hairs from elephants' tails. At his camp, on the dried-up Savuti Channel, he had made a waterhole and placed a concrete viewing bunker next to it with access from the riverbank above. In the dry season, elephants spent hours drinking at the waterhole and people could sit inside the bunker watching them from inches away. On that first visit, I sat entranced with my head pressed against one of the openings watching a group of old bulls drinking and jostling for position. Suddenly, I felt a gentle touch on my arm, as if a feather were brushing against it. I turned and saw that there was an elephant's trunk poking through the adjacent opening inspecting me. The elephants were obviously just as curious about us as we were about them.

On a visit to Zimbabwe, I had my first sense of the depth of feeling experienced by elephants. With the help of my guide, Chris van Wyk, I observed a mother elephant mourning the death of her newborn baby. Chris, a tall, lean man with a gentle manner, has now left the safari business, but once owned a delightful bush camp called Nemba, in the Linkwasha area of the Hwange National Park. He was one of the first guides to initiate bush walks for the guests. The evening I arrived, we drove to the sad little scene that was taking place not far from the camp. The dead baby lay on a patch of grass, and the grieving mother, who had long since been left behind by the herd, had her two older offspring nearby offering consolation. She paced back and forth, drooping in a melancholic manner as she nudged the lifeless little body. Chris had been watching her for two days. But on this the third and final day she would have to leave as thirst got the better of her and life had to go on. However, her genuine grief was very apparent.

I was astounded to learn from conservationist Richard Leakey's book, *Wildlife Wars: My Fight to Save Africa's Natural Treasures*, that he did not know about elephant families, their consciences or ability to communicate until elephant researcher Joyce Poole had introduced him to the herds that she and Cynthia Moss were studying in Kenya's Amboseli National Park. As head of the Kenya Wildlife Service, although Leakey worked tirelessly with terrific results to save elephants from poaching, he was nevertheless bowled over by the revelation that they were creatures of high intelligence and that they possess family loyalties. I thought that everyone living and working in the bush knew this, but, in reality, it is a fairly recent discovery, one that has come about because we are now studying animal intelligence and communication. Much of this understanding of animal behaviour has been communicated by the safari guides, who spend their lives observing animals' habits.

Many books have been written about elephants, which are perhaps the most fascinating of all creatures: the more you are with them, the more you want to be with them. Their family unit is extremely close-knit. They find it hard to survive without it and will form one even in unnatural circumstances. For example, at Abu's Camp, in Botswana, a disparate group of elephants brought together by the founder, Randall Moore, have created a strong family bond. This is a most unusual group, because adult bulls live together with the cows and young. In the wild, young bull elephants are expelled from the herd once they reach maturity and they form their own bachelor groups, only venturing into a breeding herd when a cow is in oestrus. Randall's elephants are a mixed bag of adults rescued from zoos, babies from herds culled in the Kruger National Park, problem elephants from other parks, the occasional lost wild baby and now two babies, sired by wild elephants, born to one of the females.

When I first visited these elephants, I was overcome with awe (a feeling like that never goes away). To touch them, walk with them, ride them and discover their personalities is a tremendous privilege. My most vivid memory is of the first time I watched them communicate with one another. It was a perfect Okavango morning and we set off through the delta. Miss B, about two years old, was the youngest elephant at that time and had bonded firmly with Bibi, an adult female recently arrived from a Sri Lankan zoo. It had been decided that Bibi, who was still settling in, was not to come out on the walk that morning. And Miss B was torn with indecision – should she come or should she stay with Bibi? As we set off across the water, I could see her darting in and out of the bushes, watching us and then going back to her adopted mother, undecided as to what she wanted to do. Finally, the morning's excursion won her over and she set off on her own to join us. At first, she couldn't see us or smell us and walked in a large arc around the water, her little trunk up, trying to work out which way the herd had gone. Then, suddenly she located us and ran through the water trumpeting. The other young elephants became very excited and ran towards her. An ecstatic, noisy meeting took place as they splashed, trumpeted and frolicked in the shallow water. Amid all this confusion, there came a loud, low rumble from Benny, one of the adult bulls, and immediately the young ones stopped what they were doing and got obediently into line, and walked quietly and sedately with the rest of the herd. I was astounded at what I saw. Michael Lorentz, an extremely perceptive guide who was leading this safari, told me later that this behaviour was quite normal – Benny had had enough of the elephants' raucous behaviour and had told them to stop it at once.

The lead elephant, Abu, after whom the camp is named, was a tremendous character of note, but is, sadly, no longer living. He is deeply mourned by all who knew him. Because of his gentle nature, I was exceptionally honoured to have been able to sit up behind his head. He knelt; I stood on his front knee and was given a leg up to straddle his massive neck. Once he had risen to his feet, he stood still as my bare legs slipped over his neck, and his ears came back, gently holding them in place. The crook of his ears was soft and warm, the texture of velvet. The sheer joy I felt that afternoon will stay with me always.

Michael Lorentz worked with these elephants for nine years and they clearly respected him, and even listened when he spoke. His ability to communicate with them and his great love for them were most apparent.

Even with my limited experience, I have witnessed so many instances of animals thinking through and planning their actions that it can't always be explained away as instinctive behaviour. One instance of such apparently premeditated behaviour was a fascinating incident I witnessed involving baboons in Hwange.

It was a quiet evening, and the Makalolo waterhole was drenched in golden sunlight, but not a single animal was to be seen. So, we headed down a dirt track and moments later saw a tightly packed troop of female and juvenile baboons being hurriedly herded through the grass by very nervous, large males. Suddenly, a leopard darted into the middle of the group and scattered them. The shrieks and cries were deafening as the males gave chase and the rest of the group rushed onto a large termite mound, where they sat tightly packed together. The males then spread out to vantage points to look for the now-vanished leopard. One large male, completely oblivious of our presence, stood on a termite mound right next to our vehicle with his back to us. His arms were raised and his body was rigid with tension as he defecated from the stress.

Moments later a neighbouring troop of baboons suddenly appeared from the bushes to help the first troop. Their females and young huddled together on another termite mound while the males joined in the leopard hunt. The males all seemed to communicate without a sound as they moved in a coordinated, seemingly predetermined pattern to close in on the leopard, as if following a practised military manoeuvre. However, the leopard stayed hidden, and even this highly organised joint effort failed to flush him out. Finally, the males of each troop rounded up the females and juveniles. The helpers from the second troop melted into the bush, but the first group crowded together and came towards us up the road, marching like a bunch of tightly packed protestors without banners. They parted ranks smoothly around the vehicle, without even looking at us and went off to roost in their tree by the waterhole. We were surprised that a second troop had come to help, and we watched astounded by the disciplined tactics that the baboons employed. I was with a well-known Zimbabwean guide, Fausto Carbone, on this occasion, who told me that, in all the years he had been guiding, he had never seen anything like it.

WALKING ON THE WILD SIDE

A guide once said to me, 'Looking at animals and the landscape from a vehicle is like seeing the movie; walking in the bush is like reading the book.'

In fact, it's more like *being* in the book. There is nothing on earth quite like the adrenalin rush you get when tracking a lion or walking up to an elephant. It's not easy to do these things, as wild animals are generally very nervous around humans and will disappear long before you know they were there. It takes great skill on the part of the guide to get you anywhere near wild animals.

Most guides prefer to walk with a maximum of six people – more than that makes the group unwieldy and difficult to control. He will start with a talk on how you should behave – explaining how you should keep quiet, stick together close behind him and stand dead still if charged by a lion! The guide will usually choose an open space, noting the layout of the bush he is walking through. Buffaloes often hide in thick bush and can be very dangerous if startled. A good guide will walk you through the bush listening for the sounds that tell the story: the baboons' special bark when they spot a predator, or a guinea fowl warning that something might only be a snake but it could be a leopard, although the latter is unlikely to be seen because of its extreme shyness. It is best to be downwind to get close to the animals you are tracking, but, when walking up to bull elephants, it is preferable to be upwind, so that they know you are there. Ivan Carter describes this technique succinctly a little later.

Being on foot in the bush offers so much sensual and tactile interaction that it becomes much more than just finding animals, in itself quite a challenge because one seldom gets very close because of their fear of people. What makes the experience is the countless subtle aromas – wild thyme, dry grasses, wild gardenias, the whiff of elephants or buffaloes, and many other smells that you long to identify. And the tracks in the sand tell their own stories – a lion walked here in the night; a snake crossed there; something was dragged for a few yards along a dusty track (the delicate tracery made by porcupine quills is covered by the perfect little prints of an African wildcat) – all making you aware of what a busy place this was before you came along. Guides who were once professional hunters are often the most confident trackers because of the many hours they spent tracking animals with their hunting clients. That said, many guides who have never hunted professionally seem to have a wonderfully developed sixth sense when walking in the bush.

Matusadona National Park, bordering the Kariba Dam in Zimbabwe, is an excellent walking area, perfect for tracking lions or black rhinos. The latter were recently reintroduced into the park in the 1990s after years of devastating poaching. One can only speculate what has happened to these poor creatures in the recent lawless years in Zimbabwe. The 15 000-square-kilometre park was stocked mainly with the animals that were rescued during 'Operation Noah' in the early 1960s when this section of the Zambezi Valley was flooded with water to supply the newly built Kariba Dam. In a race against the clock, stranded animals were plucked off trees and islands in an operation organised by Rupert Fothergill in a blaze of worldwide publicity. The land slopes down from the top of the escarpment to a low-lying area along the lakeshore. This region is heavily wooded. The mopane trees provide cool, shady areas for walking and their distinctive butterfly-wing-shaped leaves are a favoured food for elephants. It is over 50 years since the lake was created and the skeletal remains of drowned forests still protrude from the surface like eerie spectres from the dark depths of the lake near the shore, making perfect perches for abundant varieties of waterbirds.

It was in Matusadona that I first tracked a lion on foot, with John Dabbs, who is now retired from guiding. Early one morning, we spotted large, fresh lion spoor (footprints) in the mud on the edge of a little inlet of the lake. A big male lion had been drinking not long before we arrived and we set off to track him through the bush. It was a dry October day and his spoor was clearly visible in the sand.

After a while, we heard the angry noises of a fight coming from a patch of dense undergrowth – lions on a kill, snarling and growling at one another as each tried to get the choice bits. We stood quietly for a while, but they got a whiff of us. There were three lionesses, not our lion, their yellow backs slipping through the dry grass, lit by sunlight as they streaked away from us as fast as possible. We peaked under a tree where we had heard the noise. Lying there was the half-eaten carcass of an impala that must have been killed just moments before.

Once again, we picked up our lion spoor and walked on, zigzagging, losing then re-locating the tracks. Then John suddenly saw a movement in front of us and dropped down low to the ground; as he did so, he ordered me to do the same and to remain behind him. We inched forward on our bottoms across the dry, sandy bed of a stream. Waiting and looking. Nothing. Maybe he had moved on. We stood up to get a better view and at that moment the lion jumped out from behind a large fallen tree trunk and gave us a spine-chilling roar. My heart stopped. I have walked many times in the bush and listened to all the instructions about standing stock-still, but, on this occasion, without even realising what I was doing, I took about 10 steps backwards very quickly. John did not move though. The lion stared at us for a few moments, flicked his tail and turned to walk off. We could breathe again. Moving a few paces, we saw that he had walked on about 20 metres, and was sitting down under a tree to watch what we would do next.

'Let's go now,' said John, 'He is telling us that enough is enough and that this is all he is going to tolerate.' Who was I to argue?

Approaching an elephant on foot is only possible with someone who truly understands them. Garth Thompson, Ivan Carter, John Stevens and Michael Lorentz have a particularly special relationship with elephants. These men take great pleasure in walking up to them, and one feels overwhelmingly excited but, at the same time, absolutely safe and protected in their company. Quite unlike the feeling I once had when, walking alone to my tent in Botswana, I found an elephant standing right in the middle of my path looking at me. This time, all 5 feet 2 inches of me froze. My heart was pounding so hard I could hear it. This was it, I thought! However, he just looked at me for a while then turned and nonchalantly went off about his business. I felt so relieved and rather foolish for having been so flustered.

It takes a certain cockiness and self-assurance to walk up to wild elephants. Mana Pools National Park, in Zimbabwe, has plenty of serene old elephant bulls, which stroll through this small paradise, feeding on the acacia pods, water hyacinths and mopane trees that flourish there. They know their territory and feel secure. However, they are still wild and caution is always the keyword.

Garth, John and Ivan are past masters at interacting with elephants in this park. I asked Ivan Carter to describe to me how he would approach an elephant without ending up between its toes.

'Elephants have the most amazing body language. A lot of it is quite subtle, but, then, like humans, a lot of it is very obvious and vigorous. I think that the most important tones are the subtle ones – a slight lift of the head, a slight stiffness in the tail, a twitch of the tip of the trunk, etc., which all show that he knows you are there. Sometimes all you notice is that he has stopped swinging his tail. You notice I always say "he" – I would not walk up to cows and babies, as they are far less predictable and unless you are waiting at a waterhole or near a path, I would not by choice approach them on foot. What I do is approach the guy from two or three hundred yards with the wind straight from us to him. That is a crucial point, as I want to see his reaction as he gets our scent. Often, as the scent gets to him, his posture will change slightly and then he will relax, move on and get wary, etc. This will indicate whether I can go closer or not. What I want to see is a brief moment where the tip of his trunk gets pointed to me, and then he continues like we aren't there ... that's an ideal guy to approach. Then, without hiding in the least, I try to walk slowly in towards him, and as I get closer I talk, either to*

*him or to my guests. I think that the steadiness in our voices lets them know
we are there and that we are confident, and that is what keeps them calm.
Once I am within a hundred yards, I like to try and see where he is going and
position myself in his path, so that it is he who chooses how close he wants to
come. That way, it will be of the minimum disturbance to him. Sometimes a
few of the bulls I know well will actually veer off towards us and spend time
feeding within a few feet of us. It's the most wonderful feeling, a feeling of
great privilege and a feeling of being humbled by the great beast.*

'*In Mana Pools the acacia pods make up a huge portion of their daily
intake at certain times of the year. I like to find a particularly laden tree and
just sit under it and wait for them to come, and often they end up picking
up the pods literally within a couple of feet of us. It's the highlight of a day
in the bush.*'

Having walked up to elephants with Ivan, I understand exactly how
he feels. As he says: '*It is very important, and not only with elephants, to
be sure that you are arriving and leaving with the least impact. If you leave
him stressed and ruffled out of shape, you have failed in your approach. If
you leave quietly and look back, and see him still doing what he was doing
before you arrived, then you have achieved your objective.*'

People who go for this lifestyle start with a love of the bush. They study
from childhood and gain such tremendous insight into animal behaviour
that it becomes only natural that they should share it with others. A guide
also has to have a natural rapport with people and an easy temperament,
otherwise he will fail very quickly. Most guides have their pet subjects
– many are great ornithologists, for example – and have such a vast
knowledge in that one field that they bring people to them from all over
the world. The late David Rattray, for example, with his knowledge of
South African history, took tourism to another plane by giving his guests
at his lodge, Fugitive's Drift, in KwaZulu-Natal, a deeply emotional
experience when he related the stories of the Anglo-Zulu battles that took
place at Isandlwana and Rorke's Drift. The legacy lives on with his son,
Andrew. The Schoeman brothers offer an equally emotional experience,

only this time it concerns geology, desert life and the formation of the earth on their Skeleton Coast safaris in Namibia.

And imagine the thrill of being on a horse and galloping with wild animals – it could be across the plains of the Masai Mara with giraffes or wildebeest when riding with Tristan Voorspuy. Or perhaps through the water with leaping lechwe in the wetlands of the Okavango Delta riding with PJ and Barney Besterlink or David Foot on the edge of the Makgadikgadi Pans, in Botswana. There seems to be something special for everyone, one way or another.

Specialist guides are among the greatest drawcards Africa has: their company is congenial; I have never known the conversation to lag; laughter is paramount; and the joy of being in such company and in the bush is supremely intoxicating. It is no wonder people return again and again for what was originally intended to be a 'once-in-a-lifetime' holiday.

Many friends and clients have come back from their safaris spilling over with enthusiasm for the things they have seen and learnt, in particular the extra-special moments created by their guide.

For many years, a delightful couple called John and Jan travelled twice a year to Africa as clients of our travel company. They had met when Jan (a widow) consulted her bank manager, John (a widower), after which he invited her to dinner. Romance blossomed and they married with the blessing of all their grown-up children, and proceeded to have the time of their lives visiting Africa as frequently as they could. Every spring and autumn, we would plan new delights for them until, one autumn, they had to cancel their trip because John had become ill. The following summer he died and, soon after the funeral, Jan planned another trip. I sensed that she wanted to take his ashes to Africa. She went on this pilgrimage alone and everywhere she was met with kindness and care.

Her final stop was Nxamaseri Lodge (now known as Nxamaseri Island Lodge), a beautiful little place set among trees and reeds on the Okavango River in the Panhandle, where the river winds its way down from Angola to the delta. Early on a perfectly still sunny morning, she set off with her guide in a small boat, each knowing this was the moment. The boat slid gently through the water until they came upon a long, white sandbank jutting out from the papyrus. African skimmers were darting and swooping over the water, and a fish eagle called in the distance as the papyrus rustled in a sudden breeze.

'I think we have found a really good spot, don't you?' asked the guide. Jan agreed and he moved into the back of the boat, leaving her on her own to perform her task. The tranquillity was perfect and, with a little prayer, John's ashes were whisked away on a puff of air, dispersing in the sunlight and across the water he had so loved. Jan sat motionless, unable to stop the tears rolling down her cheeks. The guide silently moved forward and put his arms around her and held her tight. Jan had given John his final peace in Africa.

SWEET SIXTEEN

Together with another family and their two children, we did a family safari in Botswana with David Dugmore, one of three men who were running their own safari business, Kalahari Kavango. David was filled with energy and enthusiasm, and gave us a marvellous safari. However, he stopped guiding so he could make wildlife films, one of which (about Abu's Camp) appeared on the Discovery Channel. David now runs his own camp, Meno A Kwena, on the Boteti River, in Botswana; his brother, Roger, still does mobile safaris in Botswana; and the third partner, Ralph Bousfield, operates mainly in the Makgadikgadi. Ralph is featured later in this book.

During our safari with David in the Okavango Delta, our daughter, Olivia, turned 16. That was a memorable place for a birthday in anyone's book. During dinner one evening in the camp, the conversation was rattling along at such a great pace that no one had noticed that David had disappeared from the table – until someone dashed in telling us to hurry and come and see something. We all thought someone must have spotted the leopard whose tracks we had seen in the camp each morning. But no. We were taken down to the water's edge, where we stood on a sandy bank and watched in amazement as, out on the dark water, a *mokoro* (a traditional dugout canoe used in the delta), lit by lanterns, was being poled gently towards the bank by David. Sitting in the boat were the two female members of his camp staff singing a haunting melody, which was then taken up by all the male staff standing on the bank. This lyrical harmony soared across the still night air as the boat gently skimmed towards us to deliver a birthday cake to Olivia.

It was an unforgettable moment of goose bumps and tears, and the result of perfect planning by a thoughtful guide. The cake turned out to be a delicious sponge, not the usual iced elephant turd often served up on adult birthdays!

THE CHANGING FACE OF SAFARI

Africa is so well known for the vastness and infinity of its landscapes that I feel it is often this rather than the animals that brings people back again and again. To stand on a rise and see miles and miles of woodland, purple hills, desert or towering mountains, where nothing is man-made other than the vehicle track, is a breathtaking experience. Once the first excitement of seeing animals in the wild has subsided, people realise there is so much more to enjoy. The culture, the history, and the cradle of both animal and geological life are of enormous interest as well. Good guides help you understand Africa in its many and varied facets.

Sometimes the influence of the guide can even be a life-changing experience. An example is a family with three teenage children who did a canoeing trip on the Zambezi River with Garth Thompson. Their journey was a tremendous contrast to the regulated lives they led back home in England. Their adventure, which provided many an adrenalin rush as they walked up to large bull elephants or skirted in canoes around pods of hippos, and their animated discussions around the campfire with Garth altered all their previously held ideas and aspirations. After university, their eldest son gave two years of his life to a charity that cleared landmines. Their daughter studied travel and tourism at university, determined to get into the travel industry. And the youngest son, who was only 12 at the time, although not as outwardly moved as his siblings, has nevertheless been involved in development charity Raleigh International (previously known as Operation Raleigh) and has taken a keen interest in the developing world.

Journeys through Africa with specialist guides can have a significant impact on those who make them. Life is never quite the same again – you have joined an exclusive club whose members truly understand how intense and moving the African experience can be.

These exciting experiences really started with the opening up of tourism in Africa in the 1970s. Hunting was going out of fashion, and, instead, photographic safaris were becoming the vogue in a big way as far more people showed interested in wildlife and the bush. Expert guides grew out of the need to satisfy people's hunger for adventure, fun and knowledge on their safari holidays.

Chobe Game Lodge, in the north-east corner of Botswana, built in 1972 as a hotel rather than a bush lodge, became famous for hosting the wedding of Elizabeth Taylor and Richard Burton. This put Botswana on the map. Hunting was banned in Kenya in 1977 and, while some of the hunters looked for greener pastures, others stayed at home arranging photographic safaris.

People were becoming more affluent and adventurous, and travel was becoming much easier. Soon a great amount of attention started to turn to Africa. The die was cast, hunting was diminishing and, with easier access to Africa, photographic safaris were about to explode into the travel world.

THE ORIGINS OF GAME VIEWING IN SOUTH AFRICA

The traditional game-viewing area of South Africa is Mpumalanga, which means 'the place where the sun rises' in isi-Zulu. Here, in the north-east corner of the country, the world-famous Kruger National Park extends from the Zimbabwean border in the north nearly 500 kilometres south to the Crocodile River and is approximately 160 kilometres wide.

P resident Paul Kruger set land aside for a park in 1898 when he realised how quickly the wildlife population was being depleted. Wild animals had roamed all over South Africa in vast herds, from the Cape to the Indian Ocean. The speed at which they were being shot and killed appalled the president. His was an act of conservation without precedence at that time.

The eastern side of the Kruger National Park borders Mozambique and, on the west, farms, mines, villages and a series of private game reserves, originally set up as farms, straddle the length of the park. The best known is the Sabi Sands Game Reserve, which had been divided up into private farms for many years for cattle ranching until that was halted by a rinderpest epidemic, after which many owners turned to hunting. In 1962, the Sabi Sands Game Reserve was officially recognised as a reserve and hunting was banned there.

EARLY DAYS IN SABI SANDS: GETTING STARTED AT LONDOLOZI

Londolozi and MalaMala were two of the original 1920s farms in the Sabi Sands. MalaMala, which belonged to the Campbells, was the first to open its doors to paying photographic safari guests in the 1960s, followed by the Vartys' farm, Sparta (later renamed Londolozi). It was the dawn of a new era. In time, other private farms in the reserve became commercial safari enterprises and, although all of them gave their guests an excellent experience with good guides, it was Londolozi that gained a reputation for producing exceptional guides.

MalaMala had been the private hunting ground of the legendary Wac Campbell, whose hunting guests included royalty, ambassadors and cabinet ministers. A descendant of the 1850 Byrne settlers, Wac had a powerful allegiance to the British Crown. A short-wave wireless in the camp was able to pick up the BBC World Service and all guests had to sit quietly listening to the evening news, after which everyone was required to stand to attention while the Union Jack was lowered ceremoniously.

Guests also included many visiting National Party MPs, who were not exactly pro-British!

An honorary Zulu chief, Wac Campbell was much respected by his 'subjects', whose etiquette involved falling to their knees when speaking to him and never turning their backs on him. When he lay ill and dying at his home in Durban, two Zulu warriors appeared one day. They did not ask permission to enter the house, nor did they speak to anyone; they simply kept their wake, standing tall and noble outside his bedroom door, and were relieved by two others every eight hours. This continued until he died. More than 20 000 mourners attended his funeral.

When his son, Urban Campbell, inherited MalaMala, he made a tentative start at bringing in paying guests, but, in 1964, he sold the property to Mike Rattray, who turned it into the first really well-known safari lodge in South Africa.

When Wac's neighbour, Boyd Varty, died in 1969, his sons were still in full-time education. John was at university and Dave was at school when they inherited Sparta. They had spent so much of their childhood there that their passionate commitment to the place was unwavering. They decided to change the name to Londolozi, a Zulu word meaning 'protector of all living things'. In spite of their youth, or maybe because of it, with time and plenty of lateral thinking, they began to build a legend.

Over the years, as their business developed, Dave and John have set a great example throughout southern Africa by protecting the precious few wilderness areas still remaining in the region. Once they had inherited Londolozi, their priority was the conservation of the environment. Pressure of farming and a series of bad droughts in the Eastern Transvaal (now Mpumalanga) had seriously altered the land since their grandfather had bought the farm in 1927. They were intensely anxious to reverse the damage that had been done, employing all manner of experts to help and advise. Ecologist Dr Ken Tinley was one of their major advisers, and much of his work was aimed at repairing the land that had been so badly damaged by cattle grazing.

Londolozi was quite a primitive establishment at first and they learnt by trial and error the best way to operate. The camp was rudimentary and, in those days, spending a weekend in the bush had a real pioneering spirit to it. The guests were mostly the Vartys' friends, out for a good time. Dave and John were young and very energetic, and their enthusiasm knew no bounds. They drove their guests around in a couple of rattly old vehicles held together with string and a prayer. Dave would use one of the vehicles for the game drive, taking along a pretend radio (they had nothing as sophisticated as real two-way radios in those days) and would set off on a drive knowing full well that the vehicle would not last very long before breaking down. John would be waiting, hidden, along the chosen route with the spare vehicle. When the inevitable breakdown occurred, Dave pretended to call John on the radio for help, pouring the drinks while waiting for John to come to their aid. John, fully aware of what was happening, allowed a suitable interval before appearing, by which time the guests were all well into their second gin and tonics!

As the popularity of Londolozi increased, John and Dave needed to spend more time running the business and decided to hire others to take the game drives and look after the guests. They were one of the very first in the business to initiate a training programme for guides back in the days when the profession was a lot more relaxed and carefree. Numerous books have been written about them and their ecological achievements. I can only give a glimpse through the keyhole into the fun and games that went on during those early, happy-go-lucky years.

In 1976, Lex Hes, a young man who was to play such a big part in the early days of Londolozi, arrived first. He was passionate about wildlife and photography, and had badgered the Varty brothers into letting him stay and help out just for his keep. He had no role in the beginning other than counting birds and animals, but later he was roped into doing game drives while they advertised for another person to help.

In the 1970s and early 1980s, Londolozi became known for its intensive training of guides, and many of its alumni would become legendary characters. When they first started escorting customers in the bush, clients and staff had a lot of fun together. It was one big carefree party and it is perhaps surprising that no one was ever harmed or injured. Soon the guides became much sought after as a result of the new safari phenomenon that was burgeoning all over southern Africa.

Mike Myers, a Zimbabwean, was in Johannesburg around this time. He had left Wits University and had just obtained his pilot's licence, but owing to the fuel crisis and not being able to speak Afrikaans, he was having difficulty finding a flying job. In desperation, he turned to the classified columns for something, anything, to keep body and soul together, and replied to an advertisement seeking an 'officer' to lead wilderness trails. The interview took place at the home of Shan Watson, then girlfriend, and later wife, of Dave Varty. Mike, dressed in his only smart clothes, a Wits rugby blazer and tie, walked in to meet John, who was lounging around in cropped blue jeans and no shirt. John saw a solidly built, good-looking young man with a sense of humour, energy and enthusiasm – qualities of paramount importance for the job on offer – and had the good judgement to hire Mike immediately.

John and Dave's friends continued to spread the word that Londolozi was the best party in South Africa. Soon many of them were flocking to Sabi Sands Game Reserve for their weekend entertainment at Londolozi. Money was always in short supply and during the week, when there were no guests, the staff lived on impala meat and mealie-meal (maize). Their girlfriends working at MalaMala supplemented this diet by bringing extra goodies to their weekly bush parties.

Once Mike started working there, he and Lex took over the guiding, along with André Goosen, the next to join. The group consisted of the three guides, John and Dave Varty, the owner/managers, Dave's girlfriend, Shan, who looked after the lodge, the catering and the bookings, and the hostess, an ethereal fine-arts student who floated around looking after the guests. There was also George and Diana, two young cheetahs that they were hand-rearing. One of the great strengths of the Londolozi team was its ability to pick the right person for the job.

As Londolozi became increasingly popular, the old vehicles were replaced, and more staff and guides were employed to entertain and look after the guests. In 1985, Yvonne and Pete Short came in – Pete to look after guest relations and the wine cellar, and Yvonne as the catering manager. On arrival, Yvonne completely reorganised the kitchen, throwing out all the old pots and pans, buying new refrigerators and cooking utensils, and generally bringing the kitchen into the 20th century, while Dave complained that she would bankrupt him. Yvonne was a real live wire, a bundle of energy and laughter, and her arrival must have been a huge asset. After four years of working there, Yvonne gave birth to twin babies and, like all mothers, she was up and down during the night. Her windows faced onto the guides' sleeping quarters, which gave her a continuous view of their clandestine meetings. They were always puzzled about how she knew so much about what they got up to. Soon after she arrived, it was decided to improve the night watch – one old man asleep over his stick was no longer good enough. So two watchmen were employed to set up lanterns along the pathways and to take them away when the guests had gone to sleep. The nightwatchmen were given clipboards to report what happened during the night. But, instead of noting events like hyenas prowling around the kitchen, or elephants eating the shrubs, their reports went something like this: the lady in room no. 2 went into no. 4 at midnight. No. 3 joined them in no. 4. When the gentleman in no. 2 came out and asked me where his wife was, I said she was in no. 3! And so it went on.

TESTING AND TRAINING

In the early 1980s, John and Dave fine-tuned their intensive and arduous five-day selection test for the prospective guides, and there was no shortage of suitable candidates. Personality remained a top priority. They did not necessarily choose people with degrees or even previous experience of conservation. They knew that if they found the right qualities, the rest could be taught.

Most of the testing was to ascertain how the applicant stood up to pressure and whether they were quick and alert. Applicants were given a copy of Keith Coates's *Palgrave's Trees of Southern Africa*, the definitive guidebook of regional trees, and told to spend the afternoon learning about the trees, and memorising their names and uses, and they were later tested on these. The same applied to birds: half a day studying *Newman's Birds of Southern Africa* was followed by a written test at lunchtime. All this was done individually, not in a group.

Applicants had to complete various tasks devised to determine how well they would handle themselves in the bush alone. They were given a rock and a simple hand-drawn map of the property showing the old railway line that ran through it, one building and the extensive system of dongas (eroded gullies). Without guns or the help of radios, and not knowing the land at all, each prospective guide was sent out with the rock and the map, and was told to find a certain tree and place the rock beside it. His second mission was to find a water pump and a campsite, and to document this by placing them on the map and describing what they looked like.

Another test of character was to send them out together to sleep in the bush; they were equipped only with sleeping bags – no mosquito nets and, again, no guns. The next morning, they were told they were going to have to walk to breakfast, but what they thought would be a stroll turned out to be a couple of hours' route march. They were tired and hungry; some had blisters, and took off their shoes and walked barefoot. It was a hot, strenuous hike, and certainly gave an indication of their stamina and character.

A similar test was conducted during the six-week course for guides. The staff would arrange a party in the bush one evening, during which they would ply the new guides with drinks. The following morning, hung-over and hungry, the guides would be handed over to someone and taken on another long walk, only to find at the end of it the staff sitting under a tree waiting for their breakfast. The guides had to cook the breakfast and it soon became apparent that there was only enough food to feed the staff. The guides were not allowed to touch any remaining food until everyone else had been fed and the washing up completed.

Tony Adams, who was at one time in charge of training, explained how these tests truly indicated the sort of men with whom the owners wanted to work. It wasn't imperative that they pass every test, but their reactions indicated the types that were best for the job. It was extremely important that they should remain calm and cheerful should they come across rude and difficult guests.

Once they had been appointed, the guides were on probation and still had some tough tasks to perform. Each of them had to go out and shoot an impala and bring it back to camp – on foot. One man spent six days looking for his impala, going out every day. At last he found one on the farthest boundary of the property, shot it and carried it back, as instructed. But when he was just about 500 metres from the lodge, someone drove past him and offered him a lift, which he accepted. Unfortunately, this incident had been seen by John Varty, who sent him back out again to a point that was even further from where he had shot the original impala, and he was instructed to shoot another. Jackie Evans, the second female guide to join Londolozi (Tony Adams's wife, Dee, was the first), took a compressed-air horn with her when she went on her impala hunt. After many hours of stalking, she finally sighted a little herd across the dam, but at the same moment a lioness also spotted the impala and came over to investigate the presence of a human on her hunting patch. Jackie climbed a tree, frantically blowing her horn at the startled lioness, which bolted in horror. Unfortunately, of course, the impala bolted too.

Another guide went out early one morning to shoot his impala and was back by 8.30 am. Dave Varty saw him and said, *'That was quick. Did you get an impala?'*

'Yes,' he said, *'it's hanging in the tannery.'*

'Let's go and have a look at it,' Dave suggested. *'Where did you shoot it?'*

'Well,' he said, *'I shot it in the neck, then gave it another shot in the backside, just to make sure it was dead.'*

Needless to say, he did not make the grade: he was out for both lying and shooting an animal in the backside. Had he shot it in the neck to start with, he would not have had to shoot it in the backside to make sure it was dead.

The way in which the Vartys were opening up their guests' minds and hearts as to how the natural world worked soon spread like wildfire. The style of guiding they pioneered became the hallmark for other burgeoning safari operations throughout the region.

PARTIES AND HIGH SPIRITS

The motto at Londolozi was 'work hard, play hard', and they certainly lived up to it. The place was renowned for its fun and games, both for guides and guests, and once the guests were in bed the partying continued for the staff, with midnight parties in the bush. There was always an excuse for a party: fancy-dress affairs to welcome a new member of staff, birthdays and, of course, New Year's Eve. However, if a guide was not spruced up and ready for duty the next day at 5.30 am, he was fired, or if the keys to the gun safe went missing, the last guide to have them was fired on the spot.

On one occasion, the 21st birthday of one of the staff was celebrated in the middle of the bush with a *Rocky Horror Picture Show* theme party. After saying goodnight to the guests, the staff got dressed up. The party was wild and wonderful, and a great effort had gone into making the costumes. Most of the staff wore fishnet stockings and all had on masses of make-up, which the guides did not realise was going to prove difficult to remove. They were back in time for the 5.30 am wake-up call, frantically scrubbing their faces and trying their best to look alert and fresh in spite of traces of kohl and glitter. One of the first sightings that morning, much to the amusement of the guests, was a bra found hanging from a tree and, the next day, Yvonne overheard one of the guests saying to another, 'That guide we had was supposed to be such a big macho man, but I swear I saw fishnet tights sticking out from under his trousers every time his boot went on the clutch!'

Dinner in the boma would often turn into an uproarious party. Former English cricket captain David Gower was a popular and frequent guest. He normally dined in a dinner jacket and trainers, and the guides followed suit as best they could. Often, a game of cricket would be started up by the guests during dinner, something that always broke the ice. Another icebreaker was John Varty's guitar playing. As the guests tucked into their desserts, he would reach for his guitar and walk around the boma asking guests to name a tune. He then called for his support team – five attractive young ladies who worked at the lodge had the job of standing behind him waving their arms and chanting the chorus. John was not a good guitar player, but knew the words of the songs, so as he strummed away he managed to get everyone singing. This usually ended with the guests standing on their chairs doing hula-hoops before departing to the airstrip for nightcaps among the grazing hippos.

Mike Myers, an excellent guitarist, initiated some wonderful singing sessions. In fact, the music at Londolozi crops up often in people's recollections. One of Lex's enduring memories is of when Tina Turner visited. She sat on the ground by the fire one night singing to her mesmerised audience of safari guests and guides. Two young tour operators from Cape Town had no idea who the singer was and were so impressed by her voice that they told her she ought to be a professional singer!

Occasionally, there was a small initiation ceremony – as in the case of a certain Englishman who arrived with a smart new safari hat that he was extremely proud of, but which deeply bothered his guide, Map Ives. After a day of eyeing this hat, the guide grabbed it, tied it to a rope and dragged it behind the vehicle, running over it now and then. Finally, it was picked up, dusted off and handed back to its owner. 'Now, that is what I call a safari hat!' said Map.

Now, over 10 years on, in 1987, they had a good clientele and were successful enough to buy their own plane, having put in an airstrip in 1985.

On another occasion, a very special 40th birthday was to be celebrated by a woman who had booked in from Hong Kong with a group of friends.

Yvonne rang them to see if they would like any special arrangements. Their reply was, 'What can you guys in that banana republic possibly know about putting on something special?'

Naturally, this was like a red flag to a bull.

The group were to arrive on a commercial airline at Skukuza Airport, in the Kruger Park, where the Londolozi plane would pick them up for the 10-minute flight to the lodge. Yvonne hired a gorilla suit from Johannesburg and dressed the pilot in it. Only his epaulettes and cap distinguished him from any other gorilla that might be hanging around the airport in this 'banana republic'. Waiting for passengers arriving at Skukuza Airport were smart uniformed pilots from MalaMala and other safari lodges, all standing to attention and holding name boards. The Londolozi pilot, however, swung through the trees, as it were, holding a large bunch of bananas as the passengers alighted.

The other passengers dispersed with their hosts, while the Londolozi guests stood around bewildered, not sure who was greeting them until the gorilla bounded up to them scratching his armpits and grunting. He herded the visitors into the plane. As he climbed in, he held up a book bearing the title *How to Fly a Plane*, and asked if any of them could help start the aircraft. They realised it was a joke but were nevertheless rather uncomfortable. With his earphones over his arm he took off at a precipitous angle, leaving them all breathless and, minutes later, made a steep but safe landing at the Londolozi airstrip, to a great sigh of relief from the passengers.

An immaculate, brand-new vehicle and smartly turned-out guide were waiting to greet two passengers who were not part of the Hong Kong party and drive them back to the lodge. As it disappeared, a noisy old tractor emerged, decked in skins and horns, and towing a trailer with plastic chairs tied to it, escorted by scouts on bicycles wearing large hats from which dangled plastic spiders. The gorilla jumped in and said, 'Come with me to the Banana Republic Safari Lodge!'

That evening, in the warm glow of the setting sun, while sitting on the flat rocks in the river, the guests sipped French champagne and were served chilled oysters. They were given a little talking-to about never again calling them a banana republic. They laughed and loved the treatment.

Businesses started hiring Londolozi for their promotions. One of the first was the Jaguar Car Company of Great Britain. An 18-page list of instructions arrived at Londolozi, setting out how Jaguar would like the promotional weekend to run. The executives wanted to be met on the airstrip with champagne and music playing in the background, and a full choir and drums. The Land Rovers should then emerge over the horizon in a line, with trackers sitting on the front holding rifles. No problem. The first plane carrying the luggage would buzz the lodge to get the timing right. The male kitchen staff would use the pots and pans as drums, and the women would wrap tablecloths round their waists as a uniform. Choir and drums would be ready.

But it all started going horribly wrong. The morning game drives were late returning and the existing clients had not checked out. Time was short and the rooms couldn't be made ready while the guests were still eating their breakfast. Yvonne was shouting, 'Ladies and drummers, we've got to move now!' The luggage plane, meanwhile, was circling the camp. The tablecloths were whipped from under the guests' plates and off they went.

The planes kept circling and no one could understand why they were not landing. Racing to find out what was wrong, Yvonne found that a very new student guide, who had been sent to the strip to set up a table of champagne and snacks, had set it up right in the middle of the airstrip. She shouted at the guide to fetch his Land Rover and remove the table and drinks from the runway. In his panic, though, he forgot to release the handbrake and the heat and friction set fire to the gearbox, igniting the dry grass underneath. With no water to hand, the champagne had to be used to quench the fire.

Meanwhile, all the staff were tumbling out of the vehicles beating their pots and pans and fastening tablecloths to their waists. The choir was hurrying to assemble and, as many of them lived in the nearby village, all their aunts and uncles and cousins and children had come along too. The scene was absolute chaos.

Back at the camp, the departing guests, attended only by the guides, were trying to finish breakfast. Luckily, they were all driving their own cars and, after seeing them off, the guides rushed to the airstrip with their rifles and trackers to greet the new guests and retrieve their vehicles, which had been used to transfer the staff to the airstrip. Finally, everyone was sorted out and the guides were told to take the new guests on a very long game drive, under the pretence that it was miles to the camp, to allow time for the rooms to be prepared and some order restored. Oblivious to the carefully choreographed plans, the guests thought this was all normal and great fun. Africa, here we come!

There are many more tales that could be told in the same vein of this decade of light-hearted freedom. Gradually, however, the carefree attitude at Londolozi began to change as the safari business became more serious and called for greater responsibility as the market expanded to overseas guests – including those with a tendency to sue. Political correctness became the new order, and the fun and games were considerably toned down. Today, no longer are guides allowed to drink alcohol on duty, to flirt with or even touch a client, other than to offer a helping hand. Lust, which was very much part of those wild, fun-filled early days, has been outlawed.

As the years went by, Dave and Shan ran Londolozi, and John became enamoured with making wildlife films, which started when he filmed the first leopard they followed at Londolozi. He fell in love with all big cats and has been filming them ever since, while remaining a partner in the safari business.

As their business grew, John and Dave Varty, with the backing of businessmen, created new venues using their conservation and wildlife-tourism skills, and founded Conservation Corporation Africa, later known as CCAfrica. This company became a major force in the industry and launched many new lodges in southern and East Africa, some of which they own and others they manage. In this way, the Vartys have been able to spread their philosophy of conservation and good guiding that made them so well known. They emerged as one of the most innovative safari companies in style and architecture, and run their lodges to the highest of standards. They had a programme of very high-quality guide training, which took place at another of their lodges, Phinda, in KwaZulu-Natal, where the habitat is more diverse than at Londolozi. As a result of this training, the guests at each of their lodges have excellent informative safaris provided by their guides.

CCAfrica grew into a large international corporation and Londolozi was run under the management of the corporation. Towards the end of the management contract, Dave and Shan decided to give up corporate life and return to their grass roots. Managing a large company is very different from nurturing your own land and business. Their children, Boyd and Bronwyn, were now ready to take the responsibility for running their own lodge. The family business was therefore relaunched in 2007. Dave Varty's book, *The Full Circle: To Londolozi and Back Again*, details the journey they took from the early days to recovering their life back in Sabi Sands.

Phinda remained with CCAfrica, now renamed And Beyond. Shan Varty told me that the training today at Londolozi is as thorough as it ever was, but follows modern rules:

'After a vigorous interview, a candidate may make it onto our selection course. The number on the course depends on how many guides need to be replaced. We generally take on more candidates than we actually want. This allows us, as well as the candidates, to be sure of whether or not the candidates will be suitable for Londolozi.

'There are a few legal requirements that need to be covered and ideally the candidates should come with these before they even start:
- *Valid professional driving permit (PDP)*
- *Current first-aid certificate*
- *Member of FGASA (Field Guides Association of Southern Africa)*
- *FGASA Level 1*
- *Rifle-handling certification*
- *Police competency clearance for rifle handling*
- *Advanced rifle handling*

• *Trails theory for backup*

'*They then expand their knowledge by means of training, which is coordinated by the head ranger – although the training comes from many different resources. The guiding team make it their responsibility to help the new guys. They will teach them various skills that they themselves are interested in or passionate about.*

'*We have outside people who are specialised in different areas of expertise who come and talk to the team. Every year is different, and the types of resources will depend on the candidates. The length of training depends on the candidates. Sometimes we have guides that have come through with some previous experience and we have others that are starting from scratch. So this can take anywhere between three and six months.*'

Kate Imrie is Londolozi's head guide. Sadly I have never met her but have heard she is an inspirational safari guide. Her husband, Tom, has recently been voted safari guide of the year by the prestigious Africa Direct/FGASA. In my opinion, this is certainly merited.

Although time has moved on from those early days at Londolozi and the guides have developed and taken on new responsibilities, the few whom I have met who worked there in the halcyon days have certainly not lost any of their sparkle.

We follow next the careers of three of them who have remained in the industry – Lex Hes, Mike Myers and Map Ives.

LEX HES

Though he was the first guide to work at Londolozi, Lex Hes didn't actually start out as a safari guide. During his last year at school, he was sent on a wilderness trail for boys who were showing potential as leaders. The trail, which took place at Londolozi and was led by John Varty, was designed to introduce the boys to the bush and the art of survival, and to teach them to work together as a team. John's knowledge and passion were overwhelming and the entire group went away vowing they would spend their lives protecting their African heritage. This commitment never faded for Lex.

After he had finished his national service in the late 1970s, Lex had six months to spare before starting university, so he wrote to John Varty asking if he could use a little help for six months, as he was willing to do anything. His letter arrived as the Vartys were beginning to develop the farm and they were delighted to have a helper. Lex worked those six months for board and lodging, and found it completely absorbing. He was 19, the Varty brothers were in their early twenties, and together they worked and played with great intensity in an atmosphere electric with enthusiasm and joy. When the six months were up, he decided not to go to university and stayed on at Londolozi for 15 years.

Most of Lex's time was spent helping in the camp and looking after the guests. At that stage, there were four guest huts, one long-drop loo and a bucket-shower mounted on a tree. As guests came only at weekends, Lex had time to explore the bush when he was free of his chores. He walked alone for miles all over the Sabi Sands Reserve, on the Vartys' property and that of others, armed with only a pair of binoculars, a notebook and his pet parrot, Spike, named after British comedian Spike Milligan (Lex was an ardent fan of the radio comedy *The Goon Show*). His mother had instilled in him her own passion for birds and he compiled the first bird list for the reserve.

He would return each day from his explorations with plant samples to identify, noting where they grew and what ate them. He studied animal behaviour from elephants to ants. He and the Vartys learnt all they could about the ecology of the bush and how each creature fitted into it. Previously, the emphasis in guiding had been on simply tracking and spotting the wild animals, but now the guides started to educate their guests in the workings of nature. Today, we take it for granted that, on safari, we learn about the whole environment, rather than just about animals, and it now seems incredible that this had not been the case before. In the past, guides were generally great hosts and raconteurs, and they could find the animals and keep their guests amused, but they did not know very much about the bush around them.

In those early days, people hardly ever spotted leopards, which are by nature very wary of humans, having been heavily hunted in the past. People might see their footprints and their kills in the trees, or hear them grunting in the night, but the creatures were as elusive as ghosts – invisible but for the occasional glimpse, which always caused great excitement.

Three years after Lex started working at Londolozi, but while he happened to be away, one of the guides, Ken Maggs, and a tracker, Kimbian Mnisi, caught a glimpse during a night drive of something reflecting brightly in their spotlight, high up in a tree. They stopped for a better look – and there, on a branch, were the shining eyes of two small leopard cubs. They ran down the tree and into a hole in the sandbank below. Ken and Kimbian waited around but saw nothing more. But, the next day, they found the cubs basking in the early-morning sunlight outside the den. They saw them again in the evening and the next day, but on the third day they had disappeared, having evidently been moved, as their mother's tracks were visible in the sand. After this first sighting of the cubs, they were tracked and found again, and visitors spent many happy hours watching them. It would be months before their mother had grown sufficiently accustomed to the vehicles to allow herself to be seen too, but she grew more relaxed and eventually became the most celebrated leopard in Africa.

A very important project in which Lex was involved was the translocation of elephants from the Kruger National Park to Sabi Sands, where the animals were kept in a stockade at Londolozi before being released into the reserve. At this time there was a fence between Kruger Park and Sabi Sands, which only came down in 1994. This programme of translocation was run in conjunction with the Mammal Research Institute at Pretoria University, with which Lex was in constant contact. The institute provided radio collars to be fitted to the elephants so he could monitor them after their release. Until then, no data had been collected on translocated elephants.

During his long discussions with the scientists at the Mammal Research Institute, Lex learnt about their research in Antarctica and the southern Indian Ocean. He had always longed to visit that part of the world and, through his working relationship with the people who ran the institute, he managed to secure a place on an expedition to South Africa's Marion Island, in the South Atlantic, a very cold and inhospitable contrast to the African bush. The party was there for 9 months – 18 men, no women, and the only communication with home was by telex. Each man was allowed to send and receive 60 words a week.

The island's weather is harsh, with snow or rain being the norm most days. Situated in the Roaring Forties, in the path of westerly winds that blow unhindered around the globe at that latitude, the island has no trees, only low, ground-hugging vegetation. The bird population consists of rockhoppers; macaroni, gentoo and king penguins; sooty and wandering albatrosses; and a huge number of petrels. There is also an abundance of fur and elephant seals, preyed on by the orcas (killer whales) that circle the island.

Lex's function there was to study the house mouse and its impact on the island. Mice had accompanied the early sealers visiting Marion Island and had proliferated there. Someone had introduced domestic cats to catch the mice, but it was much easier for them to eat baby birds. The cat population rose to a staggering 34 000 before a programme of extermination finally eliminated them. The study of the impact of the alien mice on the ecology was extremely important, and one thing it revealed was that, unlike mice in the rest of the world, which eat grain and plants, these mice fed mainly on insects.

Later on Lex took another sabbatical to study seals on Amsterdam Island, a tiny atoll lying halfway between Cape Town and Perth in the Indian Ocean. This invaluable education in how to conduct scientific studies was to stand him in good stead in his future work at Londolozi.

Meanwhile, tracking had become a popular pastime at Londolozi. By learning from local people, who were accomplished trackers, the guides became very skilled at following and finding lions. Tracking became one of the then unusual activities the guests at Londolozi were offered. The team had never tracked leopards until that first sighting by Ken Maggs, but, then, having seen the cubs, they decided to give it a try. They followed the mother's tracks, found the new den with the cubs' footprints around it and then found each new den as the mother moved them on. As mentioned, the cubs soon grew accustomed to the vehicles and after a few months the mother showed herself for the first time. This was just about the time that Lex had returned from his first sabbatical, and he took up tracking and observing the leopard and her cubs. Cynthia Moss's 1975 book *Portraits in the Wild: Animal Behaviour in East Africa* had recently been published, setting down all that was known about the behaviour of

African mammals, but the leopard section was painfully lacking in detail. Virtually nothing of this animal's breeding biology or general behaviour was known, other than that leopards are very shy and secretive. Having learnt on Marion Island how to produce a scientific study, Lex seized on this great opportunity to record all he saw.

Over the next 12 years, he diligently recorded all his observations while developing his interest in wildlife photography. It had been easy to photograph the creatures on the island, as they had very few natural predators and were not afraid of humans. Leopards were a different story, however, as they were extremely nervous of people, but over time he built up a vast store of data on their lifestyle. The original female, known simply as 'the Mother', gave birth to 9 more litters – 15 cubs in all over the 12-year period that Lex observed the leopards. Lex watched her offspring, and their offspring in turn, have cubs. Today, when he returns to the reserve, he sees one of the mother's great-granddaughters, whom he had watched growing up as a young cub, now raising her own cubs. The spots above their whiskers easily distinguish individual leopards.

He gathered important information about what happens to cubs when they mature. Once they are adult, the female cubs establish their territory right next to their mother's in a loose family association, though they never socialise as lions do. One of the cubs at Londolozi even gave birth in the lair where she was born. The mothers and daughters seldom meet, but when they do, although there is a degree of animosity, it rarely leads to a violent confrontation. The males are distributed far and wide in order to prevent inbreeding. Leopards are loners, but they do have a social order, and discovering this must have been thrilling for Lex. His keen observations and conclusions have become widely recognised in scientific circles and led to the publication of his book, *The Leopards of Londolozi*, which contains all the information he had so faithfully recorded and illustrated with his exceptional photographs.

During his last three years at Londolozi, he took up filming and learnt how to operate a 16-mm movie camera to record in moving film the leopards he was so diligently watching. He and John Varty set up

Londolozi Productions to make wildlife films, which have been shown on television worldwide.

Lex is a tall, softly spoken man with a quick smile and an easy-going manner, who manages to get things done his way without ruffling any feathers. When I attended one of his photographic workshops, I could plainly see how his courtesy and charm make him so popular, not only with his guests but also with all the camp staff, who were eager to ensure that everything ran smoothly for him.

In 1992, he married Lynn, became the father of twins and decided to leave Londolozi to live in Nelspruit, then a small but up-and-coming town with good schools and amenities for family life, and not too far from his beloved bush. He works independently, doing photographic projects, private guiding and, with his business partner, Anton Lategan, runs a popular training school for guides. Lex took one or two trips a year for Wilderness Safaris' clients in Botswana, as well as running his own private safaris, both wildlife and photographic. He is a patient and expert teacher, and his extremely popular photographic workshops were launched when his guests pestered him for advice on how to handle their cameras and take good wildlife pictures.

Lex continued his photographic safari workshops for Wilderness Safaris for a few years but finally stopped so he could concentrate on his own tours and his ever-expanding EcoTraining company:

'I have continued to guide over most of southern Africa and other parts of Africa as well. I presently do annual, sometimes twice-a-year, trips to Zambia, Botswana and Namibia, and have been leading trips to Madagascar every year since 2010. I have just returned from a ship-based trip, where I was one of the naturalists on board, travelling down the east coast of Africa from Zanzibar and Pemba, and visiting the Quirimbas Archipelago, Bazaruto, Inhambane, Inhaca, Maputo and then on to South Africa, where we stopped at Richards Bay and Durban. The ship was the Clipper Odyssey, *which is operated by an American travel company called Zegrahm. I've been doing their African land trips since 1994. I may be doing some more ship*

work for them in the future, with Antarctica and the Galapagos as two of my goals.

'I am a partner in EcoTraining with Anton Lategan and the business has gone from strength to strength. We now have four full-time camps operating – three in South Africa and one at Mashatu, in Botswana. We also run temporary camps in Kenya at Lewa and Rukinga. We have done training all over the continent: South Africa, Gabon, Zambia, Botswana, Namibia and Tanzania, with other work coming up for the Congo and Jordan.'

Ron Beaton, a very well-known Kenyan guide who is featured in this book, has been deeply involved in guide training and has used Lex Hes's company to help with the tuition. I know from Ron Beaton that EcoTraining has been invaluable to guide training in Kenya. Lex says: *'Ron Beaton has been very supportive of us. Briefly, we started doing training of existing guides with the Heritage Group in Kenya a few years ago and, through various contacts, we were approached by Ron to get involved with the Koiyaki Guiding School. We provided a few years of consulting work to KGS and in the meantime started running some independent courses at Rukinga, in the Tsavo area. We also got more and more requests to train existing guides at various lodges around Kenya and have started running our own courses at Lewa, in northern Kenya. We are currently kept very busy doing training for various lodges, including Mara Plains, Cheli and Peacock, and for Wilderness Safaris with their new operation at Segera. We'll be running more courses at Lewa next year.*

'I have just recently started a new safari company, Safari For Real. It is my belief that many safari operators have lost the real meaning of what it is to be on safari in Africa. With so much emphasis placed on the hotel side of operations (the fancy food and spas, private swimming pools, butlers, air conditioning, etc.), the real wildlife experiences are lost in all the hype. So I started a company with a brilliant young up-and-coming guide by the name of Chris Stamper. Our focus is to give visitors real wildlife and wilderness experiences.'

MIKE MYERS

M ike Myers lives in Johannesburg, but his spiritual home is the
Okavango Delta. He was born in July 1953 in the then Rhodesia,
where a man named Nikodemus Sakarombe, who had started working as
the cook in the Myers' household when Mike was two months old, rapidly
became the most important person in his early childhood. Nikodemus
had come straight from the army, and his extensive knowledge of the
bush fired the imagination of the small boy. Nikodemus portrayed the fun
and excitement of the great outdoors, which, for Mike at that time, meant
the five acres of bush that surrounded their house on the outskirts of
Salisbury (now Harare). When he wasn't exploring the local wildlife, the
young boy sat by the fire in the staff quarters while Nikodemus cooked,
listening to the Africans talk and learning to speak their language.

At the age of 11, Mike joined the Boy Scouts and was offered the
chance to go on a field trip to Mana Pools. The Scoutmaster was an
unfulfilled game ranger who had been pulled out of his chosen career
in the National Parks to help run his father's wine-and-spirits business.
He was going to teach the boys about survival, and off they went to a
campsite on the banks of the Zambezi. Mike, a city boy who had never
been in a wilderness area in his life, had to sit up and keep watch the

first night in camp. He was in charge of the paraffin lamps, which had to be hand-pumped every 10 minutes or so as he sat through the night by the campfire, which was surrounded by a trip wire with stones attached to it to alert him if anything came near. He found the experience quite frightening, with so many strange noises in the night – whooping hyenas in the distance and crackling leaves nearby. But, worse than the animals was his fear of the Scoutmaster, whose last words before retiring to bed were: 'I will really sort out anyone who wakes me up for no good reason!'

Mike's most vivid memory of that trip was the herd of about 30 elephants that passed close by in the middle of the night when they came to the river to drink. He sat frozen, hugging his knees and with his eyes screwed shut, as they walked down the bank just a few feet away, though he couldn't resist peeping now and then out of the corner of an eye to watch them as they swayed to and fro in the water before moving silently away.

He continued to go on as many outings as possible with the Scouts until he was 18. These expeditions involved hunting, fishing, trapping and learning bushcraft. In the process, Mike also became very keen on falconry. The die was cast, and he knew that he would work with wildlife. He went to university in Johannesburg, but his heart was not really in it. The only non-academic in his family, he spent his time learning to fly, and playing rugby and guitar. Mike was an art student who found things mechanical came to him naturally. Getting his pilot's licence was not difficult, but having got it he was unable to find a flying job other than as an instructor, in which he had no interest.

His luck changed when he landed a job at Londolozi on the basis of nothing but enthusiasm. He found it the most wonderful place to develop his interests. John and Dave Varty were getting into bush clearance, community projects and conservation long before any other private landowner had started thinking along those lines. Mike formed ideas and ideals at that time that have stayed with him ever since, along with his tremendous photographic skills, acquired through his friendship with Lex Hes.

When he left Londolozi, he headed to Botswana and went to work for Brian Graham at his camp in Linyanti. He spent four months there, during which time they had just one guest, an American woman named Jessie Neal – and she stayed for only two days. Jessie owned a company called Desert and Delta, which had two camps, called Okavango and Moremi, both spectacular water-based camps. She had a reputation for hiring the best-looking young guides in Botswana and made them sign a contract that contained a clause forbidding them to 'copulate with the clients'! Her camps were very luxurious for the time: she was one of the first to introduce silver candelabra to the table in the bush. I once caught a glimpse of her bedroom at Camp Moremi when it was unoccupied, and was startled to say the least, as the walls and ceiling were completely covered with mirrored tiles, which I am sure was unique in the bush. ·

Visitors to Botswana were rare in those days and, with only one guest for months, Brian had to make sure he got his money's worth out of Mike. This meant keeping him working all the time at everything and anything. After having him paint the barge 16 times, service the Land Rover 32 times and repair the boat 92 times, Brian finally ran out of things for him to do.

So, one evening he said, 'Mike, two years ago Fred Watt left a fridge for me on the corner of the Tsetse Fly Control Road and the Chobe Park Boundary Road. Tomorrow morning I want you to take Sparky (a clapped-out Land Rover) and see if you can find it for me.'

'I was thrilled to have any reason to get out of the camp,' says Mike. 'I, Julius, the head guide, and the crew shoved a few basics into the back, together with some axes, wire and a shovel, and set off at dawn. When we reached the bridge over the Savuti Channel (still filled with water in those days), we found it to be in a very ropy state. The bridges in Botswana over the shallow waterways are made from tall, straight mopane poles, cut from the cathedral mopane forests. We set to work cutting logs and mended the bridge as best we could with wire, and drove gingerly across, jubilant to be on the other side. Sure enough, when we reached the crossroad, there was the fridge in the middle of nowhere – a stainless-steel Electrolux standing upright and waiting to be collected. I looked inside and found it to be pretty clean. The* seal was a bit loose but, all in all, it was not in bad shape, so we picked it up, loaded it onto Sparky and returned feeling very pleased with ourselves.

'Back at camp I cleaned the fridge, cut off the paraffin tank hangers, as they were rotten and attached a spare paraffin tank, which I stood on some bricks. Within four hours, we had ice. Brian kept the drinks in that fridge for the next five years. However, what we had not realised was that the fridge had become a beacon for the pilots flying to Savuti from Maun. The standard instructions were to fly up the park boundary until they found the fridge, then turn right. We heard that one pilot had ended up in Victoria Falls and another in the Caprivi Strip before the message reached Maun that the fridge had been reclaimed.'

After leaving Linyanti, Mike started his own business guiding small groups deep into the Okavango Delta. He was a real pioneer in the northern area of Botswana around Chief's Island. One of the first people to do *mokoro* safaris along the myriad waterways of the delta, he gave his guests an adventure they would never forget. He became friendly with the very knowledgeable local people, who had been plying these waters all their lives, and they taught him the ways of the delta and how to behave around animals in the wild. This was essential knowledge, as not only were they without a motor vehicle, travelling in boats and on foot, but it is also not permitted to carry a rifle in non-hunting areas of Botswana.

Each night, they slept under mosquito nets on small islands, waking to the dawn chorus of Botswana's vast variety of birds all vying to be heard in the canopies above them, punctuated by the haunting call of fish eagles and swamp boubous. Poling through the papyrus-fringed channels, they dodged hippos, found the secret places where sitatungas (marshbuck) hide and cornered bends to find elephants swimming in front of them and giant crocodiles slithering into the water.

One of Mike's guests, whose family took one of Mike's tours when she was 15, and who is now married and with children of her own, recalls the safari as being one of the highlights of her teenage years. She remembers gliding in the *mokoro* among water lilies and seeing submerged hippos below them in the clear water. They followed a greater honeyguide as it flitted through the woods, leading them to a beehive in a tree, which Mike shinned up so he could extract some delicious wild honey for them all to taste.

She recalls seeing frantic creatures of all kinds swimming for their lives from a fierce bush fire. One of them was a snake that leapt into her boat. As she instinctively flicked it back into the water, she heard Mike gasp, 'My God, that was a mamba!' Each evening, after dining on one of the six dishes Mike's mother had taught him to cook, his guests would return to the glowing embers of the campfire. Mike would be strumming quietly on his guitar and singing. Shyly at first, she sang along with him, followed by the rest of her family. The thrill, the fear, the laughter and the beauty of that perfect paradise captivated her. She fell completely in love with Mike and is certain her little sister did too!

Mike thought the natural progression from guiding safaris would be to manage a safari company. So for three difficult and very stressful years, he worked for a company called Gametrackers. I wonder if the overwhelming misery of his final year has partly blocked out the memory of the initial fun that he had with Michael Lorentz, a guide who joined Gametrackers soon after he did and who features in this book. In the end, Mike felt he was not cut out for a managerial role and was not doing what he enjoyed. He left Gametrackers and headed north to work at Chobe Game Lodge. Those were much happier years for him, as he spent all his time either guiding or training Botswanan guides, most of whom are well known and still in the business.

Living in the bush as a bachelor inevitably meant life was rather lonely for Mike at Chobe. He moved to Johannesburg, where his friends were. He would then travel to each safari guiding job, then return to his base in Johannesburg when each safari was completed. In 1995 Colin Bell of Wilderness Safaris, who had just acquired a new plane, persuaded him to fly clients for Wilderness. Mike then proposed that he should run the private guiding division of the company and fly the guests in himself whenever possible. His proposal was accepted and life took a dramatic turn for the better. He now had a new and fulfilling role that gave him true stability and peace of mind. He had a great job, was surrounded by friends and had never been happier.

A guide can easily burn out doing the same thing for too long, but, for Mike, the scope for guiding has vastly increased. A keen angler, he fishes in the Indian Ocean at Rocktail Bay, in Zululand, and is particularly passionate about bonefishing in the Seychelles and Cuba. He travels to the desert in Namibia, canoes down the Zambezi and sets time aside for his beloved Botswana. He opens the hearts and minds of his guests by involving them in conservation issues, animal behaviour and an awareness of the wilderness that has grown from the seeds sown at Londolozi all those years ago.

Mike explains his theory of guiding: *'The very top guides are the ones who work in one area all their lives and know it well. For example, Garth Thompson and John Stevens would be at their best in Mana Pools; I feel I am at my best in the Okavango Delta because I know it so very well. I have never considered myself to be the most knowledgeable guide. I have learnt about the things that really interest me as the years have gone by, applying my knowledge to the areas I am in, but I have never gained knowledge just for the sake of it. Lots of people do guide that way and are very successful at it. There is a guy called Nigel Robey, in Zimbabwe, to whom you would say, "Oh, Nigel, look at that African monarch butterfly" and an hour and half later he would still be in full flight, one thing having led to another. Ken Tinley, one of the experts who helped the Varty brothers with the conservation of their land, could sit on a riverbank and write down the names of a hundred birds before breakfast just by calling them. It's wonderful to be around guys like that, but I could never do it.*

'What has captivated me the most is the sheer physical beauty of the landscape and the animals as part of it – the big picture, linked with my photography. That has always been my bent. When I left Londolozi and came up to Botswana, I was given this unbelievable wild paradise to head into, with complete freedom. It was what I had dreamed of all my life.

I always went farther into the delta than any of the other guides. Lloyd Wilmot knew the area well, as did PJ Besterlink, but none of the others spent as much time up at the top of Chief's Island as I did. I had a brilliant poler as my guide. Although the Okavango looks flat, it isn't – the water does of course flow down, if not very noticeably. My guide knew which way to go by his understanding of the way the water flows – that is something you know only by growing up with it. Sadly, this sort of knowledge is dying out: people no longer travel the delta as they did, and there is not the same amount of water around.

'In my opinion, a great guiding experience is to approach a big herd of buffaloes on a floodplain, on foot, crouching down and hiding behind a few palm fronds. You get as close as you can while watching them come towards you as they feed and, finally, you creep away so quietly that they never knew you were there. The last pride of lions or herd of impalas that my guests see is a very different experience from their first encounter. I try to give them an understanding of the intricate way in which nature works but, above all, I want them to have fun, to go away with a light heart and a feeling of joy.'

Mike has a rollicking sense of humour and a naughty twinkle in his eye. He has found ways to have more fun in just one month than most people have in a lifetime. More than anything, he is an eloquent storyteller and no guest on any safari will laugh quite as much as they will with Mike Myers.

He is extremely busy these days, doing the marketing for Wilderness Safaris and focusing on his photography. In 2004 he co-authored *Mombo: Okavango's Place of Plenty*, a book about a very special area of Botswana, which contains many of his brilliant photographs.

Subsequently, Mike has continued to produce many of the exceptional images used in publicity brochures and advertising campaigns for Wilderness Safaris. He guides less and less now, which is a pity, as no one had as much fun and laughter as those who went on safari with Mike Myers.

'I still work full time for Wilderness Safaris and guide one or two safaris a year with guests, who are also old friends,' he says. *'Marian and I were*

married in December 2008 on my brother's farm in Simondium, in the Cape. Marian has two daughters, Elizabeth, aged 22, who is working in Johannesburg, and Sarah, who is in her final year of a BA at Rhodes. Our lives are about to change in the next few weeks, as I have bought a house in Victoria Falls and will be moving there with Wilderness Safaris.

'The reason for this move is that I am now a full-time photographer with Wilderness Safaris and will have access to five countries from our doorstep. This is going to be terrific for both of us and we are looking forward to it tremendously. I have a photographic website and am starting to sell a number of my black-and-white prints.

'I love the fact that my hobby has now become my work – I have had to learn a lot in this new digital world and feel that everything I have learned over my life will add value to this next portion of what I am going to do. Can you imagine – I will be living on the Zambezi, three hours from the heart of our concession at Makalolo. It is rather nice to be close on 60 and to have the feeling that my best years of work are ahead, and not behind me.'

MAP IVES

One would be hard-pressed to find anyone who knows as much about the Okavango Delta and the ecology of Botswana as Map Ives. He grew up in Botswana and is known as a 'delta water rat', as he is most at home in a *mokoro*, exploring the innumerable channels, his mind brimming with ideas of how to preserve and care for this unique place. Currently employed as Okavango Wilderness Safaris' environmental director, Map monitors the organisation's 20 lodges and camps, all of which are required to adhere to his minimum-standards benchmark and are subject to his environmental auditing. In addition, he monitors two large concessions, keeping accurate records of habitats, roads, fires and wildlife populations.

He supplies Botswana's Department of Wildlife and National Parks with his population figures and helps conservation groups collect data on endangered wildlife, such as cheetahs and several bird species. He presents papers at seminars on natural-resource management, the control of fires and the controversial issue of cattle fencing in the Kalahari. Map is in great demand as a lecturer:

'I am more than happy to work with all wildlife decision makers to assure the future of habitats and natural-resource protection throughout

Botswana. I am doing absolutely fascinating and important work. I know I am under the microscope and I love it.'

Francistown, on the eastern edge of Botswana, where Map spent his childhood, had burst into life when gold was discovered in the area in 1866. The town was named after Daniel Francis, one of the early prospectors. The discovery created a minor gold rush, which later petered out at about the time the rich gold strike was made on South Africa's Witwatersrand a couple of decades later. However, the town continued to flourish, as it was out of the tsetse-fly belt and therefore safe for the oxen that hauled the great wagons along the supply routes of Africa, until ox-drawn transport was rendered obsolete by the railway that was built at the end of the century.

Map's father, an engineer, was employed to electrify the town, which he converted from paraffin lamps to light switches in record time. Map grew up in Francistown as one of five children, four boys and a girl, all of whom went to boarding school when they were seven. A school in Kimberley, in the Cape Province, was chosen for the children, mainly because there was a railway route there via Mafeking, but Map and his brothers were not happy there, so they were transferred to Capricorn High School in Pietersburg (now Polokwane), which was very different. This successful government boarding school for rural children had several playing fields, a large swimming pool and high-quality teaching. It also had good rail access. School trains ran at the beginning and end of each term all over southern Africa, taking children to and from boarding schools on journeys that could take days.

The holidays were always too short. Map and his siblings spent most of their time working on the family's cattle ranch, dipping and de-horning the cattle, and wrestling with calves. Leisure time was spent wrestling with one another, swimming in the river and shooting birds with airguns, but they were only allowed to shoot doves and sand grouse. Jack Bousfield, a friend of Map's father, was strict with all the youngsters in Francistown, and if he heard of any boy shooting another species of bird he would deal with him severely. Map was in awe of Jack, a larger-than-life character who would disappear into the bush for weeks on end. Whenever Jack visited Map's father and recounted tales of the wild areas he had been to, Map would sit quietly in the corner drinking it all in, and hoping not to be noticed and sent away.

In 1973, Map left school with absolutely no idea of what he wished to do with his life. His brother had joined the British South Africa Police (BSAP) in Rhodesia (Zimbabwe), but Map was unsure of his future. He did not consider university and there was nothing happening in Botswana – no tourist industry at the time and few prospects for a young school-leaver. At that time, Rhodesia was a successful, vibrant country, with plenty of work to attract young people. Map found out about work in a booklet that listed job opportunities there, one of which was in the National Parks (an idea that appealed to him much more than a career in the BSAP), and he was invited for an interview. Armed with a letter from the mayor of Francistown and a few Rhodesian dollars, he bought a one-way ticket to Salisbury (Harare). After the interview, he was told that he would make a very good ranger and that they would be delighted to employ him in the Parks Department, and invited him to join the two-year waiting list of candidates. Rather shocked by this latter revelation, he nevertheless accepted. In the meantime, he decided that the only thing to do was to join the BSAP, even though he had to sign a three-year contract.

The BSAP training centre in Salisbury resembled a military barracks – immaculately clean and tidy. There were smart uniformed instructors who took the new recruits through the six months of basic training. Everyone knew there was a looming political problem in Rhodesia and soon Map was being trained in a variety of weaponry, counter-insurgency, horse-riding, tracking and typing skills. His first posting was to Marandellas (now Marondera), a small, sleepy farming town, where he had to investigate cycle thefts and hand out parking tickets. Luckily, his posting there did not last long. Zimbabwe's war of independence was escalating. Young, single policemen were being sent to the dangerous areas, and Map went to a post on the Mozambican border, where at times he was just metres from the border fence beyond which the ZANU guerrillas were in training camps.

He was a strong, fit young man – and he needed to be, as he was now no longer a policeman but a soldier in camouflage. It was a tough, gruelling life being part of an organised army fighting a guerrilla force. They fought hard and played hard. The Rhodesian War was going on at the same time as the war in Vietnam, and when Map sees films of Vietnam he realises how very similar these conflicts were.

He knew nothing about girls and never met any: his rest and recreation periods were spent with other soldiers in Salisbury, drinking, playing pool and becoming addicted to the same hard-rock music that blared out of the bars of Saigon.

During one of his rest periods in Salisbury, he enquired at the Parks Department, where his name was on the employment list, and found he was now at the top. He discovered that he could transfer from the police to the Parks Department in spite of his contract, as both were government departments, something he had not realised when signing up for the BSAP.

Soon after he had joined the Parks Department, an emergency call came from Chizarira National Park, in a remote area just south of the Kariba Dam. While the senior staff at the research station had been away for a couple of days' Christmas shopping, guerrillas had infiltrated, abducted the junior staff and burnt down the research building. The station staff were devastated, both by the kidnapping and because they had lost all their research documents and data, gathered over many years. Volunteers were called for – they needed young, single men, this time from the Parks Department, and preferably with some military experience. It was right up Map's street.

When he arrived, he was bowled over by the beauty of Chizarira and took to the task of replacing the lost research with delight and enthusiasm. The volunteers were to record everything they saw in notebooks, which, on completion, would be handed over to the researchers. But, first, they had to build a fort to keep the staff safe. Built of adobe clay, with several watchtowers and surrounded by barbed wire, the fort bristled with weapons placed at strategic points, and was manned by heavily armed soldiers, who were often called out to help in skirmishes. Map was twice involved in landmine explosions, luckily without injury, while driving armoured vehicles, but nothing could deter him from his newfound passion – scientific research.

Eventually, he and his friend Charlie realised that they were not winning the war and it was time to bail out. The two long-haired, bearded men, with nothing much other than the rucksacks on their backs, boarded a bus for Johannesburg. With very little money and no contacts in the city, they checked into a seedy hotel in Hillbrow, which South Africans will know as a disreputable area. But it was all they could afford. Charlie understood accounting and soon found work in a bank; Map could not find anything other than a job as a waiter.

It was 1979, the year of the Lancaster House agreement. Rhodesian Prime Minister Ian Smith had capitulated to pressure for a majority vote, and Zimbabwe was about to be born. There would be nothing for Map back in Zimbabwe and life in Johannesburg was a struggle. So when a telephone call came out of the blue from a man who had been his good friend on the police training course in Rhodesia, Map was thrilled. Ken Maggs had somehow followed Map's career, knew he had been working for the National Parks and that he was now in Johannesburg.

Map was curious and asked Ken where he was.

'I'm at a place called Londolozi Game Reserve,' said Ken, 'and the two brothers who own it are looking for people who'd like to become guides to help them run it.'

Two days later, Map was driven to Londolozi with a party of guests who were on their way to enjoy a weekend in the bush. His interview with the Varty brothers went well and he was offered a job, which he accepted without hesitation. Londolozi was the sort of place where he knew he would be in his element. Still, this was a period of adjustment for him; his life had been hard and rough, and he had no experience of the civilised niceties expected in a tourist lodge – nor had he ever worked with women.

Map was hired to replace Mike Myers, who had left to set up his own fly-in safaris in Botswana. Londolozi was still a very simple place: most of the men wore tattered clothes, but they all had one smart shirt and a decent pair of shorts or trousers to wear when the guests arrived. Dave Varty encouraged the team enormously. The resident guides helped the new recruits, and Lex Hes in particular became a very good friend to Map.

Soon after his arrival, Map discovered that he had the ability to teach. If he knew something and believed in it, he found it very easy to pass on that knowledge – an essential talent for a good guide. He was swept up by the Vartys' enthusiasm, and their adviser, ecologist Ken Tinley, also had a profound influence on Map. Dr Tinley's ideas were way ahead of his time, and, whenever he could, Map listened to the advice Tinley gave the Varty brothers. Map began to understand the importance of soil, and how drainage works and what causes it to change. His long journey into the study of geomorphology (earth sciences) began this way. But he also learnt what fun could be had in the bush, an important element in his lifelong commitment to the animals and the land.

John and Dave's approach to hiring the right people to be guides is illustrated by a story that Map told me about Chris Badger, a new guide who arrived after Map had been there for about a year. Map travelled with Chris to Londolozi for his interview. Map had been on leave and both of them hitched a ride with weekend guests travelling to Londolozi. They had just entered the Sabi Sands Reserve when they came upon a group of impalas. Chris turned to Map and asked what they were. But, in spite of Chris's complete ignorance of wildlife and the bush, he was taken on because he was such an engaging and entertaining person. However, he had to agree that, as a six-month learning initiative, he would sit in the back of the vehicle, listening and learning during the game drives, before he could take any of his own paying guests on a drive. In the end, Chris developed into a superb guide and became a great force in the safari industry. He now runs Wilderness Safaris' operation in Malawi and is married to Pam Knox, my first employee at Okavango Explorations in London.

When Map left Londolozi – he wanted to return to Botswana – he contacted Mike Myers, who was doing so well with his company, Quest Africa, that he needed another guide. Map was hired. Mike's *mokoro* trails, in which he journeyed through the heart of the Okavango Delta, perfectly suited Map, and his interest in the ecology of this beautiful wetland, which was to become his life's work, was fired on these trips. With Map as their guide, guests explored the channels and lagoons, spending nights sleeping on islands under mosquito nets and generally having the time of their lives. Sadly, though, the job was not to last. Mike had a change of fortune and found he could no longer afford to employ Map.

During their trails in the delta, Map and Mike often passed through Xaxaba Camp, an enchanting spot on the Boteti River, which was owned and run by Paul and Penny Rawson, whom Map came to know well. The Rawsons employed Map at the time their son, Dan, returned to work there and, together, Dan and Map guided and looked after the camp. The place was run on a shoestring. Map and Dan had very few possessions; they shared a tent and even clothes – it was a case of first up, best dressed.

Map was fascinated by the geomorphology of the Kalahari – the ancient lakes and rivers, the fault lines whose minuscule shifts can turn a watery paradise into a desert, and the plants and creatures that survive there. While taking the guests on walks and *mokoro* trips, Map made notes of all he saw in the area, endlessly pursuing his passion for scientific research. Eventually Mike's business closed down and he joined them at Xaxaba.

At Xaxaba, Map met his future wife, Cathy. Penny Rawson had gone to South Africa for a few days. There she met Cathy's mother, who asked Penny if her daughter could work for her at the camp. Shy and pretty, she arrived at Xaxaba to find three wild, hairy, rough-looking men grinning with glee at the sight of the 20-year-old woman as she walked into the main tent. Map has never found out what she thought of the three men that she saw sitting at the bar, but it was certain she could hold her own and loved working there. It was a good two months before she and Map realised just how much they liked each other. Cathy had a temporary work permit and at the end of her three months she had to leave. But Map could not get her out of his mind, so he took leave and went to spend some time with her in Pretoria. Within two months, they were married and on their way back to Botswana.

Once married, Map decided to leave Xaxaba – the job and accommodation were not suitable for a married couple. As luck would have it, Hunters Africa offered him the job of running their photographic camp on the Linyanti River in the Savuti, a vast and extremely remote area of northern Botswana, which, at the time, was mainly a hunting block. The camp took in part of Savuti and all of Kwando and Selinda, concessions that today each have two or three camps, but in those days there was only one six-bed tented camp to service photographic safari guests in that whole area. Map's guests would stay much longer in one camp than they tend to today, and explore a large amount of territory, especially along the Savuti Channel, which was then still full of water. Vast herds of elephants can be spotted here and, on one occasion in the summer, a period when the animals are sleek and fat, and elephant families often meet on the emerald plains, he came upon more than 500 elephants massed together.

Map and Cathy spent two years in that little tented camp. Map did the maintenance and guiding, while Cathy did the catering and housekeeping. As they had not known each other for very long before they got married, this presented an ideal time for them to learn about each another. They were happy there, but eventually Hunters Africa had to close the camp because it was too remote and did not attract enough clients.

After that they went to Maun, where David Hartley employed Map to guide at his lodge, Tsaro, in the Khwai area of the Moremi Reserve, which is where I first met him.

Map was such an extraordinary person to listen to on a game drive. Brimming with enthusiasm and knowledge, he provided an exciting insight into African wildlife for his guests and generated an interest that I have never lost. While at Tsaro Lodge, Cathy had their first baby and, as it is very difficult to combine parenthood and lodge management, they decided to leave and set up home in Maun.

Map then continued guiding on a freelance basis before starting his own company, Map Ives Safaris. With his great knowledge and experience, he should have been very successful, but his marketing skills, so vital in this industry, were not well developed enough. He would sit in his little stall at the World Travel Market or at Indaba, the major South African travel fair, watching a steady stream of people going to the Wilderness stand and wondering why no one came to him for a meeting. He did not understand the importance of networking with agents and tour operators, and was not prepared to accost people in the aisles. He did of course have some clients – people who knew him from the past and who longed to go on safari with him. But by the time he had a second child, there was simply not enough business to support his family.

After four years, he was ready to pack up his business when Wilderness Safaris approached him to help them with their guide-training programme. He enjoyed doing the training because he loves teaching, but when he heard that the position of environmental manager was coming up, he asked to be considered. It was a job made in heaven for Map and there is no one who could have filled that post better. He was able to indulge his lifelong passion for research and conservation, developed at Londolozi, to his heart's content. He is strongly optimistic about the future of Botswana and the surrounding countries.

Map and Cathy live in Botswana and send their daughter to school in Nelspruit, where she is in the same year as the twin son and daughter of his old friend Lex Hes.

As the years have gone by, Map has ceased to guide and prefers to concentrate on the well-being of the animals and the land. He is now the director of environment and conservation for Wilderness Safaris Botswana and, as they are the largest safari company in the country, with lodges in nearly all the safari areas, he has to care for a great swathe of the country. He is also in charge of the Rhinoceros Project, which is included in the final chapter. His passion for and devotion to the welfare of Botswana are immense. He still enjoys taking a few safaris each year with guests who have been with him in the past or by special request.

'The Okavango, which, as you know, is my bailiwick, is still filled with fascination. I find it humbling in many, many ways to have lived here for long enough to see some incredible natural cycles take place. The Okavango was experiencing a wet cycle when I first arrived here and which was fascinating in itself, but which appeared so normal at the time. The Savuti Channel flowed strongly all the way to the marsh; the Selinda Spillway flowed annually and the lower reaches of the delta were flooded. Wetland plants and species such as wattled cranes dominated floodplains. Pel's fishing owls, sitatunga antelope and lechwe antelope were all successful species. Then, in about 1983, things started to go dry. The Savuti Channel dried up all the way to its source at Zibadianja; the Selinda Spillway stopped its annual links with the Linyanti; and the vast areas of distal swamp became rich grasslands for much of the year. This drying period came at a time when the tourism industry really expanded and many iconic camps were built. Those wetland species decreased in abundance for obvious reasons – their wetland habitats were much reduced and predation became more widespread. This was also the time that other species did really well; there was much termite activity, island formation and increases in general predator populations, which makes it no wonder that tourism grew. Now, I find that we have re-entered another wet cycle – the Savuti and Selinda systems flow again, grasslands are back to wetlands and the species abundance has reversed again.

'Absolutely bloody fascinating and extremely dynamic! I simply cannot explain the wonder and privilege of being able to have lived here and observed these cycles. They are not really changes, as these cycles have been taking place for thousands of years and little old me has been lucky enough to have lived through one full cycle here.'

BOTSWANA'S FRAGILE BEAUTY AND HARMONY

I have a very soft spot for Botswana. There, my passion for Africa resurfaced and the memories of my first safari in the Okavango Delta linger as if it were yesterday. I can instantly evoke the sound of splashing, grunting hippos at dusk, the soft crunch of dry leaves on the ground as hyenas crept around outside my tent in the night, and the symphony of birdsong at dawn. I remember watching astounded one evening as our host, David Hartley, plucked a small crocodile from the water with his hands, holding it firmly so that we could touch it and marvel at its beauty before it was released to swim back to the bottom of the lagoon. I had no idea anyone could do that sort of thing - it was astonishing.

B otswana is about the size of France but with a population of just 2 million. Most of the country is flat, dry and dusty, but in the northwest corner there is a jewel beyond compare – the Okavango Delta.

Here, water from the mountains of Angola drains down onto the Kalahari sands, creating a unique watery paradise like no other on earth. The channels and lagoons are lined with papyrus, whose roots filter out impurities, creating crystal-clear water, home to a multitude of waterfowl, fish, crocodiles and hippos. The palm-fringed islands within the delta and the dry areas surrounding it support a diverse multitude of animals and birds.

Besides the pleasures of the wetlands, there is the Kalahari Desert. The dry salt pans known as the Makgadikgadi contain Stone Age remnants. Visitors might encounter Bushmen, and one can marvel at the vast herds of elephants in the Chobe and Savuti areas of north-east Botswana.

Visitors carry away with them a kaleidoscope of extraordinary visions – the annual miracle of the flood waters from Angola creeping over parched, thirsty lands as they increase the extent of the delta; excited flocks of birds clustered at the edge of the incoming water, gorging on grass seeds brought to the surface as the water rolls over the dry sand or feeding on trapped fish flapping in the pools when it recedes; papyrus bending towards its mirror image in the still water adorned with water lilies and lotus flowers; the head and neck of a darter rising snakelike between the lilies while a tiny malachite kingfisher flits like a living gem from reed to reed.

In the hot, dry month of October this parched land has a beauty of its own. Dust turns the sun scarlet as it sets and even the full moon appears red as it rises. Elephants move like spectres among the mopane trees silhouetted black against the grey, floating dust. Away from the forests, the open plains stretch golden-yellow under a pale-blue sky until the billowing clouds appear with the promise of desperately longed-for rain. Once the rain arrives, the land becomes emerald-green, animals turn fat and sleek, and the renewal of life is evident in the numbers of newborns in the antelope herds. Migratory birds are prolific. Thousands of herons nest in the fig bushes along the lagoons and carmine bee-eaters dig their nest holes in high riverbanks. A memorable image for visitors is the sight of carmine bee-eaters perching on the backs of kori bustards in the Savuti Channel. The little passengers fly off to catch the insects disturbed by the huge birds as they walk through the grass.

Visitors to the Okavango Delta are spiritually restored by its beauty and harmony. They spend time either in small, intimate lodges or under canvas enjoying the myriad delights of a Botswanan safari and being lulled to sleep by the roar of lions, the whooping of hyenas, the grunting of hippos or the chirrup of a scops owl.

Further south is the huge, dusty Kalahari 'thirstland', covered in scrub and acacia trees, which stretches south into South Africa, east into Zimbabwe and west into Namibia. One small seismic shift and the delta could disappear completely, as it did at Makgadikgadi. Perhaps it is this geological fragility that makes its beauty all the more haunting.

RALPH BOUSFIELD

Ralph is a Botswanan whose base is Jack's Camp, situated on the northern perimeter of the Makgadikgadi Pans, in the heart of the Kalahari. Covering an area of 12 000 square kilometres, the largest salt pans in the world once formed the bed of a great inland sea covering 80 000 square kilometres, which dried up because of tectonic movements, leaving a flat, seemingly endless white surface framed with golden grass and stately ilala palms. As you stand on the pans with the vast arc of the deep-blue sky overhead, gazing at what seems to be the visible curvature of the earth, you will experience a very rare phenomenon: total silence – no birdsong, no rustle of a leaf, nor the whisper of the wind.

From the camp, the pan's white, salty crust stretches to the horizon, completely flat and seemingly featureless, but when explored on quad bikes with Ralph it becomes a place full of interest. On one visit, my family, friends and I, all roaring with laughter, with kikoys wrapped around our heads for protection against the sun and wind, making us resemble extras out of *Lawrence of Arabia*, raced the bikes over the flat surface in V formation, with Ralph at the apex.

It would take most of the day, going flat out, to reach the other side of the pans, but in practice it takes much longer, as you stop to examine the surprising number of things that catch Ralph's eye. To explore Makgadikgadi properly, it is best to stay a couple of nights on Kubu Island, an isolated granite outcrop in Sowa Pan, about halfway between Jack's Camp and the 120-metre Mosu Escarpment, at the far end of the pans. This atmospheric place is where Wilbur Smith set his book *The Sunbird*, and it is not hard to imagine the presence of an ancient civilisation such as the author describes. A simple camp awaited us on the island, consisting of a table and chairs, bedrolls laid out under the stars and a canvas shower mounted over the branch of a baobab tree.

In the rainy season, the pans become covered with shallow water, creating a perfect breeding ground for tens of thousands of flamingos. In the dry season, the remains of flamingo nests are seen, often with the chicks that did not survive, mummified by heat and salt. On our journey across the pans, we came upon a monitor lizard lost in the middle of nowhere, blind and nearly dead from heat, thirst and exhaustion. Some water dripped into his mouth helped revive him before Ralph zipped him into his canvas bag. Christened 'Larry the Lizard' by our children, he was taken to the Bousfield Animal Orphanage in Francistown, where he lived another five years, blind but content and well fed.

The pans abound in ancient history, both human and geological. We marvelled at dinosaur footprints in the bedrock, found fossilised balls made by dung beetles and dislodged stone arrowheads and hand axes from the sand. Beads and pottery shards, relics of ancient settlements, lay scattered on Kubu Island and on top of the Mosu Escarpment.

This escarpment, which is a rocky precipice rising unexpectedly from the flat surface, marks the shore of the ancient lake, whose depth can be clearly seen about halfway up the cliff, where the smooth, water-sculpted rock abruptly becomes rough and jagged. At its base lies a forest of unusually stunted, orange-coloured baobabs. Ostriches, brown hyenas and aardvarks are among the few animals that survive in this harsh climate during the dry months. We wondered what nourishment could possibly be available for the string of thin, bony cattle that wandered through the sparse tufts of dry grass on their way to drink at a government-funded borehole.

As the afternoon drew on, Ralph, after anxiously studying the sky to judge the amount of daylight left, hurried everyone back onto the quad bikes. Once again, he was at the front as we headed towards the setting sun as fast as the bikes would go. The return to Kubu was spectacular. First, a tiny black bump appeared on the horizon; then the mysterious island seemed to rise from the earth, looming larger and larger against the blood-red sky as we moved like the wind across the flat pan, our engines pushed to their limit, until the spiky baobabs and rounded boulders welcomed us back. This exhilarating ride created a vivid and lasting impression. All guides have a great sense of theatre and Ralph is a master at using his backdrop to the greatest effect with his guests. (It is no longer possible to have a private safari camp on Kubu Island, as a public road has been built to this section of the pan and it is now open to the general public.)

From the moment Ralph's piercing blue eyes lock onto yours, you are completely swept up and enthralled by his extensive knowledge of the natural world. He is a captivating leader, who draws you into an enchanted world of discoveries. His special area of expertise is Botswana and the Kalahari, but his interests are wide-ranging. People are mesmerised by his tales of the desert, the Bushmen, ancient settlements, wildlife, archaeological finds, early explorers and a host of other topics.

He is extremely well read and has a remarkably enquiring mind, and with his boundless curiosity he questions everything. Once, in my garden in England, he tasted every single berry that was growing there; naturally, he ended up with a dreadful stomach ache, but there was no stopping him.

He has a dazzling array of artefacts and memorabilia, enough to exhibit in a museum. His house in Francistown is crammed with these treasures. They are not all to everyone's taste, unless you are a devotee of the weird and wonderful. Many samples are displayed in cabinets at Jack's Camp, where Bushmen's intricately beaded handbags and aprons lie alongside the anal gland of a brown hyena, an ostrich penis and the skull of a sabre-toothed cat.

On another shelf lies a skull cast of Mrs Ples (a 2.8-million-year-old early human species, *Australopithecus africanus*, found in caves at Sterkfontein, South Africa). There are burial pots of the Zhizo, the first Iron Age Bantu people to arrive in southern Africa, in the seventh century; a petrified porcupine, preserved in salt, with its stomach contents visible; and all sorts of ancient stone tools found in the area. Tucked away at Ralph's home are traditional medicines, stuffed animals, the largest stone tools ever found in Africa, animal skulls, shrapnel from his grandfather's war wounds, medals, a crossbow with traces of 'angel dust' (a form of hallucinogen) used by his father for trapping baboons, and a German general's sword from World War I.

Ralph's childhood in Francistown was filled with action and adventure, and his memory is filled with accounts of daring exploits. His parents entertained streams of visitors, mostly family members, whose life stories and tales of bravery captured his imagination. Ralph's family has an intriguing background on both parents' sides. Exploring, guiding, hunting and public service are wired into the family genes.

One ancestor was a Member of Parliament in South Africa and auditor-general of the Transvaal; another was Johannes Myers, the first government official to try to bring order into the unruly mining area where gold was found, thought by some to be the person after whom Johannesburg was named.

The tale of his uncle, Peter Whitehead, was to have a profound influence on Ralph. The son of a tea planter in China, Peter, having witnessed his father's beheading by the invading Japanese forces in 1937, escaped to Australia with his mother and became a sheep drover before studying veterinary medicine. However, his dream was of Africa and he joined the Northern Rhodesia Wildlife Department as a stepping stone to his career in Kenya, where he eventually became general manager of Ker and Downey Safaris.

But his real flair was with animals, and Ralph was fascinated by his uncle's stories of training the lions that featured in television series *Born*

Free and *Africa Texas Style*, a film that was a forerunner to television series *Cowboy in Africa*, where the actors had to lasso buffaloes and wildebeest. Peter also rescued some of the remaining Arabian oryxes, and created a successful breeding project for them, which resulted in the reintroduction of the rare antelopes into their natural habitat.

Another of Ralph's uncles, Gerald Swynnerton, was Tanganyika's senior game warden. He became a game ranger in 1939 and was appointed chief game warden in 1949 until his death in October 1959. He came from a family of renowned scientists in East Africa who had various species named after them, including Swynnerton's francolin and Swynnerton's robin.

Ralph's great-grandfather, Major Richard Granville Nicholson, was one of the leaders of Cecil Rhodes's Pioneer Column that entered Rhodesia and a friend of Jan Smuts, the second prime minister of South Africa. Condemned by the British as a traitor for fighting for the Boers, Granville Nicholson was due to be imprisoned on St Helena, but luckily was pardoned during the peace process after the Anglo-Boer War. Twelve years later, in World War I, he captured a German general who had disembarked in South West Africa (Namibia) with a force of 2 000 men. Leaving his own much smaller number of men hidden in the dunes, he approached the general, holding his rifle high with his white handkerchief fluttering from the barrel. He convinced the general that he was completely surrounded and should surrender in order to save lives. The general agreed, and the sword he handed over is the one in Ralph's museum.

Ralph's paternal grandfather joined the South African Army during World War I and served as a major in the Somme in 1916, where he was badly injured by shrapnel and his lungs damaged by mustard gas. He spent the rest of the war hospitalised in England, where he was nursed by a young woman named Nora. Once recovered and back home, he wrote to Nora proposing marriage. She accepted and booked her passage to Africa. Just before she departed, however, Nora's father died, leaving his mother, his wife and Nora's two sisters with no man other than Nora's fiancé to look after them. They all packed up and left for Africa with

Nora. Waiting on the quayside for his bride, the major must have been astonished when five ladies came down the gangplank to greet him. They all lived happily together in Francistown – a very long way from their home in leafy Surrey!

A loyal British subject, Ralph's grandfather resented his children being taught in Afrikaans in Bechuanaland, which was a British protectorate. So, in the 1930s, he moved to Tanganyika, where he settled with his family at Lake Rukwa. The journey took six months in a Chevrolet and a Model T Ford. He planned to mine gold and grow coffee there, but ended up in crocodile hunting, a trade his son Jack took over after World War II. They sold a record 53 000 crocodile skins to just one dealer in Paris.

After the country's independence in 1964, Tanganyika became Tanzania and the new government nationalised industry, making it increasingly difficult for the Bousfield family to live there. Ralph was still a baby when his father, Jack, moved his family back to Botswana, which obtained its independence in 1966, and he became involved in trapping animals and birds to sell to foreign zoos.

Ralph grew up in a boy's own world, inspired by the remarkable accounts of his family history. He went exploring, trapping and hunting with his father from a very early age. Ralph was the youngest of five children and the closest to his father, who had an enormous influence on him. Jack was a colourful and legendary character throughout Africa, but especially in Botswana. Ralph gained his wide knowledge of the bush and incredible sixth sense through years of training by his father.

Ralph was only six when Jack sent him out on a bird-catching expedition on his own with Samweli, his trusted right-hand man (who is still with Ralph today). Samweli's strong sense of propriety meant that Ralph had to sleep by himself in his own tent, set apart from the staff, which deprived the young boy of the fireside companionship that he craved. He begged to have his tent moved, but Samweli was adamant that it was not correct protocol. On the fun-packed expeditions with his father, however, Ralph shared his father's tent.

Inevitably, school loomed and Ralph was sent to St Alban's in Pretoria. It turned out be an excellent choice, as the staff had an incredibly flexible attitude to this boy from the wilds, and allowed him to keep animals. They even built an animal house for the jackals, snakes and monitor lizards under his care. He would spend afternoons at the Transvaal Museum's Zoological Department, where he helped with preserving and labelling. Each school holiday, the museum staff gave him a project to collect certain specimens for the museum. He was asked to find rare snakes and other reptiles that burrow in the sands of the Makgadikgadi. Once he brought them a quill-snouted snake, only the second specimen to have been found. Ralph spent a good deal of time in the bush accompanying Jack on his expeditions during the school holidays, an excellent time to search for specimens for the Transvaal Museum.

Ralph had several adventures while participating in his father's business. He tells of one frightening night when he was 14 during an outing to trap ostriches with two of his father's employees: *'During one of my Christmas school holidays, I was employed by my father to earn pocket money to catch ostrich for his farm. On this particular trip, I headed out with two fleet-footed assistants, Joseph and Milton, both not much older than me. We set out in my father's old Land Cruiser for a week's trapping expedition. We headed up the old trek route from Bushmen Pits to Sleeping Baobabs and beyond, one of the best areas for trapping. It was very flat with few holes so we could race at high speed after our quarry without danger of damaging our vehicle. By day six, we had managed to trap about a dozen or so birds and decided to head back to my father's camp.*

'The old Land Cruiser had a set of enormous eighteen-ply tyres, which an American client had given my father. Being wide, and so heavy, they never suffered a puncture. But the downside was that they were too heavy for the vehicle. While driving along in the middle of the afternoon, I noticed a wheel overtaking me. Immediately the vehicle lurched to a stop, as the result of the side shaft having sheared off.

'I had been out of radio contact with my father all that day, so we decided that one of us should stay with the vehicle and the ostriches, and

the other two should walk to the main road. There we hoped they would get a lift back to my father's camp before he got worried and angry. It was about forty kilometres to the main road – a walk that could quite easily be covered in a night. It was decided that Milton and Joseph would do the walk and I would stay behind to look after the birds.

'After divvying up the remains of our food supplies, Milton and Joseph set off in the late afternoon. They took most of the food as well as all the water that they could carry, and left me a can of baked beans and bully beef.

'The rains had been good and there was a pan not far from where we had broken down, so, in the early evening, I wandered over to get water to cook with and found it full of enormous bullfrogs. I managed to catch three of them to supplement my dinner. As there were no trees in sight, I had little wood to keep a fire going, so I was in bed soon after sunset.

'It was a very clear, bright moonlit night. I had laid my bedroll by the front wheel of the car but, foolishly, I had not set up a mosquito net. My father had always insisted on us using a white mosquito net, as he was convinced that no predator would ever take anyone from under a white mosquito net.

'Late at night, it must have been at least midnight or one o'clock in the morning, I woke up confused and not quite sure what was going on. I was aware of the most terrible smell and it took me a moment to come to. All I could see was a dark patch in front of me, surrounded by a halo of moonlight. Then, to my horror, I realised what it was. The enormous head of a lioness blocked out the moon and the awful smell was her breath as she sniffed at my face. Fortunately, it was a hot night and I was covered with just a light blanket, and was not zipped up in my canvas bedroll. As one does in a nightmare, when confronted with something incredibly frightening, one tries to sound authoritative. In an attempt to sound very aggressive – although it probably came out as a little squeak – I swore at the top of my voice and threw my blanket at the lion. This bravado seemed to work and she reeled back, leaving me absolutely starkers, and lily-white in the moonlight. Fortunately, I was right next to the door of the car and I managed to rip it open and dive in.

'Once back in the safety of the cab, I realised there was not just one lion, *but six of them. The other five were waiting in the slips for me to make a dash for it. There was no way that I would have been able to escape – at least that is what I felt at the time. In retrospect, though, they were probably just being inquisitive.*

'*The lions hung around the car until the first light of dawn, by which stage I was absolutely freezing but not cold enough to be tempted to fetch my blanket! I did try, once, to open the door to grab it, but that made them jump to attention. To my great relief, my father arrived early in the morning. Worried about not having heard from us on the radio, he had come to find us, and had met Joseph and Milton along the way. It all turned out well.*'

Ralph's first task on leaving school was to learn to fly. He got his licence in Pretoria and became an excellent pilot. However, on his first solo journey home to Botswana in his single-engine Cessna, he inadvertently flew over Pelindaba, a nuclear-research centre, and within seconds he found himself surrounded by menacing fighter jets, which forced him to land and explain himself. Flying is an excellent way of getting about in Botswana, where the distances are vast and the roads substandard, and flying was to play an important role in his thesis work as well as his explorations and bird trapping with his father. Together with Jack's quad bike on the Makgadikgadi, flying gave them greater access to a vast area.

When he left school, Ralph went to the University of Pretoria to study conservation, botany and zoology. He continued his higher education in the United States with the Endangered Wildlife Trust and wrote his thesis on the wattled crane under the auspices of the Crane Foundation in Wisconsin. Part of this thesis involved work for George Archibald, the man responsible for rescuing the American whooping crane from extinction through captive breeding and innovative vocalisation techniques. All over the world, cranes act as a barometer for the ecology in which they live and the Crane Foundation continues its work to help restore the birds' habitats worldwide.

When he returned from America, Ralph met a Zimbabwean who had come to Francistown to buy a Land Cruiser and was looking into the prospect of hunting in Mozambique. War was still raging there. However, encouraged by his mother, Ralph thought it would be an excellent idea to go with him to trap birds. With his cousin Colin and the ever-faithful Samweli, they headed east with his new hunting friend. At the border post, the officials thought they were insane, as everyone was trying to leave Mozambique, not enter the country. They travelled in three vehicles. The first had to go well ahead in case it was blown up. This was guerrilla territory and their strategy would be to blow up the first vehicle, forcing the second to stop, so that the guerrillas could kill the occupants and steal the vehicle and its contents. If the next vehicle was far enough behind, however, and the occupants saw the blazing lead vehicle, it would give them a chance to turn around and escape. Fortunately, they avoided such an incident and all got back in one piece, with new bird specimens.

Ralph had to get a job and he was still working on his thesis, so he needed to find work in an area inhabited by wattled cranes for his research. Luckily, Jessie Neal employed him in her Moremi Camp, which was home to wattled cranes. Jessie was an American from Los Angeles who had travelled extensively in East Africa and visited the Okavango in the 1970s. She returned to Botswana in the early 1980s and built two lodges in the Moremi Reserve – Camp Okavango and Camp Moremi. She gave the whole place a touch of glamour with luxurious facilities and exceptionally good food.

At Moremi, Ralph realised that research and tourism could work well together. Hitherto, researchers had always dismissed this idea, in the belief that tourists disrupted and ruined their work, but he found that the guests at Camp Okavango were extremely interested in his findings, and this added an extra dimension to their safari experience.

With his thesis completed, Ralph left his job at Camp Okavango and, together with his friends David and Roger Dugmore, hatched a plan to create a mobile safari company to operate around the delta and the Makgadikgadi area. David was put in charge of the marketing, while Ralph, along with Roger, continued to help his father in the trapping business to earn the money to support their new company, named Kalahari Kavango. A few agents supported them and Ralph led the safaris for the first two years, with either David or Roger helping until they obtained their own guide's licences. (In Botswana it became law in 1992 that no one could conduct a commercial tour without a professional guide's licence.) They did reasonably well but never earned enough money to support all three of them. They took their guests into the Moremi Game Reserve and to the Makgadikgadi, where Jack had a base and quad bikes to guide their guests on the salt pans.

Their next plan was to open a camp in the delta, which they would use to form a circuit, giving their guests experience of water, big game and the desert – all during the same safari, something no one else was doing at that time. This was before concessions were granted; if you were a Botswanan citizen, you could simply choose a place, apply for permission and build a camp.

The three friends were extremely excited about their ambitious plan. With their youth and energy, they knew they could conquer the world. Ralph's girlfriend, meanwhile, Catherine Raphaely, was spending more of her time in Botswana with him. Together with Jack, they went to inspect a site in the western delta that they thought would be perfect. They flew to the nearest airstrip, Pom Pom. But fate was about to deal them a terrible blow. After they had looked at the proposed site, they boarded the plane for the return journey. The plane had hardly cleared the trees on take-off when it lost power and crashed to the ground. Ralph and Catherine managed to escape, but just as they got out, the plane burst into flames. Jack was trapped in the back seat. Ralph braved the inferno to pull his father out, but in the process he sustained very bad burns. Jack and Ralph were flown to the Burns Unit at Baragwanath Hospital, in Soweto, where, sadly, Jack died the next day.

Ironically, because of the apartheid atrocities prevalent at that time in South Africa, Ralph found himself in the most sophisticated burns unit in Africa, where he remained for a gruelling six months, having countless skin grafts, with Catherine at his side. The 1990 referendum was imminent, and the doctors, worried that if the vote went the wrong way Soweto might erupt in violent outrage, released Ralph a month early. They were afraid that, being the only white patient in the hospital, he might become a target.

Once recovered and back in Botswana, Ralph, now in his 20s, found himself in charge of his deceased father's businesses, one of which was an ostrich farm on the Boteti River. Ostrich farms are now quite common and successful businesses but Jack's was the first ever established in Botswana, and it was not profitable. The following year, for the first time in living memory, the Boteti River ceased to flow, so Ralph closed down the farm and sold the land. He also wanted to wind down the bird-trapping business, but it was their only source of income, so that was not feasible.

Kalahari Kavango needed to support all three partners (Ralph, David and Roger) full time, so they planned a high-profile marketing strategy for their mobile safari start-up. Without Jack's financial support and influence, they were unable to get a delta camp on their own. They made themselves known to as many agents and tour operators as they could, and pooled all their resources for a trip to the United Kingdom. In 1994 these three attractive young men, with long curly hair and boundless energy, took the travel industry in the United Kingdom by storm on their first visit to the World Travel Market, the industry's annual trade fair in London. Like the three musketeers, they cut a swathe through the African pavilion, where everyone was talking about them and wanted to meet them. Their safaris, always led by one of the three owners, became hugely popular.

Ralph had a passion for the Makgadikgadi Pans and longed to set up a permanent camp on his father's favourite site. When he had returned home to Botswana after Jack's death, he had opened up a locked shed filled with crates that had remained unopened since the family's arrival from Tanzania, and found them meticulously packed with brand-new safari equipment and kit. Jack had completely refurbished his equipment in 1959 in Tanzania before their unexpected exodus to Botswana and had not touched it since. Everything Ralph needed was there: tents, lanterns, basins, silver and china, jugs and glasses, beds, chairs, bucket-showers – all beautifully made in the style of the 1950s. Kalahari Kavango, though extremely popular, had never been able to support three people. This discovery of Jack's equipment gave Ralph the impetus to stop the bird trapping, build his own camp and start making a real living out of the safari business. The Makgadikgadi, which he knew so well, was the natural place for him, and thus Jack's Camp came into being on his father's original campsite, in the elegant style of a bygone era.

Ralph and the Dugmore brothers gradually drifted apart, but Kalahari Kavango continued to operate under David and Roger. Roger still guides mobile safaris, and David has a camp on the Boteti River called Meno A Kwena. Both are excellent traditional safari experiences.

Ralph knew the pans area intimately, having explored the place thoroughly with his father and he knew this place would be a natural extension to a safari in the Okavango Delta. He and Catherine worked extremely hard to make this one of the most sought-after destinations in Botswana. Ralph delights his guests with the wonders of the desert, conjuring up one surprise after another and creating memorable experiences.

A very stylish couple, Ralph and Catherine have put a great deal of thought into the design of the accommodation and equipment. When it was time to refurbish the camp, they preserved the original ambience, designing tents that were elegant and welcoming. Today, their original camp, Jack's, is a 20-minute drive from a seasonal, more basic camp called San – whose white tents grace the edge of the Makgadikgadi like historical campaign pavilions. Their mobile unit, for adventures in the delta and further afield, was also designed with the elegance of a more gracious age in mind.

Making this destination popular has not been easy, though. The fact that the unique attractions are able to retain the interest of the guests without the delta's daily parade of big game is due entirely to Ralph's approach. His knowledge, charisma and enthusiasm, as well as his ability to instil the same passion for the area into the guides he trains, keeps the excitement happily on the boil every day. Because this area is unique, Ralph runs guide-training courses for zoology graduates carrying out research in the Kalahari – an idea he formed while engaged in his crane research at Camp Okavango. This research and knowledge also benefits the guests, as there are frequent sightings of the solitary brown hyena, especially at dens not far from the camp.

The other special thrill for visitors is walking with meerkats. A local troop has become habituated to the camp's visitors, and it is wonderful to spot them at dawn, when they keep popping out of their burrows to warm themselves in the early sun. They are quite unafraid of people as they tumble and play around the guests, but they always keep an eye out for eagles.

Perhaps the most exceptional experience is Ralph's visits to the Bushmen. He has fought long and hard to gain recognition for Bushmen in Botswana, and has become a pioneer of cultural safaris. He has formed a deep friendship with a family of Bushmen, with whom he works very closely and who take him and his guests for a few days into the world of our hunter-gatherer ancestors. On such a visit, you can walk with the men as they track and hunt animals, and collect herbs, roots and medicinal plants with the women, and, if you are really fortunate, you may witness a trance dance. This is a traditional healing and social ceremony involving the whole community. The shamans dance around the fire while the women sing and clap until finally the shamans are transported into an altered state of consciousness. While in this trance, the shamans heal people and bond the group by laying on hands. The trance dance is the experience of a lifetime.

Bushman culture is also prevalent at the camp. Families from their settlement in the western Kalahari come to stay at Jack's Camp for periods of time to entertain the guests with their expertise in bush skills.

Ralph is a mixture of sophisticated worldliness and artless charm. The breadth and diversity of his knowledge seem endless, and his deep interest in everything around him will keep you spellbound every minute you spend with him.

Over the years, his guiding has remained of paramount importance to him. Each year, in March, he takes off time from his business to run a one-month training course for the guides, bringing in specialists to enhance everyone's knowledge. One of the recent professionals was a raptor specialist and a great authority on martial eagles, the largest eagle in Botswana. The Makgadikgadi is a unique place with much diversity, but it is very different from the big-five game-viewing areas.

Ralph is very excited that the Kavango-Zambezi Transfrontier Conservation Area has been approved. This is one of the Peace Parks, and a very vital one, in that it stretches from Hwange, in Zimbabwe, to Namibia and into Ralph's Makgadikgadi land in the southern part of this conservation area. Ralph is chairman of the Makgadikgadi and Nxai Pan National Park's management committee. Peace Parks are transfrontier conservation areas, which are discussed in a later section of this book, 'Into the future'.

Ralph leads private guided tours for small groups in different parts of Africa and has had some successful helicopter trips in Ethiopia, one of which was finding where and how a group of lammergeier vultures, whose diet is bone marrow, process the bones they eat. The vultures pick up heavy bones and fly high above the cliffs of the Simien Mountains, where they drop the bones onto flat rocks, cracking them open to reveal the marrow within. The birds swallow the broken bones, which are dissolved by corrosive gastric juices, allowing the goodness of the marrow to be absorbed. Ralph's helicopter pilot on this expedition had worked for the BBC production of David Attenborough's *The Living Planet* and, luckily, had all the GPS data saved in his computer, which made it easy to find these magical spots for us all to see on the television.

In 2008, Catherine Raphaely ended her relationship with Ralph and went to live in Cape Town. She remained a partner in the business until 2014. Uncharted Africa, which has gone from strength to strength, winning many awards for its camps and especially for its guides, one of whom, Super Sande, has been outstanding. There are now three camps on the concession, and they are more popular than ever. At Camp Kalahari, visitors can take riding safaris with David Foot, who, for many years, led riding safaris on the Nyika Plateau, in Malawi.

Ralph has a new partner, Caroline Hickman, and they have a lovely son, Jack, who was born in 2012. Caroline has created her own line of stylish safari clothing, Hickman and Bousfield, which complements the elegance of Uncharted Africa's decor.

SUPER SANDE

Super Sande has been a fixture of Jack's Camp for many years. He started working for the Bousfields at their animal orphanage in Francistown in 1990. In 1991, he moved to Jack's Camp in the Makgadikgadi and has over the years become the company's senior guide for this area and Ralph's right-hand man. At 6 feet 7 inches tall, this gentle giant cares deeply about every aspect of Jack's Camp and the Makgadikgadi area in which he operates.

His knowledge of natural history is phenomenal. He knows the name of every bird, including all the LBJs (little brown jobs), and will even spot and identify the tiniest cisticola. He is a natural, instinctive tracker of all animals, but particularly cats. As a boy tending his parents' goats and cattle, Super could always find an animal that had strayed out of the fold, and he spent many hours identifying which other animals had been on the land where the cattle grazed. The early-morning tracks would reveal a host of activity from the previous night – jackals, porcupines, African wildcats, springhares and genets, to name a few. He had no idea then that he would use this skill so successfully in later years, and in so doing be able to enthral his guests by bringing to life the countless interesting aspects of this seemingly desert area with his extensive knowledge and understanding.

While my daughter and I were out on safari with Super, his tracking expertise became evident. *'I can see a very clear lion print in the sand,'* he said. *'There is not even a termite print on top of it – it is completely fresh. Two male lions walked here very recently and cannot be far away. They have walked over the vehicle tracks of the guy that left to come this way before us.'* Then, without moving his head, he said, *'The one thing you never do when tracking lions is to lean out of the vehicle. When a lion charges, it is a split second!'*

My daughter, Hetti, had stood up in the back of the vehicle and leant right out from her waist upwards to have a look at the tracks. On hearing Super's words, she jumped back into her seat like greased lightning.

'What is most important is the way Ralph has taught me to take all my skills and animal knowledge, which I know in my own language, and to describe what we are doing in English, so that I can be sure to give my guests a good time. We have to know every type of grass, plant, animal and bird. You cannot learn this in a school room; you have to be out there experiencing it all.

'The annual training for the guides, which Ralph arranges each March, is for any new guides and all of the current guides. We all learn from one another, and from the visiting specialists. If there are new guides, however experienced they are in other parts of Africa, the Makgadikgadi area is very different from most wildlife areas, and they need to learn specific skills. Four new guides were introduced to the area this year – guides who had worked well in other areas. We spent many hours introducing them to our area.'

In 1997 the Discovery Channel commissioned a series called *Uncharted Africa* to be made by Ludovic and James Lindsay. Half of the filming took place in Botswana and Namibia, the other half in Kenya and Tanzania. The film encompassed many aspects of African customs. As well as the animals and spectacular landscapes, the series featured historical stories, Bushmen healers and their trance ceremonies, strange food, interesting characters and many other unusual anomalies of African culture and nature.

Super spent time with the TV team while they were filming in southern Africa and clearly got to know them well. He featured in one or two episodes, which included his going through a guiding test with Ralph. While they were filming in the central Kalahari, one of the vehicles was involved in an accident. They were hired vehicles and this one had to go back to base in Maun, some 700 kilometres away. Super and Ludovic drove the bashed-up car with a broken roof all the way back to Maun where the car-hire company insisted that they reported the accident to the police. Ludovic was a bit anxious about involving the police, as he was unsure of exactly where in the Kalahari he was permitted to film. However, Super was able to get round the dilemma. He happened to have in his pocket some special 'anti-official oil' given to him by a witch doctor. He insisted that he must cover Ludovic's hair and forehead with this oil, as it would calm down the policeman! The officer asked to see the site of the crash, but then withdrew the demand when he realised how far away it was. He signed the statement and let them go. They drove back in a new hired vehicle. It had been a long and arduous day and they were exhausted, but happy that it had gone well.

Around the campfire that night, Ludovic described their mission to Maun, but when it came to the part of the story about the oil, a colleague helping Super with the film crew piped up and said, 'No, Super, you didn't have the anti-official oil – I have it. You have the aphrodisiac oil!'

'Ah ha', said Ludovic. 'No wonder I had such a smooth passage with that policeman!'

In November 1998, Ralph and Catherine decided that it was time to take Super to see the world that his guests came from. He had never left Botswana, and they thought the experience would allow him to gain useful personal insight. The plan was for him to attend the World Travel Market (known universally as WTM) in London, to help with the marketing on the Uncharted Africa stand at the show and to get a glimpse of the competition.

He found the thought of flying in a jumbo jet terrifying and was pretty nervous about what to expect on the other side of the world. But once he had become used to the noise and crowds of the big city, he revelled in these new surroundings. After his four busy days at WTM, he explored London, bought himself a pair of boots and visited the friends he had made at Jack's Camp. He was not really interested in grand buildings or architecture; what really fascinated him was the lights, the masses of people everywhere and all of them shopping! He met up with some people who had been on safari with him and ex-employees who had worked at Jack's Camp, as well as the film-makers Ludovic and James Lindsay. In London he stayed with a previous manager of Jack's Camp and he went to visit friends in northern England. On returning to London from that trip, he had an encounter with two London policemen:

'I arrived in Kings Cross Station from Newcastle, where I had been visiting friends. I found my way on the tube to Notting Hill. I was carrying all my kit. I was going to Lady Amabel Lindsay, Ludovic's mother, to see if Ralph was there. He wasn't there, so I walked away carrying my suitcase. On the pavement I got stopped by the police, who asked me very politely if I minded if they took a few minutes of my time. I said, "Not at all." They professionally asked me two questions, which were very relevant. They asked where I was from and I said that I was from Africa. They wanted to know what I was doing here at this house and I said that I was looking for my bosses but they were not there. They said they were not used to seeing people coming out of these houses carrying a big suitcase at eleven o'clock at night. They asked me, again very politely, if they could open my suitcase and I said yes but that, first, I would like to remove my camera and my Timberland boots, as they were brand new.

'I gave them my passport and they checked the contents of my bag. They said that all was well. I said to them, "It looks like you guys are out working hard tonight. How many times do you think I am going to be stopped?" They said that I had been kind and offered to give me a lift home. I am sure they were still working and making sure I did have a home to go to. I was staying with one of the ex-managers of Jack's Camp. When I arrived, my *friend was very surprised to see me having a lift home from policemen. I was very impressed with these policemen. Their attention to detail showed me that the English security worked and that I was in a safe country.*

'It happened once again after I had been having dinner with AA Gill and his partner, Nicola Formby. When I got back to the house where I was staying, I could not find the switch for the alarm, which was making a dreadful noise. Just as I found it, the police arrived. Then the telephone rang and it was my friend ringing to see if I was safely home again. I put him onto the police and they then understood, so all was well. It made me very comfortable to be in England with such good security.'

One of Super's regular English guests is Jan Astle, the woman who had deposited her husband's ashes in the Okavango River at Nxamaseri, described in an earlier chapter. She travels nearly every year to Botswana and always makes a stop at Jack's Camp. When I visited Kubu Island all those years ago, it was an isolated and private place where you were free to set up camp wherever you wished to explore the length and breadth of the southern area of the pans on quad bikes. However, since the building of the new road, the government has opened up the area for a community tourism project, built a tourist centre and created campsites. It is now very different from the experience we used to have, when there were no cattle or people anywhere in sight, and a shower-bucket set up in a baobab tree. Jan knew about this special place and longed to see it.

When she finally visited Kubu, it was in the early days of the new regime for self-drive tourists. She decided not to ride there on a quad bike but to take one on a trailer behind the truck in order to do some local exploring later. Her retinue comprised her guide, Super, along with a cook, a waiter and someone to look after the tent. She was lucky to have only four: once the staff found out that this trip was being planned they all wanted to go. Trips are seldom made from Jack's Camp to Kubu anymore more and everyone likes an exciting expedition. To be sure of having privacy, Super booked two campsites, which was just as well, because while they were there, a car full of people drove up wanting to camp nearby. Luckily, Super explained that they couldn't.

In the middle of the second night, Jan awoke drenched with rain. Super ran up to her with a torch. 'Never mind, Jan, I have somewhere dry for you to sleep,' he explained and drove them all to a half-finished brick building, which was part of the new tourism plan; here the staff slept in the unfinished office and Jan bedded down in the future lavatory cubicle. They felt lucky to have a roof over their heads. The next morning, they retrieved all their belongings, including Jan's small dressing tent, which had been dislodged and blown onto the salt pan with its soaking-wet contents.

Jan loved her excursion to Kubu, cooking the food over the campfire, sleeping on the ground in her bedroll beneath the stars, showering under a baobab tree and exploring on the quad bike, taking turns with Super to drive. Sadly, due to the weather, they were unable to reach the flamingo nests. It was certainly an adventure and she enjoyed every moment. But it is a pity that the cattle now roam all over the area, bringing flies and smells, that rubbish is left behind, and the wonderful feeling of space, ancient history and tranquillity that we once experienced has gone.

JOHN BARCLAY

John Barclay is the nephew of Ralph Bousfield and is working for Uncharted Africa, running the mobile safaris. When I met John in 2013 he was 25 years old and I found him to be so focused and confident that I instinctively felt he would one day be a legendary safari guide. He is already a superb guide, and in time I feel sure he is going to make quite a name for himself. I have already booked him for a mobile safari in Botswana for six of my friends.

John grew up in Botswana in a small village outside Gaborone that was used for the filming of Alexander McCall Smith's *The No. 1 Ladies' Detective Agency* stories. That was serendipity, as the Bousfields are also splendid storytellers, especially in their ability to bring back to life the adventures of Jack Bousfield, Ralph's father. Jack's daughter, John's mother, who had clearly inherited the family skill of storytelling, filled her boys' heads with the many exploits and tales of their grandfather's past. They also spent many holidays with their uncle, Ralph, at the Makgadikgadi Pans and in Francistown learning about animals in the animal orphanage and absorbing Ralph's treasure trove of memories. It was the stories of his charismatic adventurous grandfather that so inspired John to choose wildlife and guiding as his ideal profession.

When he finished school at St Alban's, Pretoria, John took a gap year travelling through the Far East. He returned to Botswana and did three months' work experience at Jack's Camp, where he learnt about the hard work and responsibility of working in the bush with guests who have very high expectations. At Rhodes University, in Grahamstown, South Africa, he studied law and management. His idealistic aspirations were to help the Bushmen and understand ecology. After graduating, he wanted to see more of the world and decided to gain experience working in London. He was lucky to be one of the last people to get a two-year working visa for the United Kingdom, as, apparently, the terrorists who had masterminded the 9/11 attacks had used South African passports, so it became very difficult for South African passport holders to get UK visas. Eighteen months into his London work experience, which he was enjoying, he had a call from Ralph, who asked, 'What are you doing there? Stop selling your soul and get back here where you are supposed to be!'

Five days later, he was back in Botswana helping the mobile-safari manager on a trip to visit the Bushmen in western Botswana at Xai, near the Aha Hills.

'In April 2010 I was managing the mobile safaris but in the back of my mind I knew I wished to get into guiding. However, I continued to be part of the management of the mobile safaris and enjoyed it enormously. The staff always arrived the day before the guests to set up the camp and we slept out of sight behind the guest's camp in small dome tents made of white netting.

'On my first evening in the Moremi Reserve I took my lantern inside my net tent to make it easier to read. The light of the lantern reflected off the white netting making it so bright that I could see nothing on the outside. While I was flicking through Palgrave's Trees of Southern Africa, I heard some soft blowing sounds close to the tent. I quickly turned off the lamp and, to my horror, I saw a whole bunch of elephants surrounding me. My heart was pounding and I clapped my hands to let them know I was there, and please don't tread on me. An enormous elephant, his trunk swishing, came right up to my flimsy netting. I watched it slowly moving upwards until my head was right back and his trunk directly above me pulling at a branch, with acacia pods raining down.

'The old stories of my grandfather's experiences came rushing into my mind, especially the one when he was trapped and gored by an elephant and the animal had knelt down to deliberately use his tusk! He was lucky to have lived. I didn't know what to do, so I picked up the nearest thing I could find that might help, a spray can of Yardley's English Blazer deodorant and squirted it at the elephant. It got such a fright that it turned and raced away into the bushes. I immediately thought they ought to remarket the deodorant as an elephant-expulsion product! That was the moment I realised how much more I needed to learn. I wanted to get involved to absorb the knowledge and to find out what is going on around me.

'While we had been setting up our tents that afternoon, one of the Bushmen chose a nice flat piece of ground under a large shady tree. As he was preparing to put up the tent, he looked up at the tree, turned round, picked up all his kit and moved well away into a rather dull open place, so I jumped in and set my tent up on his original spot, and asked him why he didn't want it.

'"You will see," he said. I certainly did. And I realised that I needed to join the guides' training programme. The Bushman knew at once that this was a night-time roost for a troop of baboons.'

The guide training at Uncharted Africa takes place every March. All the guides participate. They write an exam before they start, to make sure they are up to the mark, and another at the end, to show what they have learnt. The guides learn a lot from one another, looking at things from different perspectives, and debating many issues.

Part of qualifying for the Botswana guide licence entails a two-day exam. The applicant has to identify skeletons and bones, vehicle engine parts, plants and trees, and the sounds of animal and bird calls. There is a difficult test in which they have to reply to questions asked about a picture that is flashed on a screen for a few seconds. For example, a gemsbok standing in the distance will be visible for a moment, and the guide will need to be able to identify if it was male or female and what it was eating, etc. Then there is a final written test on subjects such as the signs that identify that an elephant is in musth, the name of the president of the Wildlife Trust and even general knowledge (such as being able to name the soccer team that won the African Cup of Nations). The final test involves a walk in the bush identifying all that the applicants see and another on how they would react to being lost. As John is well versed in survival skills, this was one of his most enjoyed moments of the testing. John passed both the Botswanan guides' exam and that of the Field Guide Association of Southern Africa, the exam South African guides have to pass, with flying colours.

'It's all very well to pass exams but the real learning curve comes from putting in many hours. For example, if you see a flock of oxpeckers flying up in a bushy area, it would probably mean that there are buffalo there, but you would not understand that on your first game drive. Experience is everything. Modern technology, though, is a great help, especially when calling up birds. As I am not very musical and cannot copy a bird sound, I have an app on my telephone with the calls of all our birds and it's brilliant at doing the job that escapes me.'

In 2012, Glyn Maude, who coordinates the researchers in Botswana, went to Jack's Camp to give a lecture during the guides' training month. Most of the researchers choose exciting animals like the cats and wild dogs or social animals like mongooses and meerkats. But Glyn's big interest is the wildebeest. His lecture was so impressive that John plans to make it his mission to rectify the injustice done to the wildebeest. The Kalahari is 900 000 square kilometres (350 000 square miles) in size, and in the 1960s there were approximately 1.5 million wildebeest living in this vast area, migrating from the southern end of the Kalahari to the north, in search of good grass and water. It was one of the world's great annual migrations. On one of the other immense African plains, the Serengeti in East Africa, there were about 150 000 wildebeest at that time. Today, through intelligent management of the land and the removal of cattle and people, the wildebeest are able to use their historical routes and have increased to approximately 2 million. And the revenue from tourism cannot be denied as a result of the increased numbers of wildebeest.

Today in the great Kalahari there are only a few thousand wildebeest eking out a sad existence, trapped in pockets of land and unable to migrate due to the fences that were strung across the country in an effort to keep disease away from the cattle. When the fences went up, boreholes were dug in the dry areas to bring them water, which worked quite well until a while ago when some of the pumps broke down and the already meagre herd was halved. It's a very sad tale and one that touched John's heart:

'I was so concerned by the plight of these animals that I truly want to do something about reversing their situation. In 2006 the fence that stopped the zebra migration between the Moremi Reserve and the Makgadikgadi was taken down, but it had been there for 45 years – that is five or six generations of zebra – and it was generally thought they would have forgotten how to migrate. Well, when the first rains came to the Makgadikgadi the following year, so did the zebra: the genetic memory had lived on.

'In order to help the wildebeest, I would have to present a well-researched document on the subject. This means I have to have a degree in zoology to be taken seriously, which can be done as a correspondence course while working in the bush, so I don't need to be away from here. I know that corridors can be created for animals unable to move into their traditional areas due to human activity. The pronghorn antelopes in Wyoming have been helped to migrate safely over wide grass overpasses where for years they diced with death crossing Highway 191. The Kenya underpass for elephants, which opened in January 2011, is beneath the north–south main road and is proving to be a great success.

'As this has been done in Kenya and the United States, why not here? I so badly would like to find a way to make these corridors through the fences for the wildebeest to migrate to their natural water and grazing grounds. To raise their numbers to what they were is my dream.'

That is the passionate vision of this young man. His intense love of the bush, wildlife and conservation, coupled with enthusiasm and fun, will surely keep the Bousfield legend alive.

MICHAEL LORENTZ

Water rippled along my legs as the elephant sank slowly into the lagoon with Michael Lorentz, the mahout and me on its back. We were in the heart of the Okavango Delta and I was swimming with African elephants! It was my first encounter with Abu, the elephant I mentioned in the 'The world of safari travel'.

Michael turned to me and said, 'What we are doing right now is unique. You can guarantee no one else on the planet is doing the same thing as we are right now.'

There aren't many occasions when you can claim that. It was extraordinary. Michael's experience with elephants is vast, intimate and all-encompassing, and his ability to share this experience with his guests is exceptional.

Michael is the only guide in this book that I did not meet through the travel business. I have had a close association with his family for most of my life. My earliest memory of Michael is in his grey school uniform with short pants that were a bit too big for him, and with no front teeth. He has grown into a man with an extraordinarily deep understanding of animals, and he feels strongly that he has as much right to walk through the bush, to be there, as an impala, baboon, lion or elephant. No more and no less.

Michael's first awareness that he really cared for animals came when he was about six years old and he acquired a white rat called Blanche, whom he loved dearly. By the age of 11 he had decorated his room in the family home in Johannesburg with a large poster of a *mokoro* being poled through the Okavango Delta, depicting his dream of faraway places. He would spend hours identifying birds or watching ants hurrying in and out of their nests going about their daily business. He found it all fascinating. But he had to wait until he was 14, when his father took him on a walking safari in the Kruger National Park, to be exposed to the real bush. That was when Michael knew exactly where he wanted to be.

However, his conventional upbringing led him to enrol at Wits University to study law – clearly the wrong thing for him, as he lasted only a year. In 1984, by sheer good luck, he landed a job as a guide at Tanda Tula, in the Timbavati Game Reserve, adjacent to Kruger. He was to take over from Bruce Measer, who stayed to help him get started and became his earliest mentor. Bruce had spent nine years as a mounted scout in Zimbabwe during the war there, only ever riding one horse. He was the first person Michael had met who had that feeling of belonging, along with all other creatures, in the bush. For Michael, Bruce shared the position of hero and role model with Jack Mathebula, a Shangaan tracker who worked at the reserve and possessed an incredible sixth sense when it came to lions.

Jack had gained fame as the tracker who found the white lions of Timbavati, made famous by Chris McBride's book of the same name. He had been away in Botswana, tracking lions in Savuti for seven years. Michael met him on his first day back at Timbavati. He realised what a gem he had for a tutor on the very first meeting when Bruce told Jack to go out with Michael. Soon they came upon some lion spoor at a river crossing. Michael said he knew which pride this was and was sure they were lying up in a wooded area to the north. 'Hmm,' said Jack. 'Maybe, but I think that they are lying at the crossing of Piggy Dam and the Rhino Loop.' Something made Michael head Jack's way and, sure enough, there they were, exactly as Jack had predicted. Jack had not been there for seven years; he hadn't met these lions and was not tracking. He just knew. Jack and Bruce were phenomenal teachers and they set Michael on the right track for life.

Jack would only work for Michael. He was a stubborn man and did as he pleased. If asked to track for another guide, he would sit in the vehicle in stony silence finding nothing. He was the most superb lion tracker Michael was ever to meet, but he didn't like anything else. He would reluctantly look at leopards, was terrified of elephants, loathed snakes and was uninterested in all small creatures. When Michael was carefully pointing out, say, a mongoose, a dik-dik or an interesting spider to his guests, Jack would speak up in Shangaan: 'Michael, stop this! People haven't paid good money to see this rubbish, they only came to see the lions.'

In 1986, Michael left Tanda Tula and went to Botswana to work for Gametrackers, a company that then had a collection of four safari camps. He was to take over managing and guiding at Santawani after a spell of three months' orientation spent at all four camps. He drove from Johannesburg with a couple of the company's managers, who were transporting a new vehicle and a drum of paint to Maun for Mike Myers, the newly appointed general manager. They stopped overnight at Francistown and left before dawn the next day so as to reach Maun in daylight. At 4 pm, after 11 hours' driving, they arrived exhausted, but pleased that they had made it. The roads were diabolical, with thick sand and potholes most of the way. During one ghastly lurch, the drum of paint fell and spilt its contents all over the floor of the vehicle. Mike Myers took one look at his brand-new vehicle, caked in dust and spilt paint, and, according to Michael, went ballistic. He tore a strip off everyone and sent Michael packing to Santawani that afternoon. Exhausted and not knowing where to go, Michael headed off in more or less the right direction. Luckily, he found that all the roads led to his destination – there was nowhere else to go.

When he first arrived at Santawani, it took his breath away. Here was a Garden of Eden, lush, fertile and packed with animals – even better than Mombo is today. Extraordinarily, the poster he had hung in his room as a child was an advertisement for Santawani. It was his childhood dream come true.

For the next three months, he visited all Gametrackers' camps, spending a little time at each, doing transfers, guiding, transporting supplies, learning how the business ran and getting to know the area well. Eventually, he settled down to run Santawani with two Botswanan guides, Buxton and Motuphi. Together they did some of the mapping for Kenneth Newman's *Birds of Botswana* and translated all the names into Setswana and Seyei (the language of the Bayei hunter-gatherers, Mothupi's tribe).

The guests came in by private charter from Gaborone or Johannesburg (there was no Air Botswana in those days) and brought with them supplies of fresh vegetables and fruit, as the little grocery shop in Maun was only sparsely stocked. They had a wonderful time. Animals were so abundant that it was not uncommon to see cheetahs, leopards and lions on the same game drive. Michael remembers a herd of about 800 elephants passing through, along with large herds of eland and sable antelopes. Today, however, the Santawani area has dried up, sagebrush and acacia scrub have encroached, and the animals have all but disappeared. As a result, the lodge is no longer used on a commercial basis.

After the unfortunate start to their working relationship, Michael Lorentz and Mike Myers became good friends and had a great time together for the first couple of years. After managing Santawani, Michael was made assistant manager to Mike, who was based in Maun. They would fly around in a Cessna 210, checking on each camp in turn and helping out with the guiding. Once, during a night drive, while guiding together with three travel agents whom they wanted to impress, they caught sight of a springhare in the tracker's spotlight. Slightly over-enthusiastically, they chased after the little creature on foot, trying to catch it to show it to the agents. As Michael ran ahead, the rodent veered back, connecting hard with Mike's boot, which abruptly ended its life. Scooping it up, he held it firmly and took it to the car, and showed the agents the teeth, the ears, the eyes, etc. He kept a straight face, all the time trying to make sure it did not look limp in his hands. Turning to put it down, they prayed the tracker would take the spotlight off it, but he kept the animal relentlessly illuminated while they placed it in a warthog burrow, assuring the agents that it was just a little disoriented and would soon come round in the safety of the hole.

Those were the halcyon days. Maun was a wild frontier town where life revolved around the Duck Inn, opposite the airport, and everyone knew Bernadette, the owner. Bernadette would not acknowledge the existence of newcomers at first and they would have to earn their stripes before winning her approval and friendship. The Duck Inn was going strong when I first went to Botswana. There was a Wild West atmosphere about the place, its tables packed with locals and visitors – jolly photographic-safari operators and their clients at one end and dour-looking hunters at the other.

Things started to go wrong at Gametrackers in 1990, four years into Michael's employment. Everyone had rather grand ideas on how the company should be run and life at managerial level became very complicated. Michael had the responsibility for running the operation, but not the authority. At this point, Michael decided it was time to have a year away from the bush and he took off for London, leaving Mike Myers to face the music in Botswana.

Michael was a fish out of water in London, dressed in a suit and tie, and working for an insurance company. Homesick and miserable away from the bush, he would watch Gametrackers' promotional videos, but they failed to cheer him up. He fell in love, got engaged, fell out of love, got disengaged and was glad to return to Botswana, having finally accepted that city life was not for him. Gametrackers was being taken over by Orient Express Safaris and he helped out where needed at their camps for a few months before starting his own company with his then girlfriend, Katie Holmes, training guides and providing relief management at various safari camps. Randall Moore and his elephants had recently arrived and he employed Michael for six weeks at Elephant Back Safaris to help him get the camp up and running.

Michael and Katie's company did not last after this first encounter with Elephant Back Safaris. His next phase was eight months with Hartley's Safaris where, along with Stephie Whitcombe, he did the marketing and helped set up the private-safari side of the business. It was the first time he had led safaris by himself and he very much enjoyed it. Some of them were quite spectacular, such as the private safari a German company arranged for their chairman as a farewell present. Hartley's sent Michael and Stephie to plan it, and they came up with several wonderful ideas, all of which were agreed to. Michael was the guide and Stephie went along as the hostess. A helicopter stood by every day to take the clients to different areas of the delta to explore on foot and by *mokoro*. Not one meal was eaten in the same place; they had different locations for breakfast and lunch, and each night they would leave camp for a bush dinner, again always in a different spot. Michael and Stephie both received an album full of photographs from the grateful clients, who had had the time of their lives.

Michael left Hartley's Safaris when Randall Moore invited him to manage and guide full time for Elephant Back Safaris. Stephie went with him for the first year, to be succeeded by Caro Henley, Daniela Bleattler and Sandor Carter. Those were the glory years: they had wonderful clients and excellent safaris, all of which were five nights long – the amount of time that they felt was needed for the guests to get to know and understand the elephants. Randall was in partnership with Ker and Downey (an established safari operator in Botswana but not part of the company of the same name in Kenya), and the original camp, though simple, had very comfortable tents with bucket-showers and long-drop loos. Later, when Randall acquired his own concession, the partnership with Ker and Downey ceased and he built a more luxurious camp on the current site.

Michael managed and worked with these elephants for nine years. He knows them intimately and part of his soul belongs to them. He did not have a share in the business, but he was a bright, intelligent employee who eventually wanted to move on in life. He does not talk of the elephants very often, but, once he starts reminiscing on the 'glory days', his face lights up as the years melt away:

'The difficulty I have in talking about Elephant Back Safaris is that what has happened in recent years, with the direction it has taken with the development and management of the herd, is such that it has rather consumed my good memories. It has really made me question whether we ever did things right – and I'm sure we did, but I find it hard to reconcile the present with the past.'

Michael made these comments before the sale of Elephant Back Safaris and what he says in no way refers to the current management.

I have already written about these elephants and how I loved them, and how privileged so many of us were to have known them. The experience was created purely by Randall's innovative idea and his hard work, but, for many of my friends and clients, and for me, the enjoyment was purely because of Michael. He made our safaris so special – for some it was life-altering, but everyone has exceptional memories of their experiences at Abu's Camp.

Many of Michael's good times were had while filming with the herd. Once, when making a film for a French company, the site chosen was the lagoon on which the current camp is situated, but at the time it was 26 kilometres from their camp. As Abu had to walk there for the four days' filming, Michael and David, one of the mahouts, took him. For Michael, it was the strangest, most magical journey. They left camp in the soft light of dawn, across the delta, two men and an elephant, the three of them part of the bush, at one with the world in which they were travelling. David rode Abu there and Michael rode him back. Hot and tired after the five-hour walk, Michael jumped up to join David on Abu's back as they plunged into the water to cool themselves and wash off the dust.

To walk with an elephant is quite extraordinary; you become like an elephant, part of the big scene; other animals usually see only the elephants and tend not to even smell humans. I was walking with Michael when we came upon three lions on a buffalo kill, less than 20 metres from us. The elephants stopped, their riders silent, as we tucked ourselves under Abu's tusks and waited. The three male lions looked up, one stood and turned towards us, staring at the elephants but not reacting to us at all. Then, completely unperturbed, the lion flopped down with his companions, doing what lions like best – dozing with their fat bellies full of meat.

Had we been walking without the elephants we would never have seen the lions; they would have scented us and run off, long gone before we got anywhere near the kill. It was a glimpse of that sense of belonging that is so important to Michael.

These outings were not always without incident. One cold winter's morning, they were tracking lions, which had been seen in the distance. All the guests were riding on the elephants and Michael was the only person walking. Following the group would have involved crossing some muddy water and, not wanting to get cold and wet, he decided to wait where he was for them to come back once they had seen the lions. Leaning his rifle against the trunk of a large tree, he sat down and lit a cigarette, relaxed and at peace with the world as the others headed off after the lions. After a while, he cannot say why, something made him turn around and look through a thick bush growing next to the tree, and there behind it was a large lion, trotting through the grass, looking over his shoulder at the elephants, which were coming along behind him. When the lion was a few metres away and still completely unaware of him, Michael, with his heart pounding and his stomach churning, opened his mouth and shouted as loud as he could, 'BAH!' The terrified lion turned and fled. Everyone on the elephants had heard the strange noise and saw the lion run off, but didn't realise that Michael was behind the bush until he jumped out and waved at them. They had followed the lion in a full circle back to the tree.

Michael has many entertaining stories of his time spent with the elephants, but I rather like his tale of walking with three city slickers on their first visit to Africa:

'About a year after I had started guiding with the elephants, three Americans arrived from New York – two men and a woman. They had never been to Africa before and were rather precious. I don't think the sun had seen their legs since they were four years old. On their first morning, they turned up in their brand-new Ralph Lauren safari kit and decided to walk with me rather than ride the elephants. All the other guests were riding and only the four of us were on foot. Suddenly, we saw lions in a palm thicket, and the herd was manoeuvred so that everyone could get a better view and we too had a great view as they ran out from under one palm thicket into another with the cubs following, not ten yards from us. Then I heard loud shouting coming from the edge of the herd. One of the mahouts was calling and instantly I realised that a wild elephant was approaching. It was without doubt the worst experience I had ever had with a wild elephant near the herd. There was one other guide with a rifle – he was on a young elephant at the back of the herd – who probably shot into the air far too soon. A young bull, in his 20s, was approaching and was definitely intent on getting into the herd.

'I clapped loudly but he took no notice. I had guests on the elephants, the baby elephants all milling around, lions with cubs no more than ten yards away and three Americans on foot. I turned to the mahouts and told them to get out of here now, quickly, and I ordered the Americans to stay within two feet of Cathy, the calm matriarch of the herd, all the way. "Joseph is in charge and he will look after you," I said. "Now go!"

'I had a dreadful ten minutes: this elephant did not want to be stopped. I fired three shots above his head, he kept trying to get around me to the herd, charging me as I dashed back and forth trying to cut him off. Finally, he realised he wasn't going to make it, but it was a terrifying few minutes.

'When I returned to the herd, which had gone about 500 yards, I found the Americans had taken me at my word! They had glued themselves to Cathy, who had gone straight through ilala palm scrub, which is covered in hooked thorns. Their clothes were ripped to pieces and blood was streaming down their legs. But the grins on their faces stretched from ear to ear. They had had one of the most exhilarating experiences of their lives. But they *would not walk again on that safari. They rode the elephants on every outing, saying that although they had enjoyed walking, nothing could have surpassed the walk they had on the first day.'*

Michael had an extraordinary and moving experience with a wild elephant, which altered his perspective on life, on communication and on who we are. He felt it was truly a link between two souls. In his own words:

'The most significant moment I have ever had in the bush was one afternoon while I was driving from the Abu main camp to my tent on the other side of the lagoon. I saw a big old bull elephant in his 40s or 50s standing thirty yards from the road, eating and just chilling out, calm and relaxed. It was a hot, still afternoon and the flies were bothering him, buzzing around the moisture in his eyes, so he was picking up a little dust from the ground in his trunk and puffing it on the flies. As I stopped, he looked at me and shook his head. I watched him for about ten minutes, talking to him all the while, as I do with our elephants. When he started to walk away, I called out, "Hey! Don't go, come here!"

'He turned and walked straight up to me, stopping about five feet from the car. My first reaction was to picture that big leader of the herd of elephants in The Jungle Book. *Looking down on me was a very big boy and I was looking up at him feeling somewhat intimidated. His body language was not threatening, his trunk was quite relaxed, the end lying on the ground. It was as if he was saying, "Well, you called me, now what do you want?" I kept talking while we just looked at each other, connecting, the most incredible energy passing between us. Two different species were actually communicating. He was letting me know that he knew I belonged there, that I was not an occasional visitor, but part of his world. It felt like hours but it was only a few minutes before he turned and walked away. I was so elated, I felt I had won the lottery and drove home with a big grin stuck on my face.*

'The next day I saw him again, not in the same place but it was the same elephant. I stopped and, once again, called out, "Hey, come here." And, once

again, he did. I kept talking and again we had this great buzz between us; it was a moment of such emotional intensity that I find it hard to describe. I told Daniela about it, she being the one person who would really understand, as she had an exceptional rapport with our elephants. We went out together to look for him. We found him, but this time he would not come up to the car. He just walked on.

'It was an experience of great revelation. I knew, right then, that I had equal rights, not just with elephants but with all the species. It started to change fundamentally the way I looked at life.'

Eventually the time came for Michael to move on. He had been in Botswana for many years and felt it was time to return to South Africa. Michael has now set up his own safari company concentrating on using top guides. He also consults for other safari companies. His business is called Passage to Africa and it has become a great success.

Many people who knew him at Abu's Camp have chosen to travel with him again. His bush walks are recognised as being extra special. Having walked on equal terms with all creatures in the bush, he feels a great empathy with them, and the people who walk with him recognise that the animals return the compliment. Michael knows Botswana extremely well, but also loves taking guests to explore South Africa, where he introduces them to little-known gems off the much-trodden tourist tracks, in the Karoo, parts of KwaZulu-Natal and the Limpopo province.

When he lived in Botswana he was married, and later got divorced. The marriage produced his beloved daughter, Tagatha, whom he sees as often as he can. He is now married to Kate McGhee and feels that his life is at last complete and he is utterly happy. Kate has a degree in zoology and botany, which, combined with Michael's knowledge, gives them both an even deeper understanding of the bush.

OUR PLACE ON THE PLANET

Michael explains his unusual philosophy of walking in the bush, a feeling that grew from that hot, still afternoon when he made contact with the large wild bull elephant:

'Reading the map of the wilderness is the first step in personal evolution on a walking safari. As you find your own pace and clear your mind of its daily baggage, leaving it strewn to blow away in the morning breeze, the world around you comes to inhabit gently the space so made.

'We have this Judaeo-Christian ethic of dominion over the planet and all its inhabitants, which is just utter nonsense. We could learn so much about humility and our role on earth from an animal like an elephant. With its communication skills, emotional intelligence, lifespan – the caring, the depth and the social bonds – it's impossible to think of ourselves as better: you really can't.

'Think of a female elephant: in her entire life of 60-odd years, she will never be more than maybe 150 metres from one of her relatives. Think of that in your terms, being born into a herd or clan, with the matriarch and the whole family structure, and all that that involves. The bonds you create day in and day out, going through the good times, the bad times, the droughts, the fruiting, the matings, the first child, expelling your sons from the herd and the deaths. Think of the intelligence required to maintain those bonds over 60 years with very little aggression or animosity. There is a little – some don't get on, some are a bit difficult but, on the whole, they manage extremely well and could teach us so much.

'I am, as we all are, fundamentally an animal. We have the same senses and we all have our strengths and our weaknesses. We are very weak of body, but we are very strong of eyesight; we are very inventive and can consequentialise quickly and effectively. If we walk into a situation, we can assess it at once, which gives us a lot of advantages. Each animal has to learn how to deal with the situations that arise. An impala has its advantages; a lion has too. If you learn to play to them and understand them, then you are not an intruder. People who go on safari think they are intruders; they are *not – at least not on foot; in a vehicle you are, undoubtedly. On foot, though, you are reacting to one another; all animals react to one another in one way or another.*

'An example of subtle inter-species communication is the way impalas react to baboons. Half the time, the two species just sit together, relaxed in each other's company. Baboons are quick to give a warning bark when danger is near, but sometimes one of the big male baboons may take a young impala – they love the curdled milk in the stomach. Impalas understand this and are on guard with their young, always aware of what the baboons are doing. Hanging out with the elephants taught me to recognise these subtleties – seeing them happening all around me in their natural environment, camouflaged by the elephants. I learnt how to walk on my own, without the elephants, knowing the animals were aware of human intrusion, but without influencing them or their reacting unfavourably to me.

'I have an unconventional attitude to walking in the bush. I feel we have a right to be there. It's all about territory; drop me into the Elephant Back concession and I walk as if I own the place, because I did, for nine years, but when you walk on someone else's land, you are the stranger and must be polite and respectful. I try to always have a gun-bearer with me when walking with clients, and prefer not to carry the rifle myself. It is best to walk as if you don't have a rifle, relying on animal body language instead.

'People, like animals, also have personalities and it is up to me to learn to understand each of my guests – which ones really want to walk, which only want a short stroll and which really don't want to leave the vehicle. I try with all my heart to make them understand that they, too, are only a part of nature and that we have to strive to live together in harmony in the ever-decreasing space on this small planet of ours.'

Over the years, Michael has continued to try with all his heart to make his guests understand the importance of living in harmony with nature. He feels that guiding is of paramount importance and he founded Passage to Africa with guiding in mind. This tour-operating company has grown considerably over the last nine years, and has offices in Cape Town,

Hoedspruit, Nairobi and Ireland. But guiding is still of great importance to Michael. He works with a group of carefully selected guides to create safaris around the expertise of the guides, rather than creating an itinerary first. Another part of his business involves servicing the needs of independent guides, booking lodges, outfitting mobile camps and arranging flights. Given his understanding of what is needed, it is a great service that he gives these clients.

Michael takes around six to eight safaris a year himself, and always looks for unusual destinations in remote areas to allow his guests to understand the tranquillity of the wilderness. He blends adventure with luxurious comfort on all his safaris. Like most of the top guides, he is exploring further afield, and takes safaris in Ethiopia, Chad, Uganda, Zambia, Zimbabwe, Tanzania and Botswana. He is probably one of the only guides to do full-scale safaris in Uganda; most arrange a quick visit to see the gorillas for a couple of days, and then continue, or return, to Kenya. Uganda has an incredible wealth of wildlife and beauty, which tends to be overlooked. Michael also visits the Zakouma National Park in Chad. Huge and beautiful, this national park is one of the last strongholds of central African wildlife and is considered a major conservation success story. Says Michael:

'I went to the DRC [Democratic Republic of Congo] this year, so now I have seen the mountain gorillas in Rwanda, Uganda and the DRC, which makes it nice to compare the different experiences. The DRC was fantastic. We climbed Mount Nyiragongo, an active volcano in the Virunga National Park, tracked gorillas a couple of times in small groups and stayed in the very comfortable Mikeno Lodge. It is much more laid back there than Rwanda and Uganda, and less expensive. The guides were excellent and the rangers were the best of all three countries, and the most committed. They have had to face phenomenal hardship to stay with these gorillas through all the conflict there. Many people have died and life has been extraordinarily difficult. It's the ones that have seen it all through who are deeply committed. The gorilla groups were fantastic, and the walking really easy, as they are mainly in the saddle of the mountains. It was starting to become much easier

to go there but now the conflict has flared up again. I haven't yet been to the Odzala-Kokoua National Park in the Republic of Congo, where they have lowland gorillas, but hope to see that next year.'

Michael has been instrumental in setting up a website called Safarious, an excellent site for lovers of adventures and safaris. He has also been a part of the formation of a society called Shackleton and Selous, about which there is more information in the last chapter. Michael is now living in Cape Town with his wife, Kate, and their three boys.

Michael would never have understood the Okavango Delta as he does without the influence of Mothupi (who features in the next chapter) when he first started guiding at Santawani. They remain friends to this day and I spent an enchanting afternoon talking to Mothupi at Khwai Lodge, on the edge of the Moremi Reserve.

MOTHUPI MORUTHA

The Bayei people have lived in northern Botswana for over 200 years, where they have traditionally plied the waterways of the Okavango Delta in *mokoro* fashioned from tree trunks. The tribe had moved down from the north and shared the area already occupied by the Bushmen, or San, whose existence stretches back into the mists of time. The Bayei used to lead a semi-nomadic life. During the dry months, they lived, hunted and fished throughout the delta, but once the rains came they returned to their villages in the dry land on the edge of the delta, rebuilt their grass huts and grew crops.

Mothupi's family hunted in the Xakanaxa area of the eastern delta long before it became part of the Moremi Wildlife Reserve. It was their place and all that they knew. Mothupi was born there, in one of the most exquisite places in that special wetland, where immense, luminous lagoons melt into the distance, giving a sense of space lacking in the more common narrow channels and waterways. With prolific stocks of game, including plenty of hippos (the Bayei's favourite meat), it was a veritable paradise for Mothupi's father, Sinokora Morutha, and his family.

When I met him, Mothupi was an arthritic old man, who walked with difficulty but concealed any sign of pain with a beaming smile that shone among the folds of his face. A natural raconteur, he told the stories of the life of Bayei hunters before the advent of tourism with humour, wisdom and wit. On a sunny afternoon, while sitting on the banks of the Khwai River, Mothupi told me how it was in the beginning:

'It was at Santawani that I started in safaris. Santawani was my hunting ground and I was there hunting. But I heard a rumour that someone was coming to put up a camp, a safari lodge. So I waited, making my palm wine, hunting and fishing until eventually somebody came. There were not many people around – just me and my friends. These new people needed somebody to help them to put up the camp, so I came with my friends. We were casual, temporary workers – we made the camp, then I was supposed to go away. But the guides came from South Africa. It was 1969 and they didn't know this area; there were no roads, nothing, so I had to go with them to show them which way to go. Then the people had to go in a mokoro and none of these white guides could take a mokoro. They asked me if I could take the mokoro and I told them that poling the mokoro is what I do.

'I was born in Xakanaxa in 1940. It was my father's hunting area. He had to move away from the village and go there to hunt because there were no animals around the village and he took my mother with him when she was pregnant. In the hunting area, we would sleep on the islands away from the lions, under a tree, sometimes with a little wooden fence around us for protection. We wore skins and hunted with snares and spears. We did not have wire snares. Now you can find wire everywhere but in my time there was no wire – you had to find the plants to make the rope for the snares. The animal would step in the trap, which would catch him on the foot, and then we would run to kill him with the spear.

'We would stay there for all the dry season, which maybe would start from May just as we finished harvesting our small crops. We didn't abandon the crops – we would dig a hole in the ground and put the ash in to protect the grain, then cover it up. No one stayed in the village. Everyone, all the children and the old people, went to the hunting areas. We would stay there until December, when the rainy season started. If it started early, we made a very small grass shelter to keep us dry – just big enough to lie *in. Then we would move back home and start to plough. Our houses at our village today are also temporary houses; we make them each year. We always use* mokoro *to move around – sometimes we kill the big animals and we take the skins in the* mokoro *too. If we want to go by* mokoro *to Maun with our skins, it is a very long way. There is a big land in between Xakanaxa and the river that goes to Maun. It is Chief's Island and we have to go all the way up, practically to the Panhandle, before we can turn down the other side. This is why we keep some* mokoro *on the other side because we can walk there and pick them up, making the journey to Maun much quicker. We had plenty* mokoro. *We kill the hippos, the leopards, the lions, all the animals, and we take the skins to Maun to sell them. But today the river is too dry: you can't go to Maun by* mokoro *any more.*

'*We came back every year to hunt the same area, until 1962. That was the last year for me. My father came in 1963 but I didn't go with him. I was working then for Tsetse Fly Control. That year, they told my father he had to stop hunting his area because it was going to be adopted into the Moremi Reserve. They gave him two weeks' notice to take everything away from there and move to a new bit of land outside the reserve. It was a good area but he was not really familiar with it. Everybody was unhappy: they didn't understand what game reserve meant – they are not educated people. I think about my* mokoro; *I have not seen that* mokoro *since 1962, when I put it under the water by the island with a small marula tree. I wrote the date on the marula tree: August 1962. One day I will go back and fetch it.*

'*I never went to school. My father taught me to read and write. A long time before I was born, my father ran away from his parents in the Panhandle to find a job in Maun. The only job he could find was to herd cattle. Maun was just mud huts and a trading store. He was employed by the man with the trading store; that man was a white man. He would buy some cattle from the local people and hire some boys to drive the cattle all the way to Rhodesia, crossing the river at Kazungula to sell the cattle. When he got there, my father didn't want to come back. He found a job with a very kind man who put him in school – otherwise he would never learn to write. There was nothing here, only bush and no one to teach. But* his parents missed him and his brother was homesick for him. His father was a chief in that area and he organised some guys to go with his eldest son to Rhodesia to find him and bring him back because he can't go alone. He was very worried when he heard people were looking for him. He thought maybe he would go to jail, but when he saw his brother he decided to go home. He took with him his two books, the Bible and a book that tells me how far it is to the moon from the earth.

'He started to teach me in 1953 when I was thirteen years. He taught me from the Bible, which was in Setswana. The other book taught me how far the moon is, but it was in English and too difficult for me. In those days, everybody learned from the Bible – that was the only book. First I wanted to learn how to read then I wanted to try to do writing, but beyond that if I could only find a place where I could go to school, where I could try the English, I would be glad.

'Then, in 1958, I went to South Africa to work in the mines. I went because I wanted to see what it was. I had heard a lot of stories and I wanted to go to school. And there was no work in Botswana. I went to Maun to sign up. I was wearing my skins, so they gave me trousers, shoes and a shirt. Then they flew me to Francistown to take a train to Johannesburg. I went with somebody who was older; he had been before, and he was the one guiding me. He helped me even with the language. You speak another language on the mines, Fanagalo. So, in my spare time, I went to the night school. I worked for fourteen months in the mines, then I went home and hunted. Then, later, I took out another contract to work in the mines again. I did that for five times until 1968, when I stopped mining.

'They looked after us very well at the mines. The work was very, very hard, but the night school was good and the food was very, very good. There was not a shortage of food. You don't have to store the food – you just eat and when you have had enough, you throw it away. I had never seen that before. I worked for Anglo American in some very deep mines, City Deep Mine, Western Area and Western Deep. Sometimes we were 2 or 3 kilometres underground, with no room to move under the low rock, where we would break up the rocks and put them onto a little belt that would ship them up to the top. We worked from four o'clock in the morning until four o'clock in the afternoon. Sometimes you would finish your work early but you had to wait in a queue to get in the cage to go up. It was a very strange place for a Bayei, especially at that time, because I knew nothing, except about the animals. I just went there like a lechwe or an impala. I had never seen a train and I had never got up into the aeroplane. The pay was not very good – three shillings and fourpence per day. Things were cheaper in those days, but it was not a lot of money. My people don't really save money because we could not keep domestic animals, as our land was covered in tsetse flies, so what I did with my money was to buy clothing and weapons for hunting, and a big trap for catching lions and leopards. My father had one gun, so I had to buy another gun for when the two of us go hunting. It is better to have a second gun, then we could help each other if one of us was attacked; the spear is not good enough.

'In 1968 I finished in the mine; I started at that camp in 1969. George Bates is the man that started the camp but he died in an aircraft crash. It was called Mekoro Trails but in 1973 they sold it to Gametrackers and it was called Santawani. My job was to tell the South African guides where to go. Now there are roads everywhere but then there was nothing. It was only the third lodge; first Khwai then Xugana then Santawani. We never had visitors from overseas; they all came from the neighbouring countries. I didn't know any birds; the South Africans taught me all the birds. My job was to do the mokoro and they were very knowledgeable about the birds. They made me stop for every one, and this is how I learned their names. And, beyond that, I took the other guides to teach them where to go with the mokoro.

'For twelve years I did the mokoro until Mike Myers came in and they decided to train me as the guide driving. In 1982 they took me to Khwai to learn to eat at the table. They trained me how to use the knife and fork, and I was the only black man eating with the guests. Even I believe I was the first, or maybe second, black man to get my guide's licence. I have worked all these years for the same company; other people have bought it but it is the same lodges. Now Santawani is not used. The water has gone away and so have the animals. But in the beginning, it was very, very lovely.

'It was in 1969 that I found my wife, Njahe. She lived in the area and we were related. We would marry maybe as the third or fourth generation, not closer than that. It was because there were not many people. It is not like the old days: nowadays we choose who we will marry. Girls would marry after fifteen years, after they start to be a lady. In our culture, when a girl turns to be a lady she is hidden in the bush for one year. Only the mother and other ladies see her. No men can see her. Men are told not to go on this side; you have to go the other way to start hunting. She has a hood over her head and the exposed parts of her body, her legs and arms and her face, are covered in clay from a termite mound.

'I had the time to approach her because her family had come to hunt in the area where I was working. I knew the family but had never seen her. She came out of hiding and I think, that is the one for me. She was dressed in nice beads, and all her skin and the skins she wore were covered in ochre. We are engaged together from 1970 and we have two daughters and one son. Ten years ago we got officially married because the rules say you must have a legal wife. I did have another wife before Njahe. She was very pretty but she was always complaining, so I left her.

'Now I live at Khwai and my wife lives at Shorobe, on the road to Maun. I work like everybody, three months on and one month off. My first daughter got married on the 29th of August 2003 and I have taken her and her husband in a powerboat I hired to see the Xakanaxa area where I grew up. Even though I asked permission from the Parks Department if I could go and find my mokoro, I did not find it because we did not have the time to get there. One day I will be going back to get it.'

Mothupi was a fount of information on the Bayei culture – their medicines, methods of hunting, superstitions and legends – and could talk about them for hours. The Gametrackers' lodges, where he spent his whole professional life, are now owned by Orient Express Safaris, and Mothupi, the treasure they inherited, was employed at Khwai River Lodge as resident storyteller.

Not long after I had met Mothupi, he decided it was time to go home and spend the rest of his days with his wife and family in his village. He was an old man who had had a remarkable life. He died in 2005, the year *Licence to Guide* was published, but it was quite a while before the news reached me. I had sent a copy of the book to Maun to be given to him but I have no idea if he ever received it. He was immensely popular and much loved. Onx Manga, the senior guide at Khwai River Lodge where Mothupi had been based, suggested that as a memorial to him, they would build a boma, which would be known as Mothupi's Boma. Onx went to Mothupi's village to talk to Mothupi's widow about this plan:

'The most challenging thing for me was to go to his wife's home to get her permission. We couldn't just call the boma after him; it had to be done in a traditional way. After I had talked to her about her family and life without Mothupi, I said I had another reason to see her and that was to ask her permission to name the boma after her husband, which she thought was a great honour. I also told her that we would like her and her daughter, along with Mothupi's uncle, who was still alive, to come to the big celebration for the opening.'

Five of the tented rooms were put aside for Mothupi's family, and the guests, who were lucky enough to be there for this gala opening, occupied the other 10. Onx made the introductory speech, and Malcolm, the Orient Express Safaris manager, explained a bit about Mothupi's connection with Orient Express, originally Gametrackers. His uncle told the story of Mothupi's early life, translated by Onx. It was a splendid affair. The wine flowed; the African food was at its best and the evening ended with a choral tribute to Mothupi's life.

A boma is a traditional meeting place in an African village, used for eating, singing, dancing and talking. It is enclosed with a fence of poles and usually has a large fire pit in the centre. In a safari lodge, a boma is used for giving the guests a special dinner of traditional African food, often with a serenade by the camp choir.

Some of the guests who were there that night have been back again and all have very fond memories of that special evening. Every guest nowadays who dines in the boma is told about why it is Mothupi's Boma.

I believe he never went back to find his *mokoro*.

ONKGAOTSE MANGA

Onkgaotse, known as Onx, was born in Maun, Botswana, on the edge of the Okavango Delta, in 1975. He grew up and went to school in this bustling little town, whose main purpose was to service the safari industry. His introduction to the spectacular beauty of the delta was on short visits with his mother to see his father, who worked for the Tsetse Fly Control Department, whenever they were working within easy distance of Maun. From an early age, he knew he had to be involved with wildlife, but was uncertain of which direction to take.

His early passion found expression in starting a wildlife club at school. Through the local Wildlife Department he arranged for guest lecturers to come to the school and the club members volunteered their time at weekends to clean up Lechwe Park, a small wildlife park outside Maun belonging to the Maun Wildlife School.

Knowing he wanted to work with nature in some capacity and having completed his O levels, he discussed his options with his father, who suggested he join an anti-poaching unit. However, he had mixed feelings about hunting. Although he abhorred trophy hunting, he nevertheless understood that a man with a hungry family might have to kill for the pot, so this was something he did not relish getting involved in.

Another option was guiding, which had far greater appeal. He enrolled at the Wildlife School near Maun, where he discovered that the knowledge he had already gained from the wildlife club and from devouring all the books he could find on the subject far outstripped that of most of the other students. For example, he knew the local and botanical names of all the trees before he joined. He was their star pupil.

When he had completed the course, he joined the Desert and Delta Safari Company for his apprenticeship, and was based at Savuti Safari Lodge – the old Lloyd's Camp, renamed when it was acquired by Desert and Delta. While in Savuti, together with the camp manager, he tested his theory of 'elephant pruning'. This is when elephants break mopane trees to about two metres so that the young elephants can feed on the new leaves at their own height after the rains. Map Ives had recently examined the same theory. Onx loves pointing this out to visitors, as it indicates yet again the clear evidence of animal intelligence.

Desert and Delta would have liked him to stay when his apprenticeship was completed but he felt he would still be considered an apprentice, and decided to move on when Orient Express Safaris offered him a job. Now their top guide, he travels between three camps, Khwai River Lodge, Savuti Elephant Camp and Eagle Island Lodge, entertaining and educating their guests.

His serious, dedicated side is ever present, and his mentor has been Pete Hancock, an ex-lecturer at the Wildlife School and a member of Endangered Wildlife Trust (EWT). Pete left the school to work as an independent nature consultant for community development and the lodges, but was quickly approached by Endangered Species to become coordinator of Birdlife Botswana – part of EWT. Knowing that Onx would be interested, Pete enrolled him to assist in their crane project. His initiation was to participate in a workshop in the Kafue Park, in Zambia, organised by a very experienced South African group. At the end of this, he became a full working member whose task is to monitor wattled cranes in the Khwai area of the Moremi Game Reserve.

Each day Onx is up before dawn to take his guests on their game drive, and returns to camp for brunch. Once his guests are happily surveying the world from the hammocks on their tent decks, he is out again taking GPS coordinates of new nest sites, and recording the behaviour of the birds and the troubles they face. These reports go via Pete Hancock to the EWT. Cranes have huge problems. There are four pairs in the Khwai area but only one chick has hatched in four years of monitoring. One of the common causes of breeding failure is predation of the eggs, particularly by pythons. But another serious cause is the threatened habitat. Onx plays a key role in community awareness, educating the communities, particularly in the Jao Flats and Xaxaba areas. He talks to the *mokoro* polers and guides, making them understand the importance of the crane in the ecosystem and engaging them to help in their preservation. Until this project began, no one had realised the importance of not burning the grass during May to August when the cranes breed. Onx is truly fulfilled in his role as guide and protector, and he is slowly getting the message through:

'I don't consider this a job – it is a lifestyle. As long as I love it, I will always do it. I don't see myself happy doing anything else. I believe as long as there are people like Pete Hancock, there is hope. If I had to sacrifice my job, I would definitely teach in the remote community areas to open the minds of the young. If I could, I would take off three months to do full-time monitoring and educating. If I could do that, I would make sure they would never burn again at the wrong time of year, but always in November, just before the rains when it can really benefit the grazing for livestock and not destroy the nests of the cranes. I am volunteering to go to Namibia for the Save the Rhino Trust during my next leave. Again, this involves community education and will extend my knowledge. I love doing voluntary work; I see it as a way of giving something back to nature. After all, I have had so much.'

In 2005, Onx was approached to join Disney in Florida to work at the Animal Kingdom. He set off on the journey from Maun to Orlando via Johannesburg and Atlanta with great excitement, and more than a little trepidation. The only hiccup on the journey was at Atlanta Airport, where they operate what is known as an automated people mover, or plane train. He needed to be transported from the main terminal to one of the satellite concourses for his flight to Orlando. Onx spent hours searching for a railway station, until, finally bewildered, he asked someone, who pointed out to him that he had just walked through the train, which to him, looked like an empty corridor!

Finally, he arrived at the Animal Kingdom, where he was to be an education officer, based at the lodge. He didn't know what to expect and was filled with curiosity. He had heard so much about Disneyland and when he saw it at last his only thought was that 'it is so fake that it's real!' He had come from Khwai Lodge, in Botswana, with just 15 rooms, to a place with 1 000 rooms.

After two weeks', training and orientation on how to do it all the Disney way, he started his lectures, which they named cultural safaris. He had taken his own material, and gave talks and slide shows three times a week to packed audiences. He managed to see a bit of the United States through friends and acquaintances from Botswana. A Texan family that he had guided on a trip in Botswana discovered that he was at Disney and flew him out to their ranch in San Antonio for a visit that was so successful that he spent Thanksgiving and Christmas with them. Days off were few and far between, but he did manage to get to see New York City. Altogether, Onx had a most stimulating and interesting 18 months, and his time there resulted in many new American visitors to Botswana – people who wanted to get a taste of the real thing.

On his return to Botswana and Orient Express, he was asked to manage one of their camps, which was in need of a manager. He enjoyed managing the camp, which led him a few months later to be sent to do a management course at Cape Town's Graduate School of Business. He thoroughly enjoyed his time in Cape Town, did extremely well on his course, made lots of friends, walked up Table Mountain and lived in one of the guest cottages at the Mount Nelson Hotel. I think most people would enjoy that.

Back in Maun, instead of becoming a lodge manager, he was offered the position of environmental officer based in Maun, but with plenty of access to the bush. He is responsible for all the guides, their training and equipment, and now, thanks to Onx, Orient Express has a very in-depth guide-training programme. Although he primarily works with the guides and the community projects, he is in fact responsible for the company's whole environmental programme:

'I brought in five new young guides and they learnt their skills from scratch. First of all, I sit down and listen to all they know. They come from very rural areas and know a huge amount about animal behaviour and the natural progress of the seasons and migrations, etc., but they know nothing else, not even football. I teach them to open their minds, to listen and learn. I send them to listen in on guests' conversations over dinner or drinks then they come back the next day to tell me about global warming affecting the polar bears, or ozone layers, or American football – in fact a multitude of subjects of which they have never heard. I also send the men to learn about other parts of Africa – for example, gorillas and chimpanzees; they watch videos and discuss them. They are gradually picking up general knowledge on new subjects that might come up – from Manchester United to deforestation.'

Onx pointed out that people will ask the guides what they think about the poaching of mountain gorillas, for example. There are no gorillas in Botswana and these young men had never heard of them. However, the point is that they learnt about issues that interested their clients, and now they guide to a very high standard as a result of their own knowledge of their environment – and they are also able to converse about other issues. And they have all read Garth Thompson's *The Guide's Guide to Guiding*, the greatest book on guiding with common sense and understanding.

The standard of guiding in Botswana has risen considerably. Every guide now has to qualify at the guiding school and obtain a certificate to work as a guide in the country. All of Onx's protégés go through this process and pass the school's exams.

Onx is always looking for ways to make visitors have unusual and enjoyable experiences with him. One of his ideas was to offer a self-drive experience in a 4 x 4 vehicle. Clients drive from one camp to another; a professional guide accompanies them, who knows the route and will take over if fatigue kicks in, which is possible travelling from Khwai Lodge in the Moremi to Savuti, a journey that takes nearly a whole day. Along with challenging roads to navigate, there are three rivers to be crossed and the Savuti Marsh. This is the type of adventure many people long for, and one that is not often on the menu. The first time Onx did this self-drive experience was with the boss of Orient Express, Sandro Fabris:

'He was so excited about the drive, when we reached the first river crossing I could see him shaking, asking, "What do I do? What gear must I use?" I said, "Just keep calm. This is what you do: keep your foot on the pedal and don't stall it." As soon as the car started to rise out of the river and up the bank, I could see this big smile across his face and he said, "You are not going to drive this car, I shall take it all the way to Savuti."

'It was October, and when we reached the Savuti Marsh it was late afternoon and the elephants were coming in, because the Savuti Marsh is flowing again and this guy was driving to the camp through a thousand elephants. He said he had never had such a thrilling day in all his life.

'There are so many people who are adventurous or like exciting activities. They always have the choice – the guide can drive as soon as they get tired, so they can just sit back and watch the scene.'

Another of Onx's innovative ideas is to take guests out on night drives equipped with night-vision binoculars. This was an idea he picked up at the Disney Wildlife Park. It has proved to be extremely popular. The night drive starts with the help of a spotlight, but once the vehicle reaches an active area the spotlight is switched off and the night-vision binoculars are used to view the extraordinarily busy night-time scenes.

I asked Onx recently about the wattled cranes he was so carefully researching in the Khwai area when I first met him. These are fragile, endangered birds that need very large pristine areas in which to breed and thrive. In fact, the presence of wattled cranes indicates a healthy, flourishing environment. He told me that the pair he had been observing since I first met him in 2002 had raised three chicks to adulthood by 2012. This is excellent news. They have great difficulty breeding, as their eggs tend to be eaten by pythons, and, occasionally, if the waters rise too rapidly, the nests can float away.

Onx is enthusiastic about the future of the ever-popular tourist destinations. He loves the fact that he still guides, as well as thinking up and implementing new ideas to make his safaris unusually interesting.

THE
WILDLIFE DIVERSITY
OF ZIMBABWE
AND ZAMBIA

The great Zambezi River divides Zimbabwe and Zambia - both fascinating countries, and each unique in its own way. The river rises in Zambia and flows south before turning east at Victoria Falls on its journey to the Indian Ocean. Professional guides in Zimbabwe are known throughout safari Africa to be the best-trained guides in the business.

T he river rises in Zambia and flows south before turning east on its journey to the Indian Ocean. Along the way, it is joined by the Chobe River, crashes over the Victoria Falls, broadens into Lake Kariba, surges through narrow gorges and widens out to flow more slowly between the wildlife areas of Mana Pools National Park, in Zimbabwe, and the Lower Zambezi National Park, in Zambia, areas of great beauty and tranquillity. From Zambia, the Kafue and Luangwa rivers flow into the Zambezi as it surges into Mozambique through the Cahora Bassa Dam.

The crystal-clear waters of Lake Malawi flow down the Shire River, entering the Zambezi beyond the dam before it finally spills over white sands and into the coral reefs of the Indian Ocean. These rivers have been lifelines into central Africa for centuries and early explorers would have been overwhelmed by the huge herds of wildlife they came upon from the mouth to the sources.

The Luangwa River meanders through a vast, fertile valley that is home to a large variety of birds and animals. The continuation of the Great Rift Valley, its escarpments reveal primitive fossils and hot springs occur on the valley floor. Some of the best walking safaris in Africa are on offer here, where walking with professional guides has always been encouraged in the national parks, particularly in the Luangwa Valley.

The Busanga Plains, in the northern area of Zambia's Kafue National Park, is a birder's paradise. From June, when the flood waters begin to recede, until the end of October, visitors might be forgiven for thinking they have entered an aviary inhabited not only by a multitude of birds, but also thousands of puku and lechwe antelope, and their predators. Zambia is not a place of mass tourism but it has a pioneering spirit and it is possible here for a safari guide to take his guests to some of the least visited places in Africa.

Of all the countries specialising in safaris, Zimbabwe has the most diverse scenery and remarkable places, whether reached in a vehicle, on foot or in a canoe. Its most famous landmark, the Victoria Falls, never ceases to astound visitors with its power and beauty. This is a country that has produced excellent safari guides, and was the first to introduce formal training and stiff exams. Wherever you go, the guiding will enhance your experience. In the north and the west are the main wildlife areas, where huge baobab, mahogany and acacia trees shelter immense herds of buffaloes and elephants. In the cooler Eastern Highlands, the rolling hills and morning mist rising over trout streams are reminiscent of Scotland. South of the heat and dust of Hwange National Park, rise the atmospheric, bush-fringed granite boulders of the Matobo Hills, near Bulawayo, steeped in history and magic. This ancient place was once home to the San people, who left behind countless cave paintings thousands of years old – an epitaph to the enigma of their past.

GARTH THOMPSON

G arth Thompson is a Zimbabwean, based in Harare, but he is happiest when he is as far from city life as possible. His favourite place on earth is Mana Pools, on the northern border of his country, where many of his guests meet him on a red-earth airstrip surrounded by thick thorn bushes a few miles from the Zambezi. The energy he radiates is contagious, filling his guests with excited anticipation from the moment they meet. Without doubt, Garth would have spotted something special on the way to collect them, making sure their game viewing began before they were even halfway through the cold drinks provided as they clambered aboard his vehicle.

Game viewing is of paramount importance to Garth. He believes this is what his guests have principally come to Africa for and not a moment should be wasted. His speciality is canoeing down the Zambezi River, where he makes every minute of the day count. All experienced guides are adept at creating memorable and special moments, knowing that the pictures in your head will long outlast any scene you have ever photographed. Garth is a true expert at 'stage productions' in his beloved Zambezi Valley.

He gets everyone into their canoes before sunrise. And how right he is – all the moaning and groaning about the early start are soon forgotten as that spectacular red ball eases up over the horizon, painting the river with pink, then golden light. Feelings of joy and exhilaration overcome us as the canoes slide peacefully through the smooth water. Roosting cormorants stretch their wings to catch the first warmth of the sun and herons glide silently by on their way to their favourite fishing grounds. Ten minutes longer in bed and we would have missed it all.

Like all good guides, Garth has an exceptional knowledge of wildlife, but when he is guiding on the lower Zambezi it seems to go deeper. This is his spiritual home, where he has personal knowledge of individual animals, especially hippos and elephants. He knows where the bad-tempered lone hippo bulls hang out, and gives them a wide berth in the canoes. He also knows many of the bull elephants, so prominent in Mana Pools, which have adopted that stretch of the Zambezi as their personal property. Some of the best game viewing may be had in the heat of the day, when thirsty animals flock to the water. Garth is adamant that an hour or two spent sitting in the shade of a tree near a waterhole is a lot more rewarding than a siesta in a zipped-up tent. He loves listening to the natural sounds of the bush, which is why he prefers canoeing, walking and riding, as opposed to guiding in vehicles and noisy motorboats. However, he understands the need for a vehicle to get up close and into the right position to take good wildlife photos. He is a good photographer himself.

Once when we were walking with Garth, he spotted a small group of elephants heading for the river. We were close to the river, so he took us into a small dip, where we were instructed firmly to crouch down and keep dead still. These wonderful beasts appeared just above us and trundled down to the water's edge only a yard or two away. Hearts pounding, we watched as they drank and swam. Their stomachs rumbled (were they acknowledging us?) as they strolled into the beds of water hyacinth for their morning snack, and we could relax and let out our breath at last!

Garth knows how to make a Zambezi canoe trip a most rewarding experience. His famous 'leg over' on the river (the canoes are held together by putting a leg over the next canoe) allows everyone to keep still while watching a baby elephant frolic with its mother at the water's edge, or a timid impala coming down to drink. Breakfast is sometimes served in the middle of the river on a sandbank in shallow water. With the table and stools pushed into the sand, everyone calmly eats home-made muesli and drinks coffee while knee-deep in the Zambezi (apparently crocodiles like only deep, dark water). Being on that river is a thrilling experience, but being there with Garth takes the experience into another realm.

Garth comes from tough pioneer stock. His Huguenot ancestors arrived at the Cape in 1688 and his great-grandparents were among the first settlers to arrive in Rhodesia 200 years later, where they farmed cattle, fruit and maize near Fort Victoria (now Masvingo), the first town to be pioneered in what became Southern Rhodesia. When Garth was born, his parents lived on the outskirts of Salisbury (Harare), by then a bustling city. His father was involved on a part-time basis in the control of problem animals in farming areas, where elephants were breaking fences and destroying maize crops, and lions were killing the livestock. Farmers regarded these wild animals as a major hindrance to their livelihood.

Garth's outdoor life began at the tender age of three when he was considered old enough to go out with his father on expeditions. Although he was not allowed to go on the hunts, and instead remained in the safety of the camp under the buck sail – a canvas tarpaulin providing shade and shelter – until his father's return, he still managed to sense the adventure. During those childhood days, the seed of excitement and appreciation of the great outdoors was sown. By the age of nine, Garth had become obsessed with the wild areas around his home and spent many hours devising interesting trails on which he took his mother's guests, who frequently came to tea. The landscape included a river, waterfalls, rocks and jungle areas, all of which provided a surprise at every turn. This was the germination of his guiding style today: he loves to create surprises.

His deep interest in nature remained with him through his teens, and he persuaded his girlfriends to explore the trails with him, rather than spending time waterskiing and dancing the night away in the local disco. During his A levels, he was employed by South African mining company

Goldfields to assist a geologist in the south-eastern corner of Rhodesia, adjacent to the Gonarezhou National Park. He had little interest in the rocks and soil that he awoke each morning at 4 am to help collect, but after nine, while the geologist was examining his finds, Garth's services were no longer required, and he had the freedom to explore this vast and fascinating area for the rest of the day.

After military service (he spent four years in the army, three on active service), he had planned to work for Rhodesia's National Parks Department, but by a twist of fate his future was sealed during a squash game. His squash partner that day was a particularly pretty girl who had caught the eye of one of the men playing on the adjacent court. One ball went astray, then another. The second time this happened, Garth went to borrow a ball from the players on the next court. The man who could not take his eyes off Garth's friend said that he would only lend him one if he could have a game with his pretty partner. While the two of them played squash, Garth sat talking to the other player, who turned out to be the personnel manager of Southern Sun Hotels, the company that owned the only three safari lodges in Rhodesia at that time. By the end of the game, Garth had landed himself a job. Three weeks later, he arrived at Hwange Safari Lodge, situated in a 26 000-hectare concession bordering the Hwange National Park. The plane he had arrived in was shot down by guerrillas on its return leg of the journey, killing all 52 passengers on board. The tourist industry, almost non-existent at that time, had suffered a major blow and 10 days after this incident the lodge was closed.

However, Garth remained in the camp training a militia force to protect the animals and the lodge. They built and repaired roads, firebreaks and boreholes, and Garth headed up the anti-poaching team on the reserve. He took this opportunity to study the wildlife and learn all he could from the experience. He would ask the local people for the names of the trees in Ndebele and then find them in the *Rhodesian Botanical Dictionary* and Keith Coates's *Palgrave's Trees of Southern Africa*. He noted what the animals ate by examining their droppings. He learnt about the intelligent behaviour of elephants, the breeding habits of birds and generally how the whole ecological system linked together like a jigsaw.

Once the lodge reopened in 1980, the company changed from Southern Sun Hotels to Zimbabwe Sun Hotels. Garth was apprenticed to Dave Rushworth, the newly appointed resident guide, and began studying for his guide's licence. Dave had a huge influence on Garth because of his knowledge not only of wildlife, but also of tourists – there had been so few in Hwange around then that most young guides were ignorant of their requirements. The Hwange Safari Lodge possessed one 1964 Land Rover to do the game drives on the estate. The vehicle had a viewing hatch above the seats behind the guide, and could comfortably seat four guests and the guide.

Dave and Garth always went on the drives together, whether it was with one guest or 14! This number may sound unfeasible, but one could squeeze into the front with Dave, three behind him, and four facing one another on the rear bench seats. Garth would be on the roof along with six other guests – three in the front and four behind the viewing hatch in the back. In those days, the game drive cost four Zimbabwean dollars per person. Although four dollars was worth a lot more then than it is today, it was still excellent value. The drive started at 4 pm and they returned at 8.55 pm, ready to take out the night-drive clients at 9 pm. The night drive was scheduled to return at 11 pm, but often they stayed out until 1 am. The $4 fee included all drinks, including alcoholic beverages.

Today, game drives at Hwange Safari Lodge cost a lot more; they start at 4 pm, only include soft drinks and return by 6.30 pm sharp.

Garth writes in his book, *The Guide's Guide to Guiding*: '*Dave Rushworth had absolutely no need of money. He was oblivious to time and did not succumb to stress or pressure. He was equally at home with the rich, the poor, old and young alike. He treated everyone as equals and gave 110 per cent of himself to everyone, all of the time! He gave the guests what they had come on safari for – a genuine wildlife experience and to really feel wanted.*'

When he gained his guide's licence in 1983, Garth was one of only eight licensed guides in Zimbabwe, of whom he and John Stevens are the only two still in active guiding. When Dave left to run a wildlife park for the King of Swaziland, Garth was made the wildlife manager of Hwange Safari Lodge and later the manager of all Zimbabwe Sun properties. At the time, these included Bumi Hills Safari Lodge and Water Wilderness.

Garth, who has always been a keen photographer, produced a number of slide shows to share his experiences with the guests at Hwange. His forte was elephant behaviour, having spent six years with what was called the Presidential Herd, which roamed in the large concession area adjacent to the Hwange Safari Lodge. That was a time when a great deal was being discovered about the behaviour of elephants and their remarkable intelligence. From many hours spent observing elephants, Garth was the first to witness what was at the time a new discovery about African elephants – that mature bulls come into musth once a year. A secretion appears from their temporal glands and they dribble urine down their back legs – the condition known as the green-penis syndrome.

The sight of a large male elephant in full musth is something to behold. He will hold his head up high as he swaggers, radiating power and arrogance. You can almost hear him saying, 'I am the greatest!', while the smaller bulls and those not in musth back off and keep out of his way. In normal circumstances, full musth is achieved only when bulls are in their 30s and it is most likely that such a bull will be the one to mate with females that are in full oestrus.

When some North American guests saw his slide shows, they invited Garth to go to the United States and Canada to present his pictures at various zoos. He travelled all over both countries explaining animal behaviour to many audiences. At one venue, in Calgary, 700 people attended. On his first trip to the United Kingdom, the World Wildlife Fund arranged for him to do a presentation that was so successful that news of it reached Buckingham Palace and Prince Philip asked to see the slides. This time, it was for an audience of just two!

At about this time, Garth was invited to invest in Ruckomechi Lodge, in the Mana Pools National Park, which meant leaving Zimbabwe Sun and running the lodge himself. He made his way to the lower Zambezi, where his love affair with the river began.

Mana Pools is a beautiful national park – an enchanted place, situated on the lower Zambezi River in north-eastern Zimbabwe with views of the mountains across the river that are the continuation of the Great Rift Valley that runs down the eastern side of Africa.

It is a gentle landscape of majestic trees with sweet-scented flowers, long vistas and hazy pastel hues that change hourly from a soft golden glow in the morning, through silvery blue at midday, to violet and pink in the evening. In the dry season it is packed with animals. Wherever you look, moving quietly as if in slow motion, there are eland, kudus, impalas, buffaloes, baboons and a constant stream of small groups of elephant families. Towards the end of the dry season, the acacia seedpods are the food of the gods to the elephants, which spend many hours shaking the trees and scuffing through the dry leaves with their trunks to pick them up. A few of these intelligent giants have even learnt to stand on their hind legs to reach them. This is a superb safari area and Garth's favourite. Although he guides all over Africa now, he keeps returning to Mana Pools.

His love affair with his wife, Mel, had started a few years before he went to work in Mana Pools. Married and expecting a baby, they arrived at Ruckomechi Lodge to run it together. Mel then went to Harare for the birth of their son, David, and returned to Mana Pools to visit the lodge when the baby was six weeks old. When he was three months old, she moved back in permanently. Interestingly, their home was a converted water tower. The bedroom was on the top, surrounded by wooden planks and consisting of their bed, a cot and a flush loo. Underneath there was a camping table, two folding chairs and a cold shower. Youth and innocence made this brave move work. The baby just had to fit in with their plans because the alternative – being apart – was not an option. Luckily for them, David was a very easy baby and the guests at the lodge hardly knew he was there. He was seldom ill except for one or two ear infections, which involved consulting a doctor by radio, then waiting anxiously for the next plane to land with new guests – and the antibiotics. Happily, problems of this kind were few and far between. Malaria is always a worry in that region, but with prophylactic syrup for babies and a little canvas cot covered with a mosquito net, David was kept free of this dreaded disease.

The real problems started when David began to crawl. His safety was paramount, so a cage was erected outside the kitchen to keep the animals out and to keep baby in a safe place. Here he happily played all day with his favourite toy, the brightly coloured rattling acacia seed pods. It was not possible to employ a female nanny, as all the staff at Ruckomechi were male, and it would have made life too difficult for one woman to live among the male staff. So, instead, an 18-year-old boy was employed, whose only duty was to watch over David all day.

They had one rather uncomfortable experience when they were returning to the lodge with a supply of frozen meat in a truck. In the vehicle were Garth, his trusted right-hand man, Johannes, Mel and the baby. They were running late and were far from any habitation when the vehicle got stuck in the mud up to its axle. Try as they might, they could not get it moving and had to spend the night in the truck. Luckily, they had brought some baby food and the canvas cot, so David, oblivious of the drama, slept peacefully all night. For the rest of them, there was only a bottle of brandy as sustenance, so they passed the night taking turns to sip from the metal screw cap. Mel spent a sleepless night, convinced that the lions roaring nearby could smell the meat slowly thawing in the back of the vehicle and would appear to investigate at any moment. But the night passed without incident and help appeared at dawn in the form of a search party from the camp. It took five hours to dig the vehicle out.

That Garth and Mel managed so well with the baby while having to spend 18 hours a day looking after guests is almost miraculous, but, finally, when David was about two and a half, they decided it was time to get him back to civilisation. For the next couple of years, Garth ran the lodge, commuting from Harare until David had to start school. In 1987, the family moved to Harare permanently and Garth gave up lodge management and all that went with it: dealing with the storerooms, rubbish pits, workshops and staff problems, and the endless repairs to generators, water pumps and all things mechanical. He started up the canoeing safaris and continued doing this for many years. He took ecstatic clients on magical mystery tours of the Zambezi, skirting hippos, walking in forests, sleeping under the stars and having many close encounters with elephants.

Ever since his move from Ruckomechi Garth has continued to commute to the bush from their lovely house in Harare. Two sisters arrived for David and all three grew up in Harare. They had horses and dogs, and were surrounded by all the trappings of a happy family life. Garth's deep love of the bush and animals has manifested itself in Danny, his eldest daughter, who occasionally helped him with his safaris during school holidays.

He created two companies: Natureways for his canoe and walking safaris, and Safari Consultants to handle lodge bookings and transport. Garth ran Safari Consultants for 20 years and Natureways for 15 years, as well as guiding many of his clients. He sold both companies when it came to the point that there was too much administration, and not enough guiding. Garth has high principles and sent his clients only to those camps and lodges that lived up to his expectations, no matter what commission they offered. Unless they were up to scratch, he would not use them, and as a result Safari Consultants became one of the most respected tour operations in Zimbabwe. His annual detailed reports on all the safari lodges and camps became a bible to the overseas operators such as us, who used him as a ground handler.

SURVIVAL COURSES

Garth's Natureways river safaris flourished and guests came from all over the world. Garth also ran 10-day survival courses for children between the ages of 10 and 15. More than 1 000 children passed through Garth's hands on these outward-bound holidays, where they were taught how to track and live off the land:

'The survival courses were to instruct young people on the most important principle in life – survival. And to be able to compete against your peers at school, at work, in sport and in love. The most important tool in survival is a positive attitude. If you have this, you can do almost anything. We taught them how to find water and food, build shelters, track each other and animals, how to make fire without matches. We taught them how to work out directions, about the stars, animals, plants and their uses, and mammals' behaviour.

'Usually on the fourth day of the course, while out tracking, Johannes would drive to our canoes and take everything out of them except for my medic's bag, fishing rods and worms. So we would come back to find the canoes empty – no clothes, food or bedding. I would explain that we were now shipwrecked and they had to imagine I was dead, so they had to choose a leader from among them. The younger kids, the ten- to twelve-year-olds, always chose wisely. But the thirteen- to fifteen-year-olds normally chose the loud-mouth bully boy, who was mostly a bag of hot air and quite useless as a leader.

'Although I was "dead", I followed them around closely to make sure no harm would come to them, bearing in mind there were lion, buffalo, elephant, crocodile and hippo in close proximity. They would put into practice the various things that they had been taught, like collecting edible plants, such as spinach and fruit; some would catch fish and others would collect firewood. That night we would all sit around the fire and they would eat what they had collected. Some were only wearing a pair of shorts, which is what they had been tracking in. When your ship sinks, you can't ask for your suitcase.

'I would set them initiative tests, like offering them coffee if they could boil water in a plastic mug. Obviously they couldn't put the cup in the fire, as it would melt. They would put river pebbles in the fire and once they were glowing red hot, they would take them out with a pair of sticks and place the incredibly hot stones into the plastic mug of cold water, which would soon come to the boil. If there weren't any stones around, they would submerge into the water the glowing ends of hardwood sticks that had been in the fire. They then strained the water through a hat to separate the ash from the water and make it cleaner.

'The following day, they were split into groups of two. Each group was given a match, the side of a matchbox and an egg. They had to use their ingenuity to cook the eggs in as many ways as possible – boiled, poached, fried or baked. By now they were all quite hungry, given the small amount they'd had to eat the day before, so they were keen to cook the eggs. There were no man-made containers of any sort – no pots or pans. Those who were able to cook their eggs successfully could eat them; those who didn't had them cracked over their heads. If cooked, into the mouth they went; if soggy, then on the head they stayed!

'The most difficult thing was to collect good tinder and wood to be able to make the fire with one match. I knew a few ways to cook an egg, but I learnt many more from their fertile minds. Here are some of the ways they would cook an egg:

- Dig a shallow hole in the sand; place the eggs in it; cover up the hole and build a fire on top. The heat would bake them.
- Pack around the egg a generous quantity of mud and place the mud-enclosed egg in the fire until it baked.
- Wrap leaves around the egg; tie them with creepers and place the leaf-wrapped egg next to the fire, turning it every few minutes until they thought it was baked.
- Place a flat rock in the centre of the fire to heat up. The temperature was gauged by the spit test, i.e. when spit evaporated quickly, the rock was hot enough to fry the egg.
- A youngster once asked me if he could have an orange to poach his egg in. I always kept a few oranges for the kids who became weak from lack of food. He sliced the orange in half and ate the fruit (a bonus for his ingenious idea). He then broke his egg into the empty half orange and placed the orange on the coals, the egg bubbled away in its tough orange skin and poached well. Once it was cooked he ate a perfectly poached egg – with a slight orange flavour.
- Some kids would take the large woody fruit from a baobab, the cream-of-

tartar tree, and cut off the top third of the pod. Some large pods could hold at least a pint of water. They filled the pod three-quarters with water and placed hot, glowing stones in it until it boiled. Once boiling, they took out the stones and added one last glowing red rock to keep it boiling and then in went the egg, timed for three or four minutes and then tested with the egg test on the head!

- *Amazingly, if you just place an egg close to the fire and keep turning it, it eventually cooks itself. You need to make sure it is not too close, though, or it will burst.*

'*They were given all sorts of other initiative tests, but these would fill a book on their own. But, in brief, once we were doing a 25-kilometre walk after the night on our "Survival Island". After 6 kilometres they were tired and whining. I told them if they could stop a tourist vehicle and tie up its occupants, they could drive the rest of the way in the abducted car. They decided to pretend a snake had bitten me (I was lying in the ditch moaning and groaning). The youngest, most angelic-looking boy stopped the car. When the driver bent over to see how I was they attacked him and tied him up. They bundled him into the back of the car. I couldn't drive because I was "dead", so one of the fourteen-year-olds drove, and off we went!*'

As time went by and the river became busier, there were quite a few hippo incidents, Garth said. They would bump boats or knock them out of the water. When one man lost his leg, Garth felt it was time to put a stop to the children's survival courses (even though no hippo incident ever occurred during a Natureways safari). Undoubtedly, there are many young men and women who feel very privileged to have had the experience of having been on one of the survival courses.

After selling Safari Consultants and Natureways, Garth guided full time on a freelance basis. He continues to weave his magic on this special river for the lucky few who manage to book a safari with him.

His interests are not confined to Africa, and Garth has explored many other parts of the world. He has a great passion for riding, which he has taken up quite late in life. As well as taking part in horse safaris and other local equestrian events, he has hunted enthusiastically with some of the best English and Irish foxhounds. He has climbed Mount Kilimanjaro, and enjoys scuba diving and skiing. Besides energetic outdoor activities, he also enjoys the theatre and writing. His curiosity has led him to explore most of the United Kingdom and Tuscany, not to mention parts of Canada, the United States, South America and Antarctica. But his heart is in the African bush, where every day is filled with the delight of new discoveries and the comfort of the familiar.

His book, *The Guide's Guide to Guiding*, is practical and amusing, and an absolute must for every safari operator.

Although he is close to his father, Garth received only one letter from him during his entire time at boarding school. This was in reply to a letter Garth had written to his father, complaining about an unjust punishment he had received. His father wrote back with the following question: 'There were two prisoners locked in a cell peering out between the bars on the window. One could only see the muddy, derelict yard; the other looked up to the stars. Which one is you, my son?'

Garth not only looks up to the stars but lives under a lucky one. He often tempts fate by going where he ought not to go. Sitting alone by a busy waterhole in 2002, he was severely attacked by an elephant. He survived, defying the medical prognosis, and within three months of the accident he was walking without as much as a limp.

The story that follows arrived on my computer one dark winters evening. It is a good example of his courage and luck. This time, the Indiana Jones-type incident took place in Mana Pools:

'*I thought you would be interested in a little bedtime story to ensure sweet dreams!*

'*It was at the end of my last safari one particular season. We had spent a night at Ruckomechi, three nights canoeing and then the last night at Chikwenya – brilliant elephant experiences, crowned by nearly an hour spent with an old cow elephant that lives on Chikwenya Island. She was* possibly the biggest female tusker in Africa. She has a single tusk, dead straight and reaching to the ground if she doesn't hold her head up, some six feet from the lip.

'Our flight was due to leave for Harare from the Chikwenya airstrip at 7.30 am. We left camp at 6.45 am, as I wanted to show the group of Wilderness Safari directors Chief Chikwenya's grave in the huge baobab not far from the lodge. What happened was without doubt the closest shave I have ever had in the Zambezi Valley.

'When baobabs get old (they live to over a thousand years), they rot naturally from the inside and form massive smooth caverns within, which have been used in the past as stores, toilets, jails, armouries, bus shelters and, in this case, a grave. This tree is about 1 700 years old. Chief Chikwenya was laid to rest here in the 1930s with his bow, arrows, spears and a large clay pot.

'During the Rhodesian Bush War, the grave was pillaged by the army, and all the memorabilia were taken, other than the clay pot. I have taken a number of people into the tree tomb over the years. It is quite difficult to get in, as the hole is only about 18 inches wide and the same height. The hole is three and a half feet above the ground on the outside of the tree. One worms one's way through the entrance and then down by means of a handstand into the base of the tree, which is a five-foot drop. From the handstand, you drop down very ungracefully and can then enjoy the coolness of this massive, hollowed tree, which can hold about ten people. I have not taken people in for a number of years because of a beehive that became active within the tomb. It takes about a minute to scramble and squeeze oneself out of the tree, which could prove fatal if you were attacked by the swarm. I have called the bees the custodians of the grave.

'I had a torch with me and when I looked in I noticed that the honeycomb had been abandoned. Because the group was so enthusiastic, I knew they would appreciate the inside of this exciting tree. I wormed my way in, did my handstand next to the pot and flopped over into a standing position. Everyone was excited and keen to join me. I shone the light up at the comb – definitely nothing there – and then down at the pot. I began to shine the light around the tree. I hadn't panned more than two feet from the pot when, there in the beam, was a seven-foot black mamba rearing up, with its black mouth wide open and swaying its head from left to right!

'Well, let me tell you, I didn't want to be in there with this new custodian of the grave, but I couldn't get out, as he was about three feet from the hole that I had to climb up to exit the tomb – and who goes clambering around a metre away from a seven-foot black mamba? I realised that my handstand had been performed less than three feet from the coiled snake. I had nowhere to run to and no stick to defend myself with. In all the other unpleasant situations that I have been in, I have had my trusty old Mauser rifle with me. Those incidents were in the open and involved mammals that are semi-predictable.

'So many thoughts went through my mind: here I was, inside the hollowed tree, with Africa's most poisonous and aggressive snake – and the world's fastest – and I had nowhere to run. Enough to spoil my breakfast. I told the guys outside about my predicament and they went to fetch a stick. During this time the snake continued to rear and weave, threatening me with its wide black gape. There are some long, thin poles in the tomb, possibly rafters from the chief's hut. I tried to climb up them but they were old and rotten, and snapped, falling towards the snake as they broke, which made it even angrier. I was less than pleased with my predicament. By now, a stick to do battle with the snake, should the occasion arise, had been passed through the entrance. It was less than three feet long, and thin – not quite the weapon I had hoped for.

'I quote from the handbook Snakes of Zimbabwe: "Black mambas inhabit termite mounds, hollow trees and rock crevices. Unlike the cobras, the mambas hunt by day. When disturbed it will rear up and spread a narrow hood at the same time opening the mouth wide to show the black interior, any sudden movement will provoke a strike, which is likely to be inflicted on the upper body or face of a human intruder. This snake has a very potent and dangerous venom of the neurotoxic type. Bites usually occur on the mid-trunk, hands, arms or head. Initially a variable burning pain is felt, cold clammy pale skin, faintness, nausea and vomiting. There is a tightening of the muscles across the throat and chest, partial paralysis of the lower jaw and tongue, drooping jaw, profuse salivation and slurred speech. The victim has difficulty swallowing, the eyelids start to droop, the pupils become fixed and do not contract in response to light, the eyeball is immobilised in the socket, producing a 'staring' effect. Muscle twitches and spasms occur, the victim shows abnormal sensitivity and pain to even a light touch on the body. Respiration and movement of the ribs becomes progressively more difficult and painful and as generalised paralysis sets in with spasmodic convulsions, breathing stops followed shortly by the heart!"

'Charming stuff! The last minute had been a stand-off. The snake continued to weave, as did my thoughts, including the possibility of him streaking forward and striking with lightning speed, and attaching himself to my left cheek or neck with those long fangs. The mamba, which I am sure was also feeling quite uncomfortable, thank goodness, then found a hole at the base of the tree, and his long and slender body began to disappear into it. What absolute relief! It continued to disappear into the base. I was informing my anxious friends on the outside of the tree of the positive developments. There was still eighteen inches of tail left when, lo and behold, the coffin-shaped head pops out of a crack in the tree about twelve inches from the hole where I had entered the tomb and was hoping to evacuate it as soon as an opportunity arose. Well this really put a damper on things.

'I thought of future tourists coming to the grave with various guides to visit Chief Chikwenya's grave – and that of some fool called Thompson who didn't make it out of the dusky cavern. The snake surveyed the scene, I felt trapped and helpless. After no more than a few seconds, its head disappeared and down it came to its original position. It began to sway in an upright position and display the black open gape of a little under 180 degrees. I thought my only way out was to kill the snake, but I didn't really feel that this was a good conservation ethic in front of all the Wilderness directors, who were standing outside giving me encouragement and moral support. I also thought that if I did do battle with the mamba, there was a good chance that I would sustain a bite along the way, which was at the bottom of my life's priorities.

'At this point, I decided to try to lift myself up on a strong stick that was leaning against the inner wall. I found a good hand grip on the inside of the bottle-necked tree cave, and told the guys I was attempting an escape, legs first. I found some incredible strength from somewhere and levered my bulk up like an Olympic gymnast and pushed my feet into the hole. The guys latched onto my ankles and pulled me through the tight hole like a rifle cleaner coming out of a barrel. Well, there was much gusto and relief felt by us all – not least myself.

'After every walking and canoeing safari, I breathe a long sigh of relief that no man or beast was hurt. I had so enjoyed this trip with such enthusiastic and like-minded new friends, and to think I was in this predicament on the way to the airstrip, having taken a ten-minute diversion. How quickly the events of life can change.

'What a very unpleasant experience, certainly one of life's worst. As I exited, we heard our aircraft circling overhead and preparing to land. What a pleasure to be going home in one piece.

'I vow never to disturb the grave of Chief Chikwenya and its custodians again. I can only thank God it all turned out as it did. Sweet dreams.'

A safari with Garth is without doubt one of the most exciting and exhilarating experiences you will ever have. Your journey with him will create everlasting memories and a strong desire to return and to live through the enjoyment again.

Garth continues to be extremely busy. He has spread his wings and includes many countries for his safaris that were once inaccessible due to conflict or political disruption. His mind is always open to new excitements, and he visits Rwanda, the DRC, the Central African Republic, Mali, Ethiopia and Mozambique, for the incredible diversity they offer in wildlife, culture and habitat.

'My attraction is… to any new and exciting destination in Africa. Most of my safari guests return again and again. Some of them go back three decades. Many of them have become safari junkies, addicted to Africa – initially for its big game, then all forms of wildlife, followed by the diversity of culture and geographical hot spots, mountains, rivers, volcanoes, lakes, deserts, and countries that have been difficult to visit in the past. For me and my long-standing guests, a safari is about adventure, the thirst for new knowledge and experiences, the intense dislike of mass tourism, overcrowded parks and the standard, mundane run-of-the-mill safaris along with their clichés. They have been coming with me on safari since the 80s. Many have been to most of Africa's crown jewels, like the Okavango, the Kalahari, the Zambezi, Sabi Sands, the East African parks and Namibia, etc. Of course, they are completely inspired and thrilled by the magic that these places offer. However, near the end of each safari they ask, "So, where to next?" And these days that somewhere isn't on the standard tourist map.

'These people belong to a very special "bank" – The Bank of Experiences! The only things you take to your grave are your experiences. These people have all seen paper money disappear overnight on the stock market and in famous bankruptcies like that of Lehman Brothers. So these groups of adventurers subscribe instead to bankable experiences before they are too old and before the experience might disappear for one reason or another. Countries like the Central African Republic and the DRC are opening up to tourism. At the moment, these destinations are still in their embryonic stage – quite undeveloped, and do not have the best food, accommodation, vehicles, roads or guides. But they have the feeling of adventure and the unknown, a sense that one is pioneering, before the package tours reach these areas, if they ever do.

'The fascination of these safaris is that you encounter people who have hardly seen a tourist, who don't pander to tourists. You can spend time with tribes like the DRC's Ba'Aka pygmies in the forest watching how they live, hunt and gather food. You can watch herds of over 50 bongos in the middle of the rainforest in the heart of darkest Africa, as flocks of grey parrots fly by or as a herd of forest elephants come out to join the bongos and the giant forest hogs and forest buffaloes. These are animals we haven't seen before. The following day can be spent with a troop of lowland gorillas where a maximum of three tourists are allowed to commune and observe a family once each day.

'The list of new attractions in Africa is long and exciting. Places like northern Mozambique, southern Ethiopia, western Rwanda, Mali, Benin, Chad, DRC, the Central African Republic and the Congo are but a few of my new "banking" destinations. I am sure it is a natural progression when you have been actively involved in tourism for 35 years that you seek out new destinations, not only for your guests' enjoyment but also to satisfy a need and hunger to learn and "experience" – as opposed to the "vacuum-cleaner" safaris, where you suck the dust of a hundred other tourist vehicles.'

Garth hung up his paddle for the last time in 2010. His canoe was attacked by a hippo – a nasty incident but, luckily, not a fatal one. However, he felt the river had become too crowded with boats and the hippo pods had multiplied over the years, so that it was no longer safe to take his guests down the river in canoes.

He still lives in Harare. His two older children are now working abroad and his youngest is at university in South Africa. He and Mel only leave Zimbabwe for holidays and work.

Garth has not for one moment lost his zest for life. His energy and curiosity are boundless. Many of the places he loved have become very popular, packed with tourists and overused, including Mana Pools, so he is always searching for new and exciting wilderness areas in Africa to satisfy his loyal following.

BENSON
SIYAWAREVA

I first met Benson Siyawareva when he was managing and guiding at Little Makalolo, a camp in a game-rich private area of Hwange National Park, Zimbabwe, that is only open to guests staying at lodges in the area. Benson's charming six-bed tented camp, tucked in a grove of trees, looked out on a waterhole set in a wide, grassy plain edged with thickets of trees. It is one of the few waterholes in the area and a vital lifeline to animals in the dry season. Benson had designed a superb hide at the edge of the waterhole, constructed of dead trees piled together to hide a shallow concrete pit, in which people can stand, unnoticed behind the branches, and watch the animals drinking and interacting with one another in the water. This particular style of hide is his own successful invention.

Benson is an exceptional man – calmly assured, pragmatic and in control. His passion is his country and its wildlife. One of the first black Zimbabwean guides not involved with the National Parks to obtain a professional guide licence, he has risen through the ranks, developing great managerial and leadership qualities, a fact recognised by Wilderness Safaris, his employer.

Benson's first brush with nature was his own birth. His mother started walking to the hospital to have her baby a little too late. He arrived when she was only halfway there and, with the help of a companion, she gave birth to Benson by the side of the road. He is certain that this must have had an impact on his choice of career – being born into Mother Nature.

He had a happy, carefree childhood in a loving and close-knit family. He was brought up in a rural area not far from the Great Zimbabwe Ruins, in the south-east of the country. His father was the headman of their village, where there were about 50 families. Benson's home was a traditional thatched hut with no electricity. Water was drawn from a nearby river. As the last-born child, Benson's responsibilities for the animals and household chores kept him at home longer than normal – he was seven before he went to school. He remembers those early school days, laughing and having fun with the other children during the seven-kilometre walk to and from school each day. English was the teaching language used in all Zimbabwean schools. This was difficult for him at first, as it was not his home language, but he was a quick learner and soon became the most proficient in the class.

Benson's childhood in the late 1970s coincided with the Rhodesian War (known as Chimurenga – 'the struggle'), and his two elder brothers were involved in the Rhodesian security forces. His eldest brother was in the army and the next eldest in the police force. As the war intensified, it became difficult to continue their rural existence. The family was threatened by the liberation forces and eventually had to leave their home. Having a brother in the army meant there was someone in a position to look after them and he arranged for them to rent a house in Fort Victoria (Masvingo), near the barracks. Moving into a house was very strange for them all. Having light at the flick of a switch and water at the turn of a tap was astonishing in itself, but the strangest new custom of all was having to go to the loo in the house. This was something completely alien to a boy who had always been taught that this was done as far away from the living quarters as possible, out in the bush. The first time he looked into the lavatory he thought it was a well.

Benson's soldier brother, whom he hero-worshiped, was very eager that he and his family should get on in life, so he encouraged Benson to work hard and achieve good grades. All the children in Rhodesia who had relatives in the army were given free education, with the condition that when the education was complete they would be inducted into the army. The education continued along lines that would prepare them for this. They joined the Boy Scout movement, which taught them self-sufficiency and leadership, and gave them practical experience in the bush. Most weekends were spent camping outside the town, where they were taught to ride horses among the animals, to put up tents, cook and generally look after themselves in the bush. Benson flourished in these surroundings. This was the beginning of his love for wildlife and the bush that was to become his life's passion.

His brother was now responsible for not only his own wife and children, but also his parents and siblings. When not on military duty, he would take Benson into the bush to hunt with him. It was technically poaching, but a necessary evil to help feed his extended family. He taught Benson the art of silently stalking animals while keeping downwind from them. They would kill duikers and hares, or guinea fowl and doves – whatever they could find for the pot.

Fortunately for Benson, the war ended as he finished his seventh year at school, so he would not have to join the army and was instead able to continue his education. With the war over, his brother wanted to get away to start a new life as quickly as possible. This was not so easy, as the new government needed to incorporate the freedom fighters into the established army and prepare them for the civil war starting in Mozambique. This was the very last thing he wanted to do, but they required the help of experienced soldiers. In the end, he obtained a discharge from the army to join some of his white military friends who, knowing how skilled he was with weapons, invited him to join them in their hunting company. His brother's new career was to have a great influence on Benson, who would go to the hunting area each weekend to help around the camp. There he learnt about tracking and camp life.

He enjoyed it, but found the killing and the bloodshed difficult to cope with, bringing the awareness that his future path was more likely to be concerned with conservation than hunting.

Just when he had completed his O levels (Zimbabwean schools follow the British exam system), Benson's plans took a serious knock. Much to his and his father's dismay, his girlfriend became pregnant. The family disapproval was severe. His brother and his father told him he could not go back to school to take A levels, as he would have to find work to support his child. He was so miserable that he locked himself in the house and cried, day after day. He could not believe what a mess he had made of everything. Eventually, a friend of the family persuaded his brother and his father that it would be in all their best interests if Benson could complete school. Once he had his A levels, he desperately wanted to go to university. This was too much for them to accept, so he had to buckle down and care for his family. He had married the mother of his first son and his only choice was to take a job teaching while he decided what to do. Meanwhile he hoped there would be another way he could provide for his family.

His brother, who had by now left the hunting group to join a photographic safari company, came to visit Benson. He felt that teaching at a poor, ill-equipped school was doing nothing to help him get on in life and tried to persuade him to leave and come to his safari camp at Lake Kariba. Benson would not go. In fact he would not allow anyone to help him. It was a low moment in his life, but he knew he had made a mess of things and wanted to work out how to resolve the situation independently.

Things changed when his brother asked Benson to escort his children to visit their father at the camp where his brother was working. After their long, hot dusty journey on foot and in overcrowded buses from Masvingo, it is not difficult to imagine what a joy the sparkling blue expanse of water at Lake Kariba must have been to those travel-weary eyes. None of them had ever seen such a vast amount of water, and here was a lake, bathed in sunlight, with fish eagles calling from the trees and pleasure boats buzzing about. On the Zambian side, the hills were barely visible through the haze, and rocky slopes, dotted with baobabs, rose from the green floodplain that edged the lake, on which huge herds of buffaloes, zebras and antelopes grazed contentedly. The shallow waters near the shore were spiked with white leadwood trees, long since drowned by the rising waters but too tough to rot. Clusters of cormorants perched on the bare branches while elephants bathed beneath.

Fothergill Island is just off the shore of the Matusadona National Park and had become a popular tourist destination. Benson arrived there by boat with his brother's children. That brief visit had a profound impact on him and he returned to his teaching job with a heavy heart, realising how different life could be.

A few months later, his brother decided to take the initiative and sent a telegram to the school's headmaster saying that Benson was to leave immediately, as his brother needed him right away. Benson left and never went back to teaching.

His life had taken the right turn, perhaps, but it was not all plain sailing. The Fothergill camp employed him, but he could not do safari guiding, as he couldn't drive. He was untrained to do anything other than teach, so he started out as the camp gofer for a few weeks. Then his employers sent him to Chikwenya Lodge, on the lower Zambezi, which was short-staffed. Again, without appropriate experience, he was of no real use there and was sent back to Fothergill, where he was now on his own, as his brother had moved on. He knew he had to get his act together and find something to do if he were to remain at Fothergill, so he learnt how to drive a motorboat and acquired a boat licence, and this was his first step to his main ambition of becoming a safari guide. The competition was fierce. Many white school-leavers were coming to Fothergill to train as guides. Most would not last the course, but Benson hung on.

Noting his evident desire to succeed, the management decided to make him a test case. They felt sure he could learn to be a guide and look after foreign tourists. But he had to start from scratch. With his boat licence under his belt, Benson studied bird books and took guests out for boat rides. Eventually, he knew about all the species indigenous to the area. He then learned to drive, took his courier licence and was then able to drive tourists. In 1991, he was granted a professional guiding learner's licence, so he could now legitimately take game drives.

He started working at Fothergill in 1989 and finally attained his professional guide's licence in 1992. It was a very proud day for all his family. He had worked extremely hard to reach that level of proficiency, and the examinations in Zimbabwe are particularly tough. Having been at Fothergill for the entire duration of his training, he decided in 1993, by which time he had become head guide, that it was time to move on. He joined a government-owned camp called Detema, where he was appointed as estate manager responsible for the vehicles, the guides and their training, the gardens and looking after the concession. He even had his own company car. He stayed there for three years until a new manager arrived, a woman who apparently did not like men at all, especially those in authority. He hated the conflict it caused, so he left and went to work for the Landela Safari Company as manager and guide, first at Sanyati, their beautiful lakeside lodge at Kariba, and then at Gache Gache. He never felt he was qualified to be a manager, as his professional qualifications allowed him to guide, but a combination of experience and necessity had made him quite capable of managing the camps.

While Benson was working at Fothergill, he had helped with a project to reintroduce cheetahs into the Matusadona National Park. His duties included getting up at five each morning to shoot an impala, which he then took to be disembowelled before feeding it to the cheetahs that were being held in a boma waiting to be released into the wild. He lived in a tree house near the boma so he could keep an eye on the cheetahs. On one occasion he thought it would be fun to suspend some of the old impala carcasses from his tree house to attract lions. That night, he awoke to a dreadful commotion. The lions, which had discovered the tempting prize but couldn't reach it, were climbing up the steps to his room for a better chance to grab the carcasses. When Benson appeared clapping and shouting at the top of the steps, they fled in fright.

He tells of what a wild young man he was, always trying to be macho and daring, particularly with lions, which he found tremendously exciting. Having been saddled with family responsibilities so young, he had never really had time to let go, to be a bit wild, to hang out with the guys and have fun. Although he took his responsibilities seriously, and had put his whole heart into getting his qualifications, Benson had a bit of a reckless side. One of his favourite tricks to impress the guests was to chase lions, making them run and snarl at him. It was just fun and games. He remembers this stage of his life with regret, though, as it took only a few very frightening moments to knock this thoughtlessness out of him and make him the top professional guide he is today. A couple of events had a very sobering effect on him. Benson recounts the first incident:

'One of the incidents that altered my outlook happened when I was taking a group of young Australians on a game drive. They taunted me with the fact that, so far, they had seen no lions on their holiday and did not believe there were any. They wanted to walk and were all rather puffed up and cocky. They got out of the vehicle, and after about five minutes I found lion tracks and told them all to stay tightly together behind me, to keep quiet and on no account to run.

'The tracks showed the lions had small cubs. We had followed the tracks for a short while when suddenly a lioness rushed out of the grass, straight at me. I stood my ground and told everyone to inch back very, very slowly, but the lion kept roaring and pawing the ground and was soon joined by another. My heart was pounding as I gently retreated while talking softly to my guests. I did not realise that there was no one behind me – they had all fled and tried to climb trees, and this is what had so upset the lionesses. Oh my God, I thought, not only have I upset a pride of lions but also I have lost all my guests. How on earth do I go back to the lodge and tell them this? I searched and found the first lady crouched under a bush with her head in her hands. The others soon appeared from behind bushes and trees. Shaking and terrified, they wanted to rush straight back into the vehicle, but, as the lions were sitting on the road between the vehicle and us, there was nothing for it but to take a long walk through the bush, circling around them to get back to *the car, where they were humbled and shaken. It was a lesson on controlling your guests when walking.'*

The other incident, although equally frightening, was not his fault. During a game drive with seven people on an afternoon in February, when the grass was very high, Benson inadvertently drove into a herd of elephants. The vehicle stalled and the elephants went mad. One large cow charged the car and broke the door but, luckily, her tusks went under the chassis rather than through the door. She lifted the vehicle and tried to push it over. It teetered on its front right wheel as it was dragged across the road. Benson was frantically banging on the bonnet while simultaneously trying to restart the car. Suddenly he got the vehicle to start, and the elephant took fright and made off. The other elephants gathered in fury, trumpeting and mock-charging, to the abject terror of the guests. It transpired that the baby elephants in the herd had crossed the road ahead of the main herd and had become separated from them by the vehicle. The last place in Africa that you would want to be is between the females and the baby elephants separated from their herd.

Strange as it may seem, the guests who had been present regard that frightening incident as one of the high points of their lives and have returned many times to go on safari with Benson. This underlines my conviction that many people go on safari in order to experience and conquer fear.

Coming close to death has a profound impact. And those events certainly made Benson regard animals in a different light. He now realises that mutual respect makes game viewing a much more satisfying experience, and engenders knowledge and understanding of our fellow creatures, and he has become adept at judging how close one can get to certain animals and still be safe.

We had a wonderful evening together at his waterhole at Little Makalolo, where, instead of going into the hide, we sat on a branch near the water but out of reach of the elephants. As the warm glow of twilight washed over the land, the elephant families came down for their evening drink, each family taking turns to approach the waterhole. They came very close, raising their trunks to sniff us, but weren't aggressive, only curious. More and more arrived, until there were about 150 in the water or nearby.

One family included a rather mischievous young bull who was too young to leave the herd but clearly wanted to. His mother and aunts were constantly warning him to stay with the family group, but he kept wandering off, doing exactly as he pleased. When he saw us, he came to shake the branches we were sitting on – but not with malice. The next day, we bumped into those elephants again. We knew it was the same family because we recognised the young male, who was still being naughty and wandering off. It was fun to see elephants trying to deal with an errant teenager with about the same degree of success as human families do!

Benson had been running Gache Gache Lodge with a Scottish-born woman, Melissa Gilchrist, who lived in Zimbabwe with her mother. He was very fond of Melissa and they worked well together, so when she left with her mother to live in Scotland, he decided, sadly, that he too would leave Gache Gache. Uncertain where to go next, he was contacted by Wilderness Safaris, who were investing in lodges in Zimbabwe and were looking for good people to run them. Melissa had recommended Benson. The company flew him to Victoria Falls for an interview and offered him a job on the spot at Makalolo, in Hwange National Park. Benson became involved in the project of rebuilding the old Makalolo Camp, which he found very stimulating.

Wilderness Safaris' intention, once Makalolo was up and running, was that Benson should start his own venture, which was to build and run a small tented bush camp. In May 1997, the directors began flying all over the area, surveying for the best spot. Benson told them to leave the plane, and, instead, to drive and walk with him. The site had to be found from the ground, not from the air. They came upon an area with a couple of small pans in which buffaloes were lying as elephants strolled by. This was the perfect spot. The four sites for the tents were carefully chosen and drilling machines came in to dig a borehole. Fortunately they found the water in one day. Often it takes longer to search for water and tent sites might have to move, but in this case they could keep their perfect spots. Little Makalolo Camp opened in July 1997; it became Benson's life and his home for four years.

In 2002, Wilderness Safaris posted him to the Linyanti area of Botswana, where, together with his second wife, Noreen, he managed and guided at Savuti Camp. A large waterhole is a significant feature of that camp and Benson excelled himself by building a hide there in the same style as the one he had constructed at Little Makalolo. This is arguably the finest hide at any waterhole in Botswana – guests can view spectacular parades of animals all day long.

Although it is highly unlikely, given his great love of guiding and the outdoors, that he would ever take a desk job, one cannot help thinking that with his common sense, vision and superior intelligence, Benson would be the greatest asset to Zimbabwe's tourism and wildlife sectors.

Benson moved smoothly from Wilderness Safaris Zimbabwe to Wilderness Safaris Botswana where he was responsible for training the guides in the Linyanti Concession which were Duma Tau, Kings Pool, Linyanti and Savuti.

When I next saw Benson, he was managing Savuti Camp as well as coordinating the guide training for the area. He told me he would wait to see where fortune took him next; he clearly hoped it would be to have the freedom to run his own independent guiding business. I am happy to report that a warm wind blew his way and his wish has come true. He vaguely mentioned to me when my daughter Jessica was drawing his portrait for this book that he thought there might be a change for the better – but no other information was forthcoming. It was serendipity that an English couple, Fiona Thompson and her husband, Graeme, while on a self-drive holiday in southern Africa, arrived at Kings Pool in Linyanti and met Benson for the first time. They became very good friends and were so impressed with his guiding that they returned to repeat the experience a couple of times, and finally booked a six-week safari with him through Zimbabwe, Zambia and Malawi. Fiona wanted to help Benson become an independent guide. She gave him the support to leave Wilderness Safaris and set up his own company, Ngoko Safaris. She created the website and handed him a computer. But she soon learnt that, clearly, Benson was not a businessman – he was never going to sit in an office creating itineraries online. She understood at once that she had to be the business partner while he looked after the guests. This partnership has worked superbly, and Ngoko is now a highly successful, small, intimate safari company with Fiona based in England and Benson in Zimbabwe.

Benson has a very loyal string of clients who want to travel with him in their quest for new and exciting experiences. One of his guests had travelled extensively before he met Benson and has asked him to create a tailor-made safari, the plan being to visit all the places he wanted to share with Benson. Another well-travelled lady has a need to visit somewhere different every year. Benson is certainly up to all these challenges that come his way.

Benson and Noreen built a house in Victoria Falls and live there with their three children. He runs his safaris from there, while his business partner, Fiona, is based in England, which makes commercial sense. Benson still has a house in Masvingo, where his first wife and children live. His oldest son, Omigo Honest Siyawareva, went to the same school in Masvingo as Benson did to study for his A levels. Benson's greatest wish is that all his children get a good education, and he works hard to achieve this. Honest followed in his father's footsteps and became a qualified safari guide. He is currently guiding with Wilderness Safaris Zimbabwe at Ruckomechi, having worked first at Little Makalolo Camp, in Hwange, where I first met Benson.

Benson, who has never forgotten the luck he had when trying to get started himself, now devotes his spare time helping education in rural areas. In 2013, he built a small kindergarten 14 kilometres from Victoria Falls called Intaba Yeingwe (Hill of the Leopard). His company, Ngoko, provides the teacher. Ngoko is also providing adult-literacy classes after requests from some of the mothers. And they have provided sewing machines, and are looking at various income-generating initiatives. One of his guests has generously offered to fund the installation of a three-kilometre water pipeline to the school. What merriment there will be when that arrives!

It is with great sorrow that I heard very recently that the Botswanan government has cancelled Benson's work permit. It is unbelievable that they fail to acknowledge the great contribution Benson Siyawareva has made to tourism in their country and sad for him that he will be unable to continue taking his guests to his favourite sites, which he knows so well.

Benson has started writing short stories that depict the momentous and interesting happenings on his safaris. He sent the following one to me:

DRAMA ON A FROSTY MORNING

A short story by Benson Siyawareva

Not too many people associate Africa with cold winters. I have lost count of how many times guests from cold regions tell me that I wouldn't last a day in their environment. As Jake the Canadian succinctly put it, 'Hey, my friend, where I come from your nuts would fall off; I go skiing at 20 degrees below zero.' I was always happy to agree with these comments until my first midwinter visit to the United Kingdom and USA. There I discovered central heating, roaring open fires and, best of all, appropriate outdoor clothing that actually keeps you warm. No such niceties in Africa. Most of us don't even possess a warm coat, let alone indoor heating. When it gets cold, we feel it.

And it does get cold. Any guest who has been on an early-morning game drive along the dry Savuti Channel will attest to that fact.

Add this freezing dry cold to the chill factor from being in an open moving vehicle and the temperatures are tormenting. We encourage guests to bring the hot water bottles from their rooms for refilling so they can take them on the game drive. Some guides quietly switch the vehicle heater on during the game drive and sit nice and cosy in the driving seat while their guests freeze their butts off in the back. Unfortunately Wessel, our concession mechanic, had completely pulled out the heating systems from all our vehicles.

It was on one such morning that I headed out on a game drive with my guests. Early mornings are normally a good time to spot elusive predators. We toiled for an hour and all we saw were a few frozen impalas and a pair of resident jackals. For the next hour or so it was so quiet that I decided we should stop for an early-morning coffee break. I was panicking about what I could do to make the drive better. One of my guests, Barbara, was carrying state-of-the-art camera equipment and I felt I had to find her at least one good sighting to put the camera to work. So while my hands were pouring coffee and handing around biscuits, my head was full of self-inflicted pressure desperate to make the drive worthwhile despite the weather working against me.

After our coffee break we tried again and found a lone wildebeest curled up to keep warm. It is one of those moments experienced by all guides at one time or another. You stop at a sighting a bit too long, verbal diarrhoea takes hold and you espouse every bit of information you can about the animal in question. You end up with guests picking up binoculars and looking at little swifts flying about in the sky – a blatant sign of boredom and disinterest.

It was one of those situations that forced me to steer off the Savuti Channel into the bush, just for a change of scenery and a bit of bush bashing. We drove up the embankment and bingo – I spotted a honey badger behaving strangely. A closer inspection reveals he is fighting with a huge python who is hissing angrily. A huge sigh of relief. Barbara's camera is put to work.

After many years working in the bush, I had finally invested in a camera and this was my first opportunity to snap some action. Click. Click. Rrrrrrrrrrr! The slide film was finished and rewinding. In my excitement I had forgotten that the camera was set on rapid fire. A real amateur photographer. I ask the guests to go wild, we have such a unique opportunity here. Barbara doesn't need encouragement, she is already too excited and zapping away and I am tugging at her jacket to keep her in the car. As the honey badger and python continue their battle I somehow gather enough courage to ask if anyone has any spare film. Barbara shoves a hand into her jacket and throws film cartridges to me.

We watched and clicked away joyfully as the badger nipped the muscles all along the snake's body. For the first time I understood the meaning of the word 'badgering'. Suddenly, the python struck with lightning speed and latched onto the back skin of the aggressor. I assume it is now all over. The python will coil and constrict the badger to death. But we notice that the body cannot coil any more, obviously the muscles are badly damaged and it is wearing down. The badger turned in its skin and scratched the python on the head, forcing it to let go. Now in retreat, the snake tried to escape by shooting up a nearby tree. This was a fatal error as the badger also climbed the tree from behind and the two antagonists met in a fork of the trunk two metres off the ground. The badger took the snake by its head, sinking his incisors into the back of the skull. The battle was over.

Our experience continued as the badger pulled the helpless rock python to the ground and started to celebrate his victory. With the snake in his mouth he lay on his side, digging up the dirt which he pawed onto his belly. Then he opened the snake's throat with a bite and we watched in amazement as he began sucking blood. The huge snake body gradually shrivelled into a flaccid powerless tube. The badger finally dragged what was left of the snake into a bush, at which time we thanked him for the show and left him in peace.

On a whim of nature, a bad game drive had become truly awesome. Sharing this experience with Barbara led to a special bond between us and a great friendship began. I had the privilege of staying with Barbara and her family in Chicago on a couple of occasions since then, and our photo collections have been added to further, with shots of me stomping around in the virgin snow, enjoying snowball fights and learning that I am never going to be a champion ice skater!

IVAN CARTER

When I first met Ivan, another Zimbabwean, I was bowled over by his extraordinary energy and sense of purpose. His youthful zest for life and vibrant energy are contagious and heart-warming. While on safari with Ivan, I was convinced I could do anything: stalk a buffalo, climb a tree, walk up to elephants and count the stars. For a quick beat of time, I felt nothing was beyond me. Mana Pools is his spiritual home, but he takes enormous pleasure in visiting all safari areas in Africa, particularly little-visited places. Ivan is spurred on by his insatiable curiosity of the unknown. He sees all aspects of life from a slightly different angle, and as a lateral thinker he comes up with alternative slants on most accepted beliefs and convictions.

On our first day together at Mana Pools, we were sitting on a sandy bank of the Zambezi at sunset. The air was still and the purple evening light lay softly on the mountains rising steeply across the river in Zambia; the sky was streaked with wisps of orange clouds reflected in the still, dark water. A crocodile silently raised his eyes out of the smooth surface of the river with hardly a ripple, noted our position and sank back. We moved a few feet back from the edge. Ivan turned to me and said, 'When you took your shower this afternoon, did you reflect on the fact that the last time one of those drops of water landed on a living creature it could have been a dinosaur?'

The constant recycling of water is only one of several unusual observations that Ivan comes up with while exploring the 'big picture' and speculating about the universe. This wonder boy of the new generation of safari guides seems to soak up knowledge like a thirsty sponge. His questioning and probing make for lively conversations around the campfire.

Born in 1970 to farming parents, Ivan grew up – like most other safari guides – exploring the bush and learning with interest about all that went on around him. His earliest letters home from boarding school, at the age of just seven or eight, were entirely about the birds he had seen and what eggs he had found. However, and also in common with most other safari guides, school was not his preferred place. Being shut in a classroom, learning things that had no relevance to his life, was boring for him. Homework was ignored and exams were failed. During his last two years of school, his A-level years, he practically skipped classes altogether. He learnt how to work the system by not turning up for classes right from the first day, so that the teacher thought it was a mistake that he was on the list. It seems extraordinary that he got away with it.

Falconry was his great passion, and, as the school had a falconry club, he could keep his bird at school. He managed to persuade one of the teachers to let him keep his dog at school too. Ivan has evidently always had tremendous persuasive powers – he even persuaded me to try to climb inside a hollow baobab tree that was full of bats. Luckily, I couldn't squeeze through the hole in the trunk!

Every morning, straight after breakfast, he would go into the fields surrounding the school with his dog and his falcon, returning just in time for the roll call or meals. No one knew he had been missing, though he was once very nearly caught out. He joined the athletics games one afternoon and won a race more than comfortably, so he was promptly put on the school team. Afraid he would come to the notice of the school hierarchy, he then had to make sure that he never won again, even in practice sessions. He was soon thrown off the team. He managed to survive two whole years in this way – naturally with abysmal academic results. Which is ironic because, a few years later, some of his erstwhile schoolteachers came looking for work in his safari business.

Ivan's ambition was to work with animals; originally he planned to become a vet. At about the age of 11, he spent his school holidays at the little rustic tented camp belonging to Hwange Safari Lodge when Garth Thompson ran it, and Garth's enthusiasm planted the seed of Ivan's love for wildlife. However, with poor exam results, studying veterinary science was out of the question. Instead, he got a job working in an animal orphanage in Bulawayo. It was not a zoo, as all the animals needed to be there, but it was open to the public and Ivan had the job of showing people around and helping to care for the animals.

A man from the Bulawayo's zoo, who visited the orphanage frequently, suggested that Ivan might like a career as a safari guide and introduced him to Hans Strydom, who ran Sanyati Lodge at Lake Kariba. That was in 1988; business was thriving, and Hans, needing another pair of hands, took a chance and gave Ivan the job.

Hans did not have a professional guide's licence, so there was very little training available for Ivan; he was just thrown in at the deep end. He had never skippered a motorboat in his life. On the day he arrived, Hans spent half an hour showing Ivan how to do it and sent him out on the lake with clients that evening. He had tremendous fun working at Sanyati and always feels that he acquired a huge amount of knowledge there simply by having to learn the hard way.

RHINO TRACKING

One of Ivan's earliest guiding memories at Sanyati was tracking rhinos in the Matusadona National Park:

'We had three English guests staying at the lodge and we departed by boat some time before first light. I was almost trembling with excitement at the idea of tracking one of these great animals. My standard briefing, once

we arrived at Matusadona, included a bit about climbing a tree – which we rather skipped over, much as one does during an aircraft safety briefing. In the unlikely event of a rhino charge, "Get up a tree!" I would tell them.

'The three guests, dressed in their best London designer safari gear, were ready and we set off to look for a track. Before long we came across a set of footprints left by a rhino during the night when she had gone to drink. I showed the guests what we were looking for and gave them their first tracking lesson, and we set off on our adventure. Before long, we bumped into an old bull elephant staring at us intently over some bushes but he lost interest and ambled off. To begin with, the rhino tracks were quite clear and we started to cover some ground, enjoying sightings of many interesting birds, but then the tracking got difficult among the fallen leaves, so I started to make ever-increasing circles to try and find the next footprint. We were all so focused on the ground and looking for the tracks that we only realised that the rhino was in front of us when we were just ten metres away from it.

'Luckily for us, the animal was fast asleep. However, the oxpeckers on its back started chirping and fussing, and the huge beast leapt to its feet amazingly fast. We kept completely still as the rhino was blinking and trying hard to see what we were and where we were. Then, with no warning, it charged off down a path huffing and puffing like a steam train. We all let out a sigh of relief and started chattering.

'The rhino, unbeknown to us, had stopped in the bush to listen and sniff out what was going on. At the sound of human voices, it came charging back to where we were. All of a sudden, the distant memory of the briefing was now in the forefront of our minds as we scrambled up various trees. I was up a small mopane and watched as the English couple tried to climb a tree whose trunk was only about nine inches thick. The man had practically run the woman over getting there but she was now in the lead and they were about three feet off the ground. The rhino was still coming and as they got to about five feet up, the poor tree started to bend under their combined weight.

'The rhino luckily passed us all by and disappeared huffing and puffing into the bush. But the screaming couple in the tree weren't aware of this, and thought that death was upon them. They were making so much noise *that they did not realise we were all down from our trees and the rhino was long gone. They were arguing and yelling as the tree slowly bent closer and closer to the ground. As it bent, they climbed higher – at least that's what they thought they were doing. This caused the tree to bend more until they were horizontal and about three feet off the ground. The rest of the group stood watching the fiasco.*

'Suddenly all was quiet as they realised that the danger was gone and the moment had passed. They sheepishly took stock of the situation and stepped down from their bent branch, now no more than two feet off the ground.

'Everyone agreed that that was enough excitement for the day. The swift walk back was accompanied by sudden outbursts of giggling as each person replayed the whole event in their minds.'

Ivan's next step was to apply for a guide licence and then find someone to whom he could be apprenticed. He asked John Stevens, one of the best-known and most highly respected guides in Zimbabwe, but John would take him on only once he had a canoe licence. Ivan managed to get the licence by working flat out wherever he was needed for various companies. John then asked Ivan to help run his Ruwesi Canoe Trails, taking clients down the Zambezi in canoes. They camped at night on the riverbank and enjoyed the abundant wildlife along the river. While doing this, Ivan became entranced by Mana Pools.

A few years later, he was lucky enough to get permission to run his own seasonal camp, Vundu, on the banks of the river within the Mana Pools National Park. He got his professional guide's licence just 18 months after he first started working at Sanyati – quite an achievement, as it can take two or three years to pass the exams. He then acquired his hunting licence and was invited to examine candidates for guide licences for the next two years. He now had a canoe licence, a professional guide's licence and a hunting licence, which gave him great flexibility in his career.

He then got as much experience as he could by working for many different companies as a freelance guide, which allowed him to learn about the different game areas of Zimbabwe.

He was keen to start up his own mobile safari company but could not find the finance. His big break came when Neil Hewlett, a businessman with a game farm and a vision, asked Ivan to work for him. Neil planned to turn his incredibly beautiful game farm into a nature reserve, which he thought would make an excellent tourist attraction. The only problem was that the land was short of big game – and that, after all, was why the tourists came.

Ivan knew the nature-reserve idea would not work and discussed an alternative plan with Neil. They came to an agreement whereby Neil would finance Ivan's mobile safaris if Ivan promised to spend half his time at the lodge on the farm. Ivan's mobile safaris became more and more popular and he was less and less at the lodge, which, because of the lack of animals, was not being booked.

Although this was not very satisfactory for Neil, he agreed to release Ivan from his obligation to run the lodge and continued to fund his mobile operation. It was a difficult period for Ivan – borrowing money at that time came with 30 per cent interest.

He wrote a business plan for himself and asked a safari client – a Scottish financial adviser – if he would take a look at it. This man was so impressed with the 40-page handwritten document, which had come right from the heart, that he decided on a hunch to back him. With this new support, Ivan bought out Neil, which allowed him to concentrate on growing his own safari operation, but he is eternally grateful to Neil for opening the door for him. He could now kick-start his company, which began to grow very rapidly.

Within two years, he had enough equipment for 3 safaris to be out at the same time – 11 Toyota Land Cruisers, 2 Bedford trucks and 2 boats, and he used a charter company with 3 small aircraft to transport his clients between the camps.

Ivan was also responsible for 35 members of staff – camp hands, drivers, boatmen, guides and office staff, as well as 3 or 4 freelance guides at any one time. Ivan was just 25, and the owner of the most successful mobile safari company in Zimbabwe.

His was the first company to install showers and long-drop loos at the backs of each tent, making night visits less scary. His safaris were personalised to such an extent that, if the guests were there at Easter, for example, as clients of mine had been, they all received Easter eggs with their names written on them in icing – a much-appreciated personal touch. His immensely popular safaris travelled between Hwange, Matusadona National Park and Mana Pools.

As the safari company grew, so did the responsibilities, and Ivan found he was spending more and more of his time on administration rather than on the safaris. The logistics side occupies more time than practically anything else in the safari business. The boats and vehicles supplying Matusadona and Mana Pools were based in Kariba, and the Hwange Camp was supplied from Victoria Falls. His mother, Claire, managed the bookings.

It's strange how often one small incident crystallises what you had been thinking all along. Ivan remembers well the day he heard that the guide who was taking one of his safaris in Matusadona had left behind a case of Coca-Cola, which had been particularly requested by the guests. A boat had to be sent back to Kariba to fetch it. The three-hour journey meant that those Cokes turned out to be more expensive than a case of champagne. That Coca-Cola incident was the trigger, the moment Ivan decided to close down the company and work for himself as an independent safari guide.

It had not been easy for him. Administration was getting him down and he longed to spend more time guiding. It was also the year of a tragic accident that occurred in one of his camps, when a young man employed by the company had been killed by lions, which, unsurprisingly, had an enormous effect on all concerned. (The incident is related below.)

Closing down the business took great courage: first, there was the sadness of putting so many people out of work; secondly, all the tour operators had to be informed and, finally, a crippling debt had to be paid off because all the money that the company had made had been ploughed back into the business to improve facilities. However, Ivan does not lack courage.

A HEARTBREAKING EPISODE

In 2000, a tragedy occurred when lions killed a young Englishman working for Ivan Carter Safaris. This had a huge impact on Ivan's life, because the man was not only an employee, but also a friend. The following are Ivan's own words on how he dealt with the tragedy in the bush:

'The way I can describe it is that, out here, when you are in the bush you are at any moment in danger of becoming part of the big picture. That is one of the attractions: the slight element of danger is what brings people back. Possibly, the element of danger is why everyone wants to see cats. People think that every lion wants to eat you at any moment. Everybody knows somebody who knows somebody who has been killed or injured in Africa.

'Then, all of a sudden, it happens to you and the only way to deal with it is to face it absolutely head-on. It is very easy to hide behind all kinds of excuses, all sorts of make-believe, all kinds of reasons – but there is no hiding. You have just got to face it and, as with any tragedy, you have to think, what is the best way for me personally to deal with this? Having said that, it is very important to deal with the people involved as sensitively as possible. This, of course, is the hardest part of all.

'When the accident happened in one of my camps, I cancelled all my safaris so I could be there to help the people involved in the best way that I knew how. The young man's mother came to Zimbabwe and I personally took her to the spot where the accident had happened, and talked her through it. I then went to England for ten days and spent time with the family. They paid me the greatest compliment – and I hope I did them justice: they got me to write and read the eulogy at the funeral, truly the hardest thing I have ever done. But I am really glad to have been able to do that. It was the most horrible and difficult thing I have ever done in my life but it helped me too. When I recently visited them, I saw they had put a quote from the eulogy on the gravestone, which I felt was a great honour. No matter what you do, you feel a huge responsibility. It would have been all too easy to hide; and some do.

'Time is a great thing from many perspectives, but one thing is definite: whenever an accident happens, one day the blame is going to shift onto you; you are never going to be blameless. While time may heal the overall problem, someone is going to say, "I wonder if Ivan was careful enough. I wonder if this guy did enough or that guy did enough." I think we are all on the brink of something like that happening to us out here. Dreadful accidents can happen – a client can fall off the roof of a vehicle in the Ngorongoro Crater; hyenas can crawl into half-closed tents; somebody can get trampled by an elephant, or an elephant can fall onto someone after it has been shot by a guide – that has happened. Hippos attack canoes and crocodiles jump out of the water. But when it does happen, it is so horrifying – suddenly it's happening to me. Help! I am now part of the story and so many people are quick to point fingers, quick to try to reconstruct in their own minds what happened, to condemn you. But, on the other hand, there are more people who know you and who will support you. Provided you have done the right thing.

'I think a lot of accidents are the result of guide error but, also, they are just one of those things. It is a huge learning curve dealing with the human element afterwards. I hope I never have to go through it again, but if I did, I don't think I would do it any differently.

'The hardest part of the whole thing was having to answer for another guide. I wasn't there at the time of the accident and, as with any profession, you wish deep down that you had been. It probably wouldn't have been any different but you can't help thinking it might have been. I have wished from the absolute centre of my soul that I had been there, just because to go and answer for myself rather than on behalf of someone else would have been so much better. It is something you have to deal with and get through; it's everyone's horror to have something happen to a client on safari. It stays with you always.

'It is incredible that there are not more accidents. There are lots of non-professional guides out on safari and just the thought of walking in big-game areas unarmed does not appeal to me at all. I have seen people do the most stupid things and get away with it. I think nature is very forgiving, but it can also be completely ruthless.'

At this low point in Ivan's life, he gained comfort from his empathy with nature and his high degree of bush knowledge. As he says, if you walk for six to eight hours a day stalking a buffalo or an elephant you have to be very aware of all that goes on around you. Animals are so different in the hunting areas, much more aggressive. He believes that if you guide only in photographic areas you get a false sense of security, especially with the extremely relaxed, big bull elephants in Mana Pools. It would be easy to forget that this is not natural. His hunting safaris help to pay off his loan and the number of clients he has for both hunting and photographic safaris keeps him working most of the year. However, it is my own belief that elephants become aggressive only when threatened and national parks contain little to threaten them.

Ivan has always enjoyed photography. His ability to see unique angles in familiar subjects produces fascinating images. He is now a professional photographer, and has had very successful exhibitions in Edinburgh and London, with exhibitions in America to follow soon. He takes time to help his guests with their photography, allowing them to catch a bit of the spirit of what is going on. Instead of their taking animal portraits, he tries to help them capture the atmosphere of the habitat around the animal. Many of his clients then go on to take photography lessons and return.

His skills as a guide are remarkable. He has a large following of clients who ask him to guide them wherever they go in Africa. He enjoys seeing new areas through the eyes of resident experts as he travels in Botswana, Zimbabwe, Zambia, Namibia, Kenya, Tanzania, Uganda, Rwanda, South Africa and Madagascar. He was the first guide to take groups into the newly established Niassa Game Reserve, in Mozambique. He likes to stay in one place as long as possible, so that his guests can truly learn about an area. He walks as much as he can to allow his clients to experience the closeness of nature and that quiver of apprehension that one gets from the unknown. His idea of making the most of an active waterhole is to stay there all afternoon, if not all day, to get a feel of the cycle of life and the daily pattern surrounding the place.

Ivan was fast becoming one of the best-known guides in Africa. He created an exhilarating, thought-provoking safari for people of all ages. He tried to plant a seed of inquisitiveness, to make his guests think about the natural world and to keep on wondering and dreaming about all these things when they get home.

Ivan had an extremely unhappy episode in Zimbabwe during the land grabs, when he was badly beaten up. His mother was staying in Harare and he had gone back to the family home to collect personal belongings. He did not want to live with the violent situation in Zimbabwe, so he moved his mother to the Bahamas and he went to America for a while before settling in the Bahamas. In 2006, he married Ashley George, a Zimbabwean, and they live in the Bahamas with their two children. Although Ivan leads selected photographic safaris, his main income is now from hunting. This saddens me.

ANTHONY KASCHULA

How often have I heard the following comments: 'If only I could go on safari as I did the very first time I went into the bush. I'd like to have a tented camp set up just for me. I don't mind stepping out of the tent for my shower and loo, as we used to do. How incredible it would be if I could see miles of Africa and its animals without seeing hordes of tourists. Just for a moment in time the world would be my oyster.'

Well, you can. Anthony Kaschula, known as Ant, will see that you do; for a small group of four or six people, your wishes will come true.

I lay in a hammock under a shady tree in the heat of the day thinking about that. A golden-tailed woodpecker was knocking on the branch above me; nearby, the haunting tones of a tropical boubou rang out through the hot afternoon air, while an old bull elephant gently dug for water in the vast sandy bed of the Runde River. Another bull elephant silently came through the bushes very close to my hammock, walked down the steep bank to the riverbed, turned right and disappeared. He had no idea that I was there.

It was siesta time in the Gonarezhou National Park, in Zimbabwe. I was on safari with one of the brightest new generation of guides that you could find. Ant has all the enthusiasm and passion that is paramount for good guides, and a great knowledge of all that is going on around him. His home turf is now Gonarezhou, a national park that he knows like his own backyard; but he also spent five years in Kenya during Zimbabwe's troubled times, working and guiding safaris there and in other African countries.

Gonarezhou, being in the south-east part of Zimbabwe, is slightly out on a limb, and was not part of the original tourist circuit, which is in the north, with Victoria Falls, Hwange and Mana Pools being the most popular destinations. But Gonarezhou (a Shona word meaning 'place of many elephants') is a magnificent, wild area, unspoilt and fresh. It is bordered by Mozambique and the Malilangwe Wildlife Reserve, both of which are part of the vast Limpopo Transfrontier Park. Ant is determined that eventually a spectacular southern circuit will be launched for intrepid and discerning travellers who revel in real wilderness areas. Meanwhile, he practically has the place to himself. No one else operates in this park, but, of course, some knowledgeable self-drive campers do make their way to this beautiful and sparsely used landscape.

While driving to the camp, we stopped to watch a small herd of elegant kudus in the glowing evening light, a magnificent old male with six or seven females grazing around him. Suddenly, from across the valley there came a loud and distinctive call of a leopard. A few impalas in the valley below, which must have caught his attention, scattered. Ant searched with his binoculars and caught a glimpse of the leopard; we sat waiting in the fading light when, all of a sudden, the leopard walked out of the thick bush and sat watching us. It was a memorable moment in this very wild place where cats are rarely seen.

Ant's excitement lifts in every bend of the road, and he has a knack of finding something interesting wherever we stop, especially when it is one of the big bull elephants that live in the park. He stops the car, turns to his open window and starts speaking to them with a low rumble that you would swear had come from an elephant! The elephant stops and listens curiously. When Ant starts talking to him, he turns his head; another tummy rumble reaches this ears; he is not sure, but he is not afraid either. Being in such a wild place, the elephants are not used to humans, especially kind ones, who mean no harm. Hunting areas border this park and woe betide any elephant with tusks that wanders over the boundary. Ant truly wants them to relax in the park, to be calm around tourists and allow people to have time to watch them. I certainly saw two or three that have got his message.

His eyes seem to pick up everything. He plucked a cicada off a tree – and they are spectacularly camouflaged – held it in his fingers for me to see its bright-green body and exquisite, delicate wings, and turned it over to show me how it rubs its little legs together to make the whistling noise you hear on hot summer days. He then gently returned it to its perch.

While driving through an overgrown little-used road through the park, Ant suddenly stopped and jumped out of the car, and picked a tiny white frog off a shrub. It was a grey foam-nest tree frog (*Chiromantis xerampelina*), which live in trees and become well hidden as they change colour to match their surroundings like chameleons. This one was very vulnerable, sitting bright white in the sunshine, and I expect about to become something's dinner! Ant, ever to the rescue, tucked it under a leaf on another shrub.

On a morning walk, while following two elephants strolling along plucking acacia pods, we came upon the bones of a long-dead elephant. Ant bent down and picked up a few small pieces of white bone – or at least I thought that's what they were. In an instant, he had put the pieces together as in a jigsaw and he was holding an elephant's tooth. Now, I have seen elephant's teeth in the skull, but never in complete bits on the ground. How incredible to recognise these pieces among all the skeletal clutter.

On another morning walk, he decided to find me a scorpion. There were many scorpion holes in this particular area, so, taking a bit of wood, he started digging. After a while, having dug a rather deep hole, the tunnel, which the scorpion walks down to reach his nest, was clearly visible, and eventually he found the creature. It was a very large shiny burrowing scorpion (*Opistophthalmus glabrifrons*), which Ant carefully held in his hand, while we examined it from nose to tail. Luckily, I was not asked to hold it. He then started licking it:

'Licking a scorpion was a trick I learnt from Cobra, a Bushman at Jack's Camp. This helps one to see the true colour of the scorpion, as they are often covered with dust if one ends up having to dig them out, like we have. With smaller specimens, it's best to put the whole scorpion in your mouth but, in our case, it would have been a bit of a mouthful and would likely have attached itself to my tongue, which would have been interesting ...'

Ant loves walking safaris, and, I must say, there is nothing nicer than getting out of a vehicle and walking with all the sounds and smells of the bush around you. It is possible to walk in all of Zimbabwe's national parks, and it's a great joy. During Ant's safaris, he sometimes takes his guests away from his main tented camp to walk in a different area and stay overnight in a fly camp at a chosen picturesque spot. Fly-camping with Ant is a real treat. He has wonderful little net tents and comfortable bedrolls. A hot shower is provided by means of a bucket slung over a branch; there is a warm campfire with steak grilled over the fire served with baked potatoes, salad and a glass or two of rich red wine; a scops owl chirrups in a nearby tree. It is rare to savour such blissful peace.

There are always a number of interesting moments when out walking in the African bush. If you keep quiet and blend in well, you never know what might be around the corner.

A MONGOOSE MOMENT

Mongooses are very shy and skittish creatures, so this encounter in Gonarezhou was extremely unusual:

'On an early morning walk along the sandy river bed in September 2009 with two American guests, we came across two little banded mongooses running around in the sand and scratching leaves about 40 metres away.

'They hadn't seen us, so we quickly couched down very close together as if one, and I started to make squeaking noises, which I often do to bring

in little predators. The two little mongooses pricked up their ears and ran straight to us. They stopped inches away from me and looked up and around to see what it was. We were camouflaged in brown and green clothes, and kept dead still so they couldn't make out what was making the squeaking noise. A moment later someone moved and they bolted away. But I had never ever had an experience like that. When they were gone, I turned my rifle down from my shoulder to the ground and the point of the rifle touched their footprints. They had been that close. Occasionally, you think something has been very close and you say half a metre but in fact it is often more like two or three metres, but here were the prints and we hadn't moved; they had come right up to us to investigate the sounds.

'It was such a wild place and these wild animals were completely unused to humans, and were very curious about the squeaking noise.'

Ant is a third-generation Zimbabwean, born in Harare, where he grew up and occasionally went on bush holidays with his father. (The family's annual holiday was never in the bush because his mother would only go to a place where she could use a hair dryer.) As a young boy on holiday at Kariba, he remembers fishing on the lake and seeing elephants on the shore of the Matusadona National Park.

He was very intrigued by wildlife, so much so that when he read on the school noticeboard that Shearwater Adventures were offering a camping holiday at Ruckomechi Camp, on the Zambezi River, for boys of 11 to 13, he begged his mother to let him go. These were the trips started by Garth Thompson in 1984, which continued for many years. Ant loved being in the bush and had already decided he would like to work for the National Parks Department, though his father had assured him there would not be a future in that.

The trip to Ruckomechi was a life-changing journey for Ant:

'About a dozen children piled into the back of a 3.5 ton lorry, which had a couple of mattresses in the back, our bags and resupplies, and a wooden bench down each side (no seats – or seatbelts, for that matter). The adventure, which started with a seven-hour drive to Ruckomechi Camp, began.

'Before Wilderness Safaris took over management/ownership of Ruckomechi, it was run by Shearwater and during the off season they took groups of about a dozen on a five-night trip. The purpose of these trips was to expose younger children to the bush and teach them about wildlife, birds, plants and bushcraft skills. I was completely in my element and hardly slept a wink so as to make the most of this precious time. I still have vivid memories of many aspects of this trip.

'Troy Williamson happened to be one of the lead guides responsible for running these trips and to us "littlies" he was a bear of a man with a mane of long, golden-blond curls. He was extremely confident and gave the appearance of someone in control of everything. To us young children, he was fearless. (He actually was, as I later found out, as he dared to spearfish in the Zambezi.) There wasn't anything about the bush worth knowing that Troy didn't know. Sadly, he was tragically killed in a head-on collision in Harare a few years later.

'Troy's enthusiasm and charisma rubbed off on me, and I immediately wanted to follow in his footsteps, realising that it would be possible to find a career that would allow me to live in the bush and do what he did.

'Anyhow, it was on this trip that I learnt about my first bird, a lilac-breasted roller, my first tree, a Y-thorn torchwood, and learnt the basics of tracking animals and bushcraft. To this day, making string out of baobab fibre is something I can't stop myself from doing, and I confess that I've actually become addicted to experimenting with making string from many different types of plant fibre – and spiderwebs.'

After this trip, Ant decided he wanted to go to Peterhouse, a boarding school in Marondera, which at that time offered over 60 sports and activities, including a snake club, rifle club, conservation, archery and falconry. He managed to persuade his parents to send him to this school. Most importantly, there were some adventurous teachers who took groups of boys on organised trips around the country. They travelled the length of the country to raise funds for research into wild dogs; they climbed the Chimanimani and Mavuradonha mountains and read rain gauges in

Matusadona. However, a truly significant activity was a walking safari in Gonarezhou that Ant did in 1993, when he was 14.

'It was on this trip,' said Ant, 'that I was captivated by the sheer ruggedness and wild beauty of the park, which has resulted in me concentrating our safari business in Gonarezhou.'

On a trip to Matusadona with apprentice guides looking after the boys, Ant understood what was involved in becoming a guide. He prepared himself to take his learner-guide exams as soon as his A levels were over and wrote to several professional guides to see if he could work for them for three to six months to gain experience, but he had only one positive reply. That was from Ivan Carter, who was prepared to take him on as a full-time apprentice until he had his guide's licence. Ant had wanted to get going in his gap year before going to university but realised he might have to complete his guiding course after university. Ivan told him that most guides took three to five years to qualify, but that it was possible to get the licence in two years.

That was enough of a challenge. Ant had already passed his learner-guide exams, and so, later in the year, he attempted to register his full written licence, but the authorities said it was too soon. Ivan Carter stepped in and assured them that he would pass, so they allowed him to register. He took the exam and attained the highest mark. He is truly indebted to Ivan for his help:

'Ivan was a very hard taskmaster and expected one to give more than 100% all of the time – which is something I thrived on. He paid peanuts but this didn't worry me, as I gained a huge amount of practical experience, especially on the dangerous game-hunting side, which is crucial for all guides in order to get their full licence.

'By October 1999, I was ready to do the final practical exam, or proficiency test, as it is also called, as it demonstrates to the examiners that one is proficient in being able to safely conduct walking safaris.

'The time between writing my learner's licence to when I did my proficiency test was nineteen months. At the time, there was no written rule

stipulating the minimum amount of time required to be an apprentice guide. But on arrival at my proficiency test – a five-day exam where one needs to host one's examiners in a tented camp, as one would do with paying guests – I heard rumours that the minimum time was two years.

'*Nevertheless, I was there and I'd gone to the effort and expense of attending the test, and my tutor felt that I was ready. So, despite this unwritten 24-month rule, I went ahead with the test in the knowledge that there was a good chance that I might be failed on a technicality anyway.*

'*At the beginning of the proficiency exam, there is an in-depth interview followed by a shooting test. I had luck on my side – despite being the youngest candidate in the proficiency test and having only been in training for nineteen months, I got the fastest time and the highest score in the shooting test, which is a major part of the proficiency and held me in good stead for the rest of the test.*

'*Without going into too much detail, the proficiency exam went well and National Parks, who issue the licence, agreed that they would give me my full licence when the two years were up – which was February 2000.*'

Ant went to study for a degree in ecology and environmental and geographical science at Cape Town University. During the university holidays, he spent time discovering the safari world of other neighbouring African countries, and did a little freelance guiding in Zimbabwe, as he had already set up his own company called Private Guided Safaris. This work was very limited because tourism in Zimbabwe had crashed at the time of the political and economic upheaval in the country.

After graduating, he travelled to America with friends and found work as a bellman at the Ritz Carlton Club in Aspen, Colorado. After a happy time in America, he decided he should return to Africa to get on with his chosen career.

A guest he had guided at Matusadona during his university years got in touch with him and asked if he could take her to Rwanda and Kenya. Having never been to either country, this was quite a challenge, but if there is one thing that Ant relishes, it's a challenge! The client was right to have enough faith in him to pay for this, his first fully arranged and guided safari, which was a huge success. He was 23 years old.

After leading one or two more safaris, Ant decided to do a master's degree at the University of Zimbabwe in tropical resource ecology. His thesis was titled 'Elephants and their impact on the woody component of sandveld vegetation communities in the Malilangwe Wildlife Reserve, SE lowveld Zimbabwe'. The Malilangwe Trust gave Ant a grant for his postgraduate research. When he had completed his master's, Zimbabwe's tourism was still in the doldrums, but, with another stroke of luck, he heard from school friend David Westwood, who had a proposition for him. At Peterhouse, Ant had been the captain of rowing, and David was the first team's coxswain. David was working for an Italian called Filippo Molinari, who owned a yacht, which he was planning to sail with paying guests from Europe to Zanzibar. The yacht owner needed someone to organise the safari activities en route.

Filippo was planning to make this trip into a tourism business. They would sail through the Suez Canal and then down to Zanzibar, stopping now and then to fly into a safari area – that part would be arranged and guided by Ant. He left Zimbabwe for Kenya to start making arrangements, and then went to the United Kingdom to man a stand at World Travel Market that had been booked by Molinari. David advertised through the African Travel and Tourist Association for someone with African travel experience to administer the London office and help with the marketing. A girl called Marian Mason applied. Remarkably, Ant knew her from Cape Town, where she lived next door to him and dated his best friend.

Marian was the ideal person to join them, as she had diving knowledge because her father operated diving safaris in East Africa. Marian was hired to help on the stand, and remain in England to take bookings and market the company, which they named Sail Africa.

After the London travel show, and many visits to tour operators, including Cazenove and Loyd, Filippo sent Ant to Switzerland to buy a 4 x 4 vehicle and drive it to Nairobi. He drove to Nairobi with an old family friend via Tunisia, Libya, Egypt, Ethiopia, Eritrea and Sudan.

When he arrived in Nairobi, he was to set up the safari aspect of Sail Africa. Filippo sent Marian to Zanzibar to run the office there and he sent Dave to Italy to help with the building of another yacht called *America*, a replica of the original boat that won the America's Cup, so no one was in England to follow up on the marketing. Filippo seemed to have many schemes on the go and after all Ant's hard work eventually the Sail Africa project fizzled out.

Ant, however, was now settled in Kenya. While he was in London, he had met Rawana Luke, a good friend of Marian. Rawana came from Kenya; her mother, Patricia Luke, is the sister of Richard Bonham and partner in his safari business. Richard and Patricia started Bonham Safaris 30 years ago, when they built Ol Donyo Wuas Lodge in the Chuylu Hills, now one of the best-known and loved safari destinations in Kenya. Ant and Rawana's romance started in England and continued despite many separations, in Kenya, until the Sail Africa project folded and Ant was at a loose end. At this time, Ant and Rawana were offered the job to manage as a couple Borana Lodge in Laikipia, which meant a two-year commitment. Ant really wanted to guide, but was aware that he would have difficulty establishing himself in a country with so many professional guides. So they accepted the position, and had two very happy years, at the end of which Zimbabwean tourism was beginning to come out of the doldrums.

Ant has an incredible affinity with animals. All the guides I have written about have this to a certain degree. Michael Lorentz has a strong bond with elephants and feels very much that we are only part of a huge animal family on this special and, so far, unique planet. Michael describes this concept well in his chapter earlier in this book.

Ant has a very similar philosophy but is also extremely talented at communicating sounds that alert and interest animals. I have witnessed his calm and steady approach with elephant bulls and the rumbling sound he makes, which is indistinguishable from the real thing. Here he describes an encounter with a friendly elephant:

'While working at Borana, I spent many hours guiding the visiting guests but the most unusual afternoon was with two English ladies. There was an elephant I had seen quite a few times who was easy to recognise, as he had thin, straight tusks, rather like a forest elephant, which stuck straight down, so I named him Toothpicks. He was quite a large elephant about 25 years old. I had talked to him on a few occasions, and got out of the car and walked up to him, scuffing my soles on the grass while rumbling and talking gently to him. In the beginning, the minute I started scuffing my feet on the ground his head would shoot up and his whole demeanour became tense but, slowly, he became very used to me being around. I had started walking closer to him than I was to the car, trying to make him aware of me on the ground rather than as part of the familiar vehicle.

'On this particular day, the two ladies wanted to have a walk, so we drove off to find a nice place to start and as we moved down the valley I saw an elephant in the distance and through my binos I saw that it was Toothpicks. I thought it would be interesting to go and have a look at him. He was not very close, about 400 or 500 metres away. We walked down the hill and when we got closer we were upwind to him. I positioned us behind a large termite mound, which was between us and the elephant. I had given the women the safety briefing: if he came up to us, they should keep still, not run away and keep quiet.

'Now he was about 40 metres from us, and the wind was blowing straight from me to him. I started rumbling and speaking gently to him, at which he immediately started walking towards us. I thought he would walk to the other side of the termite mound – but, no, he had his own ideas and came around the mound and stood about 10 metres away from us. He walked slowly; there was no sign of alarm or aggression; his head was not up and he was eating grass. We kept quite still watching him as he wandered about. He picked up a stick and threw it on his back, and then turned his back on us, which meant that he was completely relaxed in our company.

'I suggested to the ladies that we sit down and watch him for a while. They sat behind me and I crouched down with my rifle over my knees. Then came the heart-stopping moment. He started to wander towards us. At about

7 or 8 metres away, he went down on his knees and then he lay down flat on the ground, his four legs stretched out and his head facing us. It felt like a long time but was probably only about fifteen or twenty seconds. When he got up, he shook himself and just stood looking at us for a few more seconds, then went to feed on a nearby bush. I had no idea what was going on. Was he being submissive? Did he want to join us on the ground? It was something I had never seen before, but he was definitely interacting with us.

'When he walked away, I had a hunch we should move off quickly back to the car. We retraced our steps and were going as quickly as we could down the track and back up towards the road when I heard a trumpet. I looked at him through my binoculars and saw his head and trunk were up in the air searching for us. He found our scent and followed us up, moving fast, then as we reached the car and jumped in he came onto the road and just stood there, looking at us. When I started the car up, he turned and walked away. He knew we were gone. He clearly had lost us, and wondered where we were.

'We had been in a way intimately close and he wanted to find us again. I don't know what the answer is and I never saw him again. The elephants have a huge area to move around in Borana, Laikipia and Lewa. I don't know if maybe he had had human contact in the past. Perhaps he had been an orphaned elephant, I just don't know. But it was the most incredible encounter I have ever had.'

Meanwhile, Zimbabwe had abandoned the Zimbabwe dollar and had adopted the US dollar and South African rand. The dollarisation had made the economy more stable, so Ant decided it was time to go home and build his business there. Before they left Kenya, Rawana and Ant got married in Chyulu Hills, home of Richard Bonham, and they now live in Harare with two small children.

Having grown up in the safari world, Rawana was well informed on the business side of travel, and had worked for two years in her mother's office in Nairobi. She has now started up a ground-handling company with a friend of hers, which is flourishing and much needed, as tourism to Zimbabwe is picking up.

Ant is building a great reputation as a top guide. His own tented camp at his favourite campsite is a must for anyone visiting Gonarezhou, but he also lengthens his itineraries by visiting Singita Pamushana, a lodge in the Malilangwe Conservancy, and other parks, such as Gorongosa, Mana Pools, Hwange and, of course, Victoria Falls.

NORTH AND SOUTH LUANGWA AND THE ZAMBEZI VALLEY

The Zambian safari community is small and personal. Mainly Zambian-born, these professionals, whose passion for the bush and wildlife, are mostly camp owners and they are first and foremost guides, who stamp their own personalities on their safari operations. One of the great joys of safaris in Zambia is that walking in the National Parks has always been permitted and there are many beautiful and diverse areas that are wild and unspoilt.

A long with Robin Pope, another exceptional guide is John Coppinger of Remote Safaris, who raises his guests' experience to dizzy heights by giving them a bird's-eye view of animal behaviour by means of microlight flights.

There is also Rod Tether who spent 9 years in North Luangwa, but is now an independent private guide, and Grant Cumings in the Lower Zambezi Valley, who guide in areas that complement South Luangwa (they feature in the next chapters). These are people whose lives are interwoven in this small safari community. Rod's passion for North Luangwa first began when he took mobile safaris there in 1994, and the Lower Zambezi wormed its way into Grant's heart as a child on many fishing expeditions with his father.

John Coppinger originally joined Wilderness Trails in 1984 for two years, and worked at Nsefu while Robin Pope was the manager. After Robin left to set up on his own, John and his wife, Carol, managed Nsefu for eight years, during which time he opened in 1990 Mwaleshi, a camp in North Luangwa exclusively for walking safaris. The Wilderness Trails shareholders had felt it was not feasible to run such a remote camp for so few people, so when John left in 1995 to strike out on his own they allowed him to keep Mwaleshi. He built Tafika Camp in South Luangwa, a beautiful place by the river with spacious, airy, reed-and-thatch rooms so typical of Zambia, and far more accessible for safaris than Mwaleshi, which he kept for those who wanted a bit more adventure.

ROBIN POPE

Robin is a born naturalist, and has a wide range of interests and many talents. When you are with Robin, all creatures appear to you in a new light as he concentrates your attention on even the most familiar animals. You learn to appreciate the subtle and exquisite colours in the feathers of a dove, how to assess the size of a lion by studying its spoor on a dusty road or discover that mongooses can climb trees. We spent an enthralling two hours following a young leopard that had recently left her mother – but not her mother's territory. Robin explained how the cub was skirting the perimeter of her mother's territory, weighing up when and where to make the break and go it alone.

Most of Robin's adult life has been spent in the Luangwa Valley, in Zambia, and his observations of the changes that have occurred there over the years are fascinating. The Luangwa River meanders through a wide valley in large sweeping curves, flowing serenely when the water is low, but becoming a roaring torrent in summer, which constantly alters the landscape as it swirls around the bends, eating away the banks and toppling colossal, ancient trees like puny saplings. Changes to the course of the river create oxbow lakes – tranquil pools that are home to hippos and a multitude of birds for a time, and which eventually dry up to become grazing land for plains game. The process takes many years, but, slowly, new trees take root in this fertile ground – first acacias, then hardwoods, until, eventually, hardly a sign is left of these forgotten curves of the great Luangwa River.

Robin is a softly spoken, gentle man with a disarming smile that lights up his face, drawing you into his world with a feeling of warmth and comfort. He communicates his understanding and enthusiasm in a quiet, intimate manner, so that each of his guests absorbs his unique insight into the way the natural world fits together. Intrinsically shy and reticent, he has overcome this by being superbly confident in the knowledge he has acquired over the past 30 years. He is most definitely a guide for the connoisseur. He has an encyclopaedic knowledge of birds – it might be just a black dot against the bright sky, a flash of wings in a bush or a call heard in the background of at least 10 other calls, but he recognises it immediately, revealing an understanding of rare depth. When we were on safari in the Luangwa Valley, there was nothing he couldn't identify, but I was also astounded by how quickly he was able to identify things and how he never made a mistake (and we verified his identifications later in a guidebook). In this department, he outshines every other guide I have met.

One morning we left in the dark, wrapped up in blankets against the chilly pre-dawn air, for the long drive from Tena Tena, Robin's base camp, to the salt pans. These are not like the Makgadikgadi salt pans, which are flat and dry, but are caused by hot water boiling up from underground and filled with minerals that, when dry, create a white, salty crust along the edge of the pools. There was much to see along the way. To start with, we had a rare sighting of a bat hawk, streaking silently in front of us on a hunt. There were numerous herds of blue wildebeest, eland and Burchell's zebras. The incredible dawn chorus of the Cape turtle doves occurs as the sun rises and, although we had left camp long before dawn, with the many distractions along the way we were only just in time to hear them. Through the dark trees on the edge of the wide plain the blood-red ball of the sun rose, as thousands of doves performed their morning ritual. We are accustomed to hearing lone turtle doves emitting their '*work HARder, work HARder*' call, but few know that thousands calling in unison make the air vibrate like a squadron of jet fighters revving their engines in preparation for a dawn flight.

Robin's range of skills once again came into play. A dab hand with the frying pan, he cooked a most delicious breakfast of eggs, bacon, sausages and tomatoes for a group of ravenous people.

Robin's maternal grandfather, Cuthbert Jenkins, was educated at Trinity College, Dublin. He was an officer in the Royal Dublin Fusiliers in World War I, and fought at Gallipoli. In the 1920s he joined the British South Africa Company and moved to Ndola, in what was then Northern Rhodesia (Zambia). He transferred to Livingstone and was later posted to Fort Jameson (now Chipata), near Zambia's eastern border with what was then Nyasaland, now Malawi. This was an arduous journey at that time. It entailed a passage by boat up the Zambezi and Shire rivers to Port Herald, from where they travelled via Lilongwe to Fort Jameson on bush tracks in a Model T Ford and trailer.

Cuthbert had met his future bride while on board a ship from Durban to Southampton. She was on her way to the United States with her father to look at cattle, but romance intervened. They married in England and he took her back to live in Fort Jameson, where Robin's mother, Rosemary, was born. Robin has a charming photograph of his grandparents fording the Luangwa River in their Ford. Standing on the pontoon is his grandmother, wearing a long white dress and holding her baby daughter in her arms. Earlier, this had been the principal slave- and ivory-trade route down the Luangwa and Zambezi rivers to the Indian Ocean. The last Arab slave train passed through Fort Jameson in 1909, 15 years before the arrival of Robin's grandfather.

Robin's grandmother was descended from the 1850 settlers of Natal – a group of Scottish families who escaped the depression of 1848–1851 to find a new life in Africa. Many of them became prominent, successful Natal families, including the Campbells, who originally owned Mala Mala Game Reserve in South Africa.

Robin and his elder brother were born in South Africa, where his father, John, grew up. John Pope joined the Transvaal Scottish Regiment at the beginning of World War II. Fighting in East Africa alongside other regiments, such as the King's African Rifles, they defeated the Italians and relieved Addis Ababa in April 1941, giving the Allies their first major victory of the war. John travelled north to fight in the Western Desert before transferring to the air force, and was in Yugoslavia when the war ended. Returning to South Africa, he went to university, obtained a mining degree and married Rosemary Jenkins. While Robin and his brother were still small, John took the family to Northern Rhodesia (Zambia), the country of his wife's birth, where they were blessed with two more sons. Their home was to be the area of the copper mines known as the Copperbelt, near the Congolese border, which were a hive of activity, as copper was in great demand due to the post-war rebuilding of Europe. John worked as a mining engineer in Kitwe, Bancroft and Broken Hill. A few years before they arrived, the skull of an early hominid, *Homo rhodesiensis*, had been discovered in a mine chamber in Broken Hill, causing much excitement. John ended his career at the Lusaka head office of Anglo American, which, after nationalisation, became the Zambia Consolidated Copper Mines.

Living on the Copperbelt in the 1950s and 1960s was great fun for the children. They were surrounded by the bush – a paradise for little boys to explore, especially with frequent visits from their knowledgeable grandfather, Cuthbert. However, it was their parents, who had a great love for the bush and the country, who influenced and shaped their passion for nature. John and Rosemary took their sons on many holidays in the Luangwa Valley and the Kafue National Park, where they would stay in self-catering government camps. The family adored these holidays, and they set the tone for the future lives of the boys. Two of Robin's brothers are still involved with wildlife in Zambia and the youngest is in a similar career in Australia.

For Robin, the strict regime of boarding school in Rhodesia was an alien experience. He simply could not understand half of the baffling rules that were enforced, especially the policy of having to fold his clothes into neat, equally sized piles whose dimensions were measured by a prefect. At first he felt like a square peg in a round hole, but eventually he conformed, worked hard and got into university. His first year of higher education was spent at the University of Zambia, in Lusaka, which he enjoyed, but this was the height of the Cold War in sub-Saharan Africa and political conflict at the time made it very disruptive. The endless student meetings and marches in support of the various political events in the subcontinent were unsettling, making it hard to study, so he decided to transfer to the University of Natal in Pietermaritzburg, where he completed his degree in geography and zoology.

His great wish on returning to Zambia was to work for the Department of National Parks, but jobs in the public sector for young white Zambians were not easy to get. However, as luck would have it, he had an introduction to Wildlife Conservation International, an American organisation that was attempting to turn a game reserve on the banks of the Zambezi River into a national park. Robin was taken on to work for them as paymaster for the scouts. It was a very important project because the lease for a game reserve can be revoked, whereas a national park would require an Act of Parliament to close it and alter the land use. It was therefore of paramount importance to succeed and protect this special area. The organisation was putting in systems and training scouts as rangers, but these efforts were eventually thwarted by the increasing intensity of the war across the river in Rhodesia. Robin worked in this spectacular area opposite Mana Pools on the lower Zambezi for 18 months. It was an exciting time for him; he learnt a lot, not only from the scouts, but particularly from the man in charge of the project – Erick Balson, formerly wildlife warden of Tanzania.

Robin has had many exciting moments through the years, but he recalls one especially frightening experience while he was with Wildlife Conservation International:

'The war in Rhodesia was intensifying during the time I spent on the Zambezi. Because of this, we had to operate without weapons. All the wildlife

officers had their guns taken away in case we were mistaken for Rhodesians or guerrilla fighters. We did a little fishing in the river to supplement rations for the scouts and to sustain ourselves. On one occasion, while walking down to a sandbank with some of the lads, who were carrying a large net to fish in the river, I saw some vultures on the ground about three or four hundred yards away. I was walking with a scout and carrying our only weapon, a large stick. Thinking they must be at the end of a kill, I wanted to see what had been killed. When we had crossed the sandbank I suddenly realised that the birds were not on the ground but sitting on top of a ridge and as I approached they flew off. I thought to myself as I climbed the ridge that there would not be much left of the kill. How wrong I was! Peering over the top I confronted eight lionesses on a waterbuck. They growled and bounded off to my right.

'For some reason, the game scout and I decided to go and have a look at the kill. Not really thinking very clearly, we negotiated around a small lagoon to get there. While we were looking at the carcass, I heard some strange noises coming from the riverbank beyond us. I thought maybe it was hippos fighting. As I turned to discuss this with the scout, a huge lion charged from the bushes with an ear-splitting roar. His mane spread out and his tail rigid in the air, he came straight for us. The river was on my right and the lagoon on my left. The scout shouted, "Don't run!" I couldn't run back, as that is where the lionesses had gone but I also had no intention of standing still! I ran into the lagoon and swam across as fast as I could, the scout following me and the lion following both of us! Luckily, we were the faster swimmers and had gone quite a long way when the lion arrived on the bank. After shaking himself off, he decided to go back to the kill.

'It was a very close call, but we did learn a thing or two at the kill. We saw that the stomach and gall bladder of the waterbuck had been buried in the sand and the carcass dragged well away. This meant there must have been cubs nearby, as these are parts of the body that would be bad for the cubs, hence they had been removed from the animal before they came to feed.'

After 18 months, Wildlife Conservation International had to close down the project because of the increased military action across the river. The Zambezi National Park was created in 1983 as the conflict came to an end following Zimbabwe's independence in 1980.

Robin was now out of work, so his friends suggested that he apply for a job with Norman Carr Safaris and Wilderness Trails, based at Chibembe Camp in the South Luangwa National Park. This operated as both a hunting and photographic safari outfit; it was well known and in an area that Robin had often visited with his family. He joined them as a walking-safari guide in 1976. Norman Carr was already the best-known and most highly respected man involved in Zambian wildlife and tourism. He worked tirelessly to improve the parks, introduce tourism and involve the local communities.

Both Norman Carr and the manager of Chibembe Camp, former Wildlife Department ranger and warden Phil Berry, inspired Robin to pursue a career as a walking-safari guide. However, it was the wildlife scouts who really saw him through those turbulent and exciting early years. Norman had been in the King's African Rifles during World War II and had with him a loyal group of ex-military scouts – superbly disciplined men who had experienced battle and were completely at home in the bush. They taught Robin everything they knew about tracking, self-sufficiency and adaptability, for which he is extremely grateful. Norman had 24 professional hunters working for him at that time, all of whom had had to serve a two-year apprenticeship before they could take out a client. They spent this time mainly walking in the bush and learning their skills from his excellent scouts – a regime that was strictly adhered to by Norman, which gave Zambia an excellent reputation as a hunting destination.

Although he did not train to be a hunter, Robin was fortunate enough to participate in this exceptional training with the scouts and with Phil, who was already an experienced safari guide. The clients who came there on safari knew little about the bush or the names of the birds, but Norman insisted that anyone working for him had to be thoroughly appraised.

They had plenty of clients, mostly British, for both photographic and hunting safaris.

In 1979, Robin was invited by some British clients to join them on a safari in the Selous Game Reserve in Tanzania with Richard Bonham. Richard is another of Africa's great safari guides. He became well known for his walking safaris supported by porters in the Selous Game Reserve and has two exceptional camps – Sand Rivers, on the Rufiji River in the Selous Game Reserve, and Ol Donyo Wuas, in the Chyulu Hills, Kenya. Robin did not wish to go as a guest, but was keen to visit the area. In the event, one of Richard's guides had to back out, which gave Robin the opportunity to drive a Land Rover on the safari. American writer and environmental activist Peter Matthiessen and photographer Hugo van Lawick travelled with them to research a book about the experiences of a game ranger in East Africa. The book, *Sand Rivers*, published in 1982, is one of the most exquisite books ever published on this vast and beautiful area.

The Luangwa Valley was known as the Valley of the Elephants. There used to be an estimated 100 000 elephants there, along with 6 000 rhinos. Commercial poaching, however, started in the mid-1970s and proved to be a conservation disaster. Towards the end of the decade, the Save the Rhino Trust, in which both Norman and Phil were involved, was formed to help the National Parks Department combat the destructive poaching of these animals in the Luangwa Valley. It proved very difficult to halt. At the height of the killing, it was estimated that 27 elephants were being shot every day. By the early 1990s, when poaching was eventually under control, there were almost no rhinos left and the elephant population had been reduced to 20 000.

Norman Carr employed Robin in 1977 at Chibembe, Chinzombo and Nsefu to take walking safaris for Wilderness Trails, the photographic side of a hunting company called Zambia Safaris, in which Norman was a director. This was the first time that Robin had been employed in the tourism industry. In 1980, Norman left the hunting company to concentrate on photographic safaris under his own name, Norman Carr Safaris. He later built Kapani Lodge in the Mfuwe area.

Robin remained in the employment of Wilderness Trails, who asked him to renovate and manage Nsefu Camp, a cluster of thatched rondavels that had been a self-catering government camp since the 1950s – a place he had visited as a child. Although it had become run down, it was beautifully situated on a broad bend of the Luangwa River and, once renovated, it became very popular, as it was in an excellent game area.

In 1982, Robin was granted permission by the then National Parks and Wildlife Services to open Tena Tena, a tented fly camp, 12 kilometres south of Nsefu, to be used as a satellite camp for walking safaris. The camp consisted of a circle of tents, a drum-shower (which has greater capacity than a bucket-shower) and a long-drop loo. It provided a three-day optional walking safari for guests based at Nsefu who were interested in really getting out into the bush. During the early days of these safaris, black rhinos were still frequently spotted in the area.

In 1985, Robin left Wilderness Trails but retained Tena Tena Camp, as Wilderness Trails was acquired by Eco Safaris and the latter did not want to operate Robin's camp. So he set up his own company, Robin Pope Safaris, which took the lease over in 1986. His was one of the first companies to open in the Luangwa Valley after the government's nationalisation programme of the 1970s and early 1980s ended. The logistics of running such a remote camp were a huge challenge. A convoy had to travel from Lusaka to Tena Tena at the beginning of the season with supplies – a long, tedious journey that had to be repeated at least once more during the season, depending on the cash flow. Robin dreamt of having a base at Mfuwe, the hub of the Luangwa Valley, to ease his transport problems.

In fact, Robin's head has always been full of dreams and ideas but, as he was so popular and therefore constantly busy with clients, he had little time to realise them. He needed an energetic, dynamic person to turn them into reality. That person would be Jo Holmes.

It was 1988, and Jo Holmes, head of the locations department of a film company, was living in Glasgow with her long-term boyfriend. Although life seemed perfect on the surface, for some reason she was less than satisfied, so when her sister was offered a catering job at Robin Pope's camp, Tena Tena, in Zambia, but couldn't take it up and asked if she wanted to take the job instead, Jo didn't hesitate. She knew immediately she must not let this opportunity pass her by.

Robin met Jo at Lusaka Airport and took her straight to the supermarket. She simply could not believe the lack of stock she was confronted with. That was a low time in Zambia's economy. Jo lamented that she would not be able to cook any decent meals with the limited ingredients available, but Robin assured her that she would. Once the vehicle was loaded with three months' supplies, they took off like a couple of hillbillies on the long journey to the camp. As they arrived, a hippo walked up the bank as if to greet Jo. Right away she felt at home at Tena Tena, and within a month she had also fallen head over heels in love with Robin. He kept his distance for a long while, though, convinced she had a touch of khaki fever and that it would soon wear off.

Jo was an exuberant addition to Tena Tena; she brought life and sparkle to the camp with her own brand of joie de vivre. Her laughter rang through the camp, and her passion for dancing was incorporated into the evening activities. Guests arriving for a peaceful safari, many of them grey-haired old ladies who had not danced for years, found themselves joining in Jo's rock 'n' roll sessions by the Luangwa River, entering into the spirit of it and having a marvellous time. Life at Tena Tena took on a new vitality. And Robin's personal feelings for Jo also grew.

Jo also learnt about the bush. She acquired her guide's licence in 1990 and frequently went on game drives with Robin as his 'spotter'. However, she spent steadily less time on safaris and became more involved in running the business, particularly marketing Robin's safaris. Her first sortie into the commercial world of travel was attending Indaba, South Africa's annual pan-African trade fair in Durban. When she walked in, she was asked if she was a seller or a buyer, so she could be given the correct badge. Unfamiliar with the industry, she told them she was there to persuade agents to send their clients to Zambia; she received her exhibitor's badge and, placed on the Air Zambia stand, she pulled everyone wearing a red delegate's badge over to her desk. She literally stood in the aisles and accosted them. It was not long before it was the other way around: people lined up at the travel trade fairs to get an appointment with her.

As her role evolved and she became aware of how important it was to awaken the world to the qualities of Zambia as a tourist destination, Jo became an ambassador for Zambian tourism, travelling the world and spreading the word. She gathered the other tour operators around her, and took some of them with her on her travels, and always supported their products while selling her own. It is to her great credit that, although there is always a degree of competition in any business, no group of independent operators is as close to one another as are the Zambian companies.

Robin would discuss his ideas and plans with Jo, who then implemented them. 'How lovely it would be,' he said, 'if everyone in the valley could get together and sing carols at Christmas on the bridge into the South Luangwa National Park.' Jo passed the word around and from then on it became an annual Christmas Eve tradition. Carols are sung by candlelight for the guests at all the local lodges, their staff and anyone else who wants to join in.

Whenever Robin had an idea, Jo would sell it, and then, together, they would work out how it should be implemented. To give an example, ever since the occasion Robin had flown over the northern section of the park to help a producer with a film she was making, he vowed he would come back to explore the area of the Mupamadzi River, which had looked so beautiful from the air. On hearing this, Jo decided to market walking safaris in that area and sold six of them for the following year. They then had to work out the logistics, buy the equipment, find the campsites and, most importantly, get a road made. This proved a challenge. It took two years to complete 100 kilometres of road that is used for only three-and-a-half months a year and has to be regraded at the beginning of every safari season. The rains and the black cotton soil make it impassable for half the year, so, once the rains are over, Robin sends a team of men to dig the gullies and clear the way for the grader to do its job. It's a mammoth task, but the joy of walking in such a remote place is a great reward.

Robin is the dreamer and perfectionist; Jo is the architect of the vision. They are an incredible team, one of the best that Zambia has. In 1991, Mike Shirley-Bevan, a well-established British tour operator, put together the Safari Guide Company, a group of the best guides in Africa at the time. The first meeting was held at Victoria Falls in 1990; Robin was chosen as the Zambian representative. The others were Søren Lindstrom, Jan van der Reep, David Foot, Richard Bonham, Charlie McConnell, Roland Purcell and John Stevens. The association, designed to help with marketing and share joint problems, continued for eight years.

THE LOVE MATCH

Robin still thought that Jo was suffering from khaki fever, even though she had become very involved in his business. After he had turned down her advances, she said that it would be difficult for her to remain in Zambia indefinitely if he did not want to make a commitment.

In 1991, they took a trip to America to see the whales at the Baja Peninsula, followed by a visit to Yellowstone National Park. At the famous waterfall in the park, which was frozen solid, as it was midwinter, Robin asked Jo to become engaged to him. 'Are you asking me to marry you or just to be engaged to you?' she asked.

'Well,' he said, 'I thought we would just try the engagement bit for a while, but I do want to marry you.' He made her a ring of ice from the falls to pledge his love.

A long engagement proved not for them. That year, when they had a cancellation at Tena Tena, they decided to use the time to get married.

The marriage service was held under the wide canopy of an ancient fig tree by Baka Baka Lagoon, not far from Tena Tena. Hay bales were placed in rows for pews; a table with a white cloth under an arch crafted from elephant grass served as the altar; and a Roman Catholic priest from an upcountry mission came to administer the service.

The priest was a delightful man but a bit forgetful due to a bad knock on the head he had received in an accident, and required a little prompting during the service. At one point, he looked at Jo and asked, 'What comes next?'

'It's time for the Lord's Prayer,' Jo said.

'Of course. What language do you want it in?' he said, reeling off a string of African dialects.

'English will do,' said Jo.

The party at Tena Tena went on all night. The beating of drums and throbbing music carried down the river and could be heard for miles. It didn't matter, because everyone within hearing distance was at the party. It was not only a joyful occasion for Robin and Jo, and all their friends and families, but also a blessing for Zambia.

Robin's dream of having some land at Mfuwe was finally realised after years of negotiations. He had searched along the riverbank south of the bridge for the finest piece of land, and found it on a beautiful sweep of the river, with huge, mature trees and magnificent views across to the national park. His permission to purchase was granted in 1991, four years after he had applied for the land. The property, named Nkwali, is his on a 99-year lease and includes, along with the attractive lodge, the administrative headquarters of Robin Pope Safaris and a newly built house for him and Jo. Their original two-bedroom house by the river has become a hideaway and can be booked by anyone wanting peace and privacy during their stay in Mfuwe. The company's recent acquisition of Nsefu Camp, now newly renovated without losing its traditional character, has added another dimension to Robin's safaris.

The local community also benefits in many ways from Jo's involvement. The government clinic in Mfuwe became inadequate for the expanding population in the area. Jo has been on the clinic committee for many years and has helped raise money to enlarge it and improve conditions. She also runs a scheme that has brought in a doctor who is financially supported by the safari lodges. The doctor works mostly at the clinic and takes care of guests at the lodges who become ill. It is vital for the community to benefit from local tourism.

Jo has supported the rural Kawaza School for 15 years, not just financially but also through her approach to expanding the minds and skills of the pupils. Because the children live in, and will probably also work in a wildlife area, she ensures that they learn about conservation from an early age. She has introduced art at the school. Her safari guests have donated crayons and pencils, but paper, a precious commodity, is not easily available in Mfuwe. When Jo first arrived at the school with a huge stack of paper from Lusaka and told the children to start drawing, they would draw on a small corner of the page to preserve the paper. It took months to get them to use a whole page for their drawings. Three years later, the children entered an art competition in which they won first prize, and one 12-year-old is showing considerable talent. Another educational tool – a video machine and television run off a solar-powered battery – keeps many little souls mesmerised. They sit on the floor in front of the black-and-white screen, gazing at wildlife programmes and children's stories. For the older children, the favourite game in the school is Scrabble. Fiercely competitive, they play individually or in teams. The government used to provide 3 teachers for 430 pupils, but Jo has persuaded them to provide 5, and 6 more are paid for by Robin Pope Safaris. Having 11 teachers in a rural school in Zambia gives these children a rare advantage.

Day trips are arranged to Kawaza Village for tourists who want to see how the local community lives. The visitors have lunch with the locals, visit the school and spend the night in the village if they wish. All profits earned in this way go to support 12 disabled residents and the orphanage. Robin and Jo feel strongly that as much as possible should be put back into the community, not in cash handouts but in ways that benefit them all, improving people's quality of life and providing them with future opportunities.

Robin plans to explore the Chendeni Hills, some 20 kilometres south of Nkwali, a place of ancient history, fossils and rare birds. This, along with his established trips to Kasanka and Lake Bangweulu, will give his devoted followers plenty of opportunity for variety. He also has a dream of taking safaris in the Sudan. The best season to visit the Sudan would be during the rainy season in Zambia, which means he could keep his business ticking over all year with new and interesting 'products'. Jo was conceived in the Sudan, which has always made her curious about the country. And we know what happens when Jo fixes her attention on Robin's dreams.

The Luangwa Valley is one of Africa's greatest treasures. It has had some very dedicated people protecting it in the past and there is no shortage of young people in Zambia to continue this work. The wide, meandering river, with its pale, shifting sandbanks, grunting hippos and abundant bird life, is the main artery of the national park. The place throbs with life, and, for me, having been able to explore it with such an expert as Robin Pope was a special honour.

Robin continued to guide for the next few years. He and Jo established some excellent new venues, the most beautiful being Luangwa Safari House, not far from Nkwali. It is tucked away and can only be booked for personal groups, providing a sense of privacy. The house is equipped for eight guests in four luxurious bedrooms. It is an enchanting place where elephants silently walk by on their way to the river and personal safari guides are on hand to care for clients at the house, and to accompany them on drives and walks.

When Robin and Jo were developing Pumulani, a guesthouse on the banks of Lake Malawi in 2006, they met Ton and Margaux de Rooy, who are part of a Dutch travel company called Molecaten, which was keen to get involved in an African travel venture. Ton and Margaux became partners in Robin Pope Safaris in 2006 and eventually took over the business in 2010 when Robin and Jo moved to Lusaka. No longer running a very busy safari company, Robin and Jo now have time to visit other parts of the world such at Titicaca, Machu Picchu and the Amazon Jungle for their own personal leisure.

Robin still guides in Liuwa Plains through Robin Pope Safaris, and spends three months a year there. Liuwa is a magnificent wilderness area in western Zambia where there are no lodges and very few visitors. It is Robin's favourite place. He takes small groups early in the wet season to witness the wildebeest migration, and in the dry season for the prolific birdlife. This is a safari for all bush lovers, and a surprise for those who think they have seen it all.

Jo is the chairman of Project Luangwa, a charity she set up before they retired, which supports schools in the Luangwa Valley. Jo started supporting Kawaza School in 1988; now there are eight other schools benefiting from the charity, which has made a substantial improvement to education in the valley. 'We believe as a charity operating in Zambia that by developing and improving education in schools and creating training opportunities we can help families have the chance of a lasting and sustainable income,' she says.

ROD TETHER

B orn in Uganda, Rod Tether moved to Zambia with his family during the Idi Amin regime when he was three. Growing up in Zambia meant going on family holidays in the bush, as Rod's father, a geologist, was familiar with the remote parts of the country and was determined that his family should also get to know as much of it as possible. Nsefu was a popular destination with the Tether family during the time that Robin Pope managed the camp. Robin was a great inspiration to Rod. At 17, having finished his A levels, Rod applied for a gap-year job at Chibembe Camp. Norman Carr had moved on from there to build Kapani Lodge at Mfuwe, and Wilderness Trails, which was short-staffed at that time, took on Rod as a guide. He worked for the photographic-safari part of Chibembe, which was still primarily a hunting camp in those days.

Three years studying politics and international relations at Southampton University did not sway him from his lifelong passion to live in the bush. Rod spent the university summer vacations in Zambia working for Wilderness Trails, leading three-day walks. He obtained his guide's licence in 1990, the first year of formal examinations for guides in Zambia. Jo Pope, the first woman in Zambia to obtain the guide's licence, sat the exam with him.

In 1994, Rod took a break to explore South America, then returned to run tented mobile safaris for Wild Zambia Safaris in the remote areas of North Luangwa, Shiwa, Bangweulu and Kasanka. During these safaris, Rod became familiar with the wild, majestic beauty of North Luangwa. The journeys were thrilling, but because they were in places far from civilisation, the stress and responsibility were great. Fortunately, nothing went seriously wrong, but if it had they could have been at least a day away from help.

The Wild Zambia Safaris operations were based at Kapani, near Mfuwe, the lodge built and owned by the legendary Norman Carr, the most influential man in Zambia's safari and wildlife business during the mid- to late 20th century. Norman had introduced tourism to Northern Rhodesia and initiated walking safaris there. As a member of the state's Game Department, he helped create wildlife parks, and he founded the Save the Rhino Trust and the Wildlife Society of Zambia. Many of Zambia's guides began their careers at Chibembe Lodge, which Norman ran. His final years were spent at Kapani, overlooking a lovely oxbow lake, where he entertained his visitors with his stories and shared with them the wisdom he had acquired in his 40 years in the bush. Kapani is a bustling lodge with tourists coming and going, and visitors popping in for a chat. It was a great place for Rod to unwind after a strenuous mobile safari. It was also at Kapani, during the last year of Norman's life, that Rod met and fell in love with Guz Thieme, who had returned to Zambia, having left the country at the age of 13, to work as the caterer at Kapani. Guz is a marvellous cook.

It was at this time that John Coppinger approached Rod to run Mwaleshi Bush Camp together with his resident guide, Bryan Jackson, while based at Tafika. That was the perfect move for Rod, who had wanted to move on from the mobile safaris and Guz went with him to Tafika, where she had been offered the position of caterer. They were extremely happy there, as it is not just a safari lodge but also the home of John and Carol Coppinger, and their two daughters, which gives visitors and employees that special feeling of being part of a family. Rod and Bryan shared the guiding at Tafika, taking it in turns to go to Mwaleshi for the four-night walking safaris, while Guz remained in charge of the Tafika kitchen.

The drive from Mwaleshi to Tafika was an arduous six-hour journey over very bad roads through thick pockets of tsetse fly. The reward was travelling through glorious forests of cathedral mopane and marvelling at the scalding turquoise waters of the hot springs. Clearly, the destination would become more popular if there were an airstrip to fly visitors in. Once permission was granted, far more guests were tempted to visit Mwaleshi. Rod and Guz were delighted when, after their first season at Tafika with Rod intermittently guiding at Mwaleshi, they were sent to Mwaleshi to run the camp together for the season.

The season in North Luangwa lasts only about five months because the thick, sticky black cotton soil makes it impassable for vehicles in the wet season. The African staff are happy with these working arrangements and enjoy being at home, as they traditionally farm in the wet season, growing crops for themselves and for market. Rod and Guz needed to find alternative employment, and spent their time in the wet season working in a ski resort in the Alps. Guz had already established herself as a chalet cook in the off season when Rod took a job at the same resort.

After two seasons at Mwaleshi, they felt it was time to create their own camp in the North Luangwa National Park. The park had only two tourist camps and the idea of a third was welcomed by the Parks Department when Rod submitted his application for Kutundala. The agreement was made verbally, but it took eight months for Rod to obtain the written permission required to get going, which was finally granted in April 2001. Many of their clients came through Robin Pope Safaris and without Jo Pope's support it would have been far more difficult for them to start the camp. Mwaleshi continues to operate, as does one other camp, belonging to Mark Harvey, grandson of Stewart Gore-Browne, who built Shiwa Ngandu, a grand English manor house not far from North Luangwa, in the 1920s.

Kutundala is across the park from Mwaleshi, reached by the single road that runs through it. On arrival, vehicles are parked on the riverbank, and shoes are taken off and trousers rolled up in order to wade across the clear waters of the Mwaleshi River (too shallow for hippos) to reach the camp. The four delightful reed huts overlook the river, and a giant Natal mahogany tree shades the dining area and the library, where Rod keeps his collection of books on all aspects of Africa. This small, exclusive destination accommodates only six people at a time, because this is the number that guides choose as the maximum for bush walks.

Rod and Guz married in August 2002 in the chapel attached to Shiwa Ngandu. Their first son, Louis, was born in 2003 and spent the first few years of his life with them at Kutundala. Their house was a replica of the guest cottages, except that, instead of the unrestricted view from the front, it had a barrier of chicken wire for safety – a lion could easily mistake the cry of a baby for that of a distressed bleating lamb! From her open-air kitchen, Guz produced by far the best food I have ever eaten in the bush – and she was at least seven hours' drive from the nearest shop. The kitchen was enclosed by a reed fence; the oven was a hole in the ground; and a wood fire heated a hotplate on which her mouth-watering delicacies were created. Herbs, lettuce and other fresh vegetables were grown in traditional clay pots, all overlooked by a monkey's skull attached to the reed fence. (Skulls are traditionally placed in the vegetable patch to ward off theft.)

Elephants wander through Kutundala, pukus prance across the river and it is not uncommon while walking to get quite close to a herd of buffaloes or even to find lions on a kill. The game viewing may be excellent, but it is the walking that attracted Rod to this park. He prefers to view the bush and its inhabitants on foot. The joy that this brings is being able to melt into the bush, to have the smells and sounds all around you and never hear a car engine or the drone of an aircraft. In fact, it is so far off the beaten track that not even contrails streak the sky here. This is certainly Rod's favourite area. He is the only person recording the wildlife in North Luangwa. Having completed the identification of all the trees in the park for the Royal Botanic Gardens at Kew, he is now compiling a bird list.

It was not always a place of peace and tranquillity, however. Some of the heaviest poaching in Zambia took place here. Thousands of black rhinos were slaughtered; the last remaining one was killed in 1984. Having exterminated the rhinos, the poachers then turned to the elephants and, had it not been for an extremely effective anti-poaching unit, they would have probably gone the same way. Rod recalls the horror he had felt at Chibembe, when the sound of gunfire inevitably meant they would find eight or nine dead elephants every day.

The Frankfurt Zoological Society, which partly funded the anti-poaching unit run by Delia and Mark Owens, American conservationists who operated successfully in the 1980s, is still involved there today. The society doesn't manage the park – that mandate falls to the Zambian government – but it does manage projects, the latest of which is very exciting: the reintroduction of black rhinos. The society provides technical support such as vehicles, GPSs and fuel. Rod is thrilled they are there, as their presence, along with increased tourism, is generating new life in the park and, as he says, has virtually eliminated poaching:

'Poaching would be very difficult to start up again – the lines of communication are broken, and the local people have regular work and take great pride in their achievements. Working in a safari camp knowing you have a monthly wage to send home to your family is much easier than poaching. And carrying a backpack on walks and keeping the camp clean and tidy is certainly more pleasant than lugging tusks or dead animals over long distances.

'When Guz and I go to Lusaka and leave the staff in charge, nothing is locked up: all our possessions are right there on the shelves. After seeing the petty pilfering that went on in the ski resorts, I realise how lucky I am to be living in Zambia with staff that I trust implicitly.'

As tourism increases in this large area, Rod believes there is a need for another camp, as there are so many other places to see, such as the top of the escarpment, where one can picnic by pools and waterfalls, or the petrified forest and numerous fossil sites. Guz's father, also a geologist, loves the area. Together with a friend, an Oxford professor, he has discovered many sites yielding fossils of dicynodonts – mammal-like reptiles that existed before the dinosaurs.

Rod became an independent safari guide when he moved to Lusaka from North Luangwa in November 2011. Rod and Guz had continued living at Kutundala with Louis and two more children, Daniel and Sasha, until Louis was eight. Guz home-schooled both the boys, but the time came when they realised the children, Louis in particular, needed a more conventional school life to be able to socialise with others of their own age and participate in sports.

So, with heavy hearts they packed up and left Kutundala for Lusaka after 11 idyllic years. It had been a tremendous experience for them all, especially their guests, who were intrigued and delighted to find a family living happily in such a remote place.

Rod is now an independent private guide and puts together trips for 2 to 10 people. All the itineraries are tailor-made. At first, he concentrated on safaris in Zambia but has recently spread his wings to include Zimbabwe, Tanzania and Kenya, as many of his regular guests have requested visits to other parts of Africa. The next destination will be Madagascar and he is currently researching the potential for safaris in that diverse and magnificent country.

Rod designs his safaris around places when they are at their seasonal best. For example, Bangweulu is spectacular in the early dry season but not as appealing at other times of the year. Having spent 20 years in the Luangwa Valley, mainly the northern region, he has hugely enjoyed visiting the rest of the country from Kasanka to Kafue and he still visits Luangwa. Accommodation during his safaris is in the form of permanent camps or private, mobile tented camps – it all depends on the wishes of his guests:

'I really enjoy the planning aspect – bouncing ideas back and forward with the client and working out the logistics. However, the trips themselves

have been a revelation. I see my role first and foremost as a guide, interpreting the bush for my guests, and after over 20 years spending each dry season in Luangwa, it has been incredibly liberating to visit other areas that, in the past, I could only visit in the rains, or fleetingly.

'I am enjoying a renewed love affair with many areas of Zambia like Kasanka National Park and the Bangweulu, but none more so than the Kafue National Park, which is the size of Wales and contains more antelope species than anywhere else. The park gets a bad rap for its lack of game concentration and tsetse flies. What I feel people never emphasise enough, though, is its incredible diversity: the rivers change character from swamps, to lovely wide tree-lined channels, to rapids, to lakes, and there are plains, hills, mopane, riverine forest and miombo woodland. I use existing camps en route and these too are varied, normally owner-operated, sometimes whacky and all wonderfully unformulaic. The common theme of the camps is a passion for the park, but there is no complacency here, as everyone is aware that you have chosen to visit an unusual destination. Driving through the park from camp to camp is the perfect mode – long, beautiful drives, often quiet, but then, suddenly, you will get an outstanding sighting of a pack of wild dog, a cheetah, a family group of elephant, a day-time leopard or a herd of sable antelope – for everything is here.'

His knowledge, expertise and calm character make Rod one of the most exceptional safari guides you could ever choose.

ANXIOUS MOMENTS: LIFE IN THE BUSH WITH CHILDREN

'It was actually surprisingly easy bringing up our kids in the bush, thanks mostly to our wonderful, all-male staff, who were great at entertaining them and sufficiently bush-savvy to keep them out of harm's way – most of the time. There were of course the occasional hairy incidents. We'll never forget the time we had just finished supper and were still chatting around the table, when the waiter came down and said, very calmly, "Excuse, bwana, sorry

to disturb, but Shadreck [the nanny] says that there is a black mamba under Sasha's cot."

'I leapt up and one of the guests asked if he could come too. We ran to our house and into Sasha's little room. I got a torch and shone it under the cot: no black mamba – but there was a huge black-necked spitting cobra coiled up. Shining the torch had disturbed it, and it proceeded to make its way up the cot and inside the mosquito net, so there was nowhere for it to go except on top of Sasha, who was fast asleep and blissfully unaware. I threw the mosquito net back and yanked Sasha out by the arm and handed her to a member of staff who was standing behind me watching, but who, being absolutely petrified of snakes, was not going to get any closer. The snake was now in the net, so I pulled the cot out of the way and asked the staff to hand me a big stick, which they invariably carry when there is a chance of having to confront a snake – not on this occasion though and I was passed a foot-long flimsy twig. It had to do. Fuelled by adrenalin, I made a frenzied attack on the snake with this thoroughly inadequate tool but it thankfully did the job. The snake was dead, cot replaced, Sasha put back in it (she had not woken up) and mosquito net thrown back over.

'The kids and I dissected the cobra the next day, which was a fun biology lesson.

'Louis, our eldest, took a great interest in fishing from a very early age. This was a fantastic way to entertain him and it kept him quiet for a couple of hours, as his patience for sitting with a hand line was endless. He liked to catch different species and identify them in the book, and then keep them for a few days. One season there was a drying pool near Kutundala with lots of catfish floundering around in the mud. Even the storks seemed to have had their fill and it was apparent that they were all doomed so, armed with a couple of buckets, we set about a rescue mission and collected about 30 good-sized catfish that we then set free in the nearby Mwaleshi River. Louis couldn't resist keeping a couple of particularly fine specimens, so they were put in a big bucket of water in our bathroom and seemed happy enough. Later, however, Guz had to get up in the middle of the night and trod barefoot on one of these slimy creatures, both of which were wandering around the bathroom floor. Guz is not a fan of fish at the best of times and, needless to say, that was the end of keeping pet fish in the bathroom!

'Louis's happiest discovery probably came in our last year at Kutundala when he caught an electric catfish. This innocuous-looking fish gives an amazingly high voltage shock, which it uses for defence and stunning prey. Louis would delight in showing his "pet" to our guests and then ask if they wanted to stroke it. Other memorable pets included a pair of scorpions, christened Mary and Joseph. They were of the Hadogenes variety, so although they looked like something from a science-fiction film, being over six inches long with huge pincers and glossy black bodies, they are pretty benign and can be handled, even by small children, with none of the risk of some of the other species. The reason we kept them was that it was apparent that Mary was pregnant. These scorpions have an amazing life cycle with an eighteen-month gestation, after which they give birth to live young, which are totally white and for the first few weeks ride around on their mother's back. Further research, however, turned up the fact that if the mother is unduly stressed she will re-ingest her babies, so after a couple of weeks of being prodded by three children under seven who like to get a reaction (scorpions are not the most dynamic of pets), we decided to let them go from the large sand pit that we had created for them. A couple of weeks later, Kelson, our waiter, was setting the chairs by the fireside for sundowners when he called for us all to come. There was Mary with a dozen youngsters clinging to her back, so it seems we didn't unduly stress her after all.

'Our children had some amazing experiences. Charlie, a big bull elephant, regularly brushed up against our little grass house while we read them bed-time stories. They watched prides of lion take on buffalo in front of the camp and on one occasion wild dogs popped out of the grass right next to them and proceeded to kill a puku not 20 metres away while they were playing on the beach in front of the camp. They also created their own camp in the thickets next to our hut, where they would hoard treasures of bones, skulls, seed pods and snail shells, and create elaborate bucket showers to cool themselves down, emerging hours later caked in dirt and blissfully happy.'

Rod and Guz have decided to live in Mauritius and, from there, Rod will commute to wherever his safaris take him. But, most excitingly, he plans to specialise in Madagascar, definitely an under-exploited destination:

'I am now creating and guiding trips all over Africa, and have a special interest in Madagascar, a place I feel that everybody with a strong interest in natural history should visit at least once. It's a wildlife hot spot second to none, home to a quarter of the world's primates, half of all chameleon species and an incredible 111 endemic bird species. Madagascar also throws up some unique challenges and a safari there really is a journey to an exotic island "continent" with incredibly diverse geography that will never be forgotten.'

GRANT CUMINGS

Grant Cumings operates in the lush areas of the Zambezi River in the Lower Zambezi National Park – a magnificent complement to a safari in the Luangwa Valley.

Born and raised in Zambia, Grant experienced his first brushes with the wild in the form of a bite from a tsetse fly when he was only three weeks old and a bite from a baboon when he was just over a year! Undeterred, he grew up spending many weekends exploring and fishing with his father, listening enthralled to tales of his years in Tanganyika (Tanzania) prospecting for diamonds in the bush. Grant's enthusiasm for game spotting started when he was very young and has never diminished. As a child, he always had his face pressed to the car window, searching for wildlife – even when his mother told him that there was no likelihood of seeing anything other than a goat.

He did a degree in economics in the United States, and returned each summer to accompany professional hunters in Kafue and Luangwa. After graduating, he thought his career path would lead to hunting, so, after completing a two-year apprenticeship in 1989, he took hunting safaris in Luangwa, Kafue and the Bangweulu Swamps. However, it was not long before he realised that he would much prefer to take photographic safaris and started combining them with his hunting trips.

Grant and his father had spent many happy hours fishing and walking along the Zambezi River, where they camped at their preferred special spot on the bank. This was the obvious site for Grant to establish his first small tented camp, and later his permanent tented lodge, Chiawa, which he set up for photographic safaris. As the photographic side of his work became busier, the hunting diminished, and stopped altogether in 1994.

Chiawa is a lovely camp, constantly visited by passing elephants, which step carefully over the wooden railings as they walk into the camp. They follow the pathways, never disturbing the stones that border them (buffaloes kick the stones all over the place when they visit), take a branch from a tree and walk on. A wide, dry riverbed borders the camp and is used as a highway by all manner of animals coming to drink. Grant likes nothing better than to walk around this area with his guests, mingling with the abundant wildlife.

He has now opened Old Mondoro Bush Camp to complement Chiawa. A simple, down-to-earth camp further downriver, in an area of vast floodplains and open woodland, it is the ideal place for walking and game viewing.

Grant's passion for the Zambezi National Park has never waned and he is intensively involved with its care. He has been an honorary ranger since 1989 and has personally conducted numerous anti-poaching patrols to make the park habitable for wildlife and visitors alike. He is the co-founder and chairman of Conservation Lower Zambezi (CLZ), a non-governmental organisation that protects the wildlife and habitat of the area, and provides logistical support for the Zambia Wildlife Authority's anti-poaching units.

He recently started an environmental education programme for the local village communities to promote conservation awareness and raised $500 000 in just over two years for this project. CLZ also conduct aerial surveys and detach snares from lions, elephants, wild dogs and other species, and have been extremely effective in dramatically reducing poaching in the Lower Zambezi. Grant spent many months compiling a comprehensive safari guide's manual for the Lower Zambezi National Park, which is now in use. He also implemented the safari guide evaluation and examinations programme for the Lower Zambezi, and is responsible for conducting practical and written exams for aspiring walking guides. This is a breathtaking list of achievements for one man.

Grant's dedication to the safari industry in his area is phenomenal. The buzz of his motorboats may irritate some people on the Zimbabwean side of the river, where they are forbidden in Mana Pools, but, although they can disturb the peace, this is a small price to pay given that, thanks to his tireless efforts and those of the CLZ, many can now visit the park. (Incidentally, I was interested to observe that, when approached silently by canoes, hippos sink underwater, but when they are approached by a motorboat they just turn their heads and watch it go past.)

In April 2004, Grant married Lynsey Kane in Scotland. Lynsey has been living at Chiawa, where she is a great help to Grant, putting the skills she gained as a British Airways cabin attendant to use by making the guests feel totally at home there.

Like John Coppinger's daughters and Louis Tether, Grant and Lynsey may add to the generation of 'bush babies' who will grow up in the wild and help protect Zambia's priceless heritage.

Guiding is still very close to Grant's heart – as it is with all the top guides. He seldom guides any more but he oversees all the training of his guides. He commissions various experts to help broaden their knowledge – ornithologists, ecologists, professional photographers and first-aid specialists – whenever he feels the need.

He is still actively involved with Conservation Lower Zambezi's anti-poaching efforts and with the community:

'This year, 2013, for whatever reasons, not one elephant has been poached in the national park – the first such year on record. The only dead

elephants we have found so far this year expired from natural causes with their tusks intact. This is due to the clearly successful support rendered to the authorities by Conservation Lower Zambezi. Chiawa and Old Mondoro are CLZ's biggest supporters in cash and kind, and by leading with such an example, others follow so that CLZ's resources will enable much more effective law enforcement and environmental education compared to other programmes elsewhere.'

Although he has now moved to live in Lusaka with his wife and children, Grant spends half of his time at his camps to monitor the operations and ensure that conservation remains a core activity.

THE
ENDURING IMAGERY
OF EAST AFRICA

The conventional images of Africa come from Tanzania and Kenya, and these countries have fired people's imagination since the times of the earliest explorers to the modern day. The immense and glorious landscapes of East Africa, and the vast numbers of animals that live there, first captured the early travellers' imagination.

The East African region, which also includes Uganda, has the richest diversity of animals in the world. This, along with the great variety of landscapes – from jungle to desert, open savannah, rolling hills and snow-capped mountains – has made the region every tourist's African dream. And the East African guides are well aware of this heritage. This is the region where safaris began and where the word 'safari' actually comes from: 'safari' is a Swahili word meaning 'journey'.

Thanks to literature, films, paintings and television, few people are unfamiliar with the imagery of this region – the vast plains, the Ngorongoro Crater, snow-capped Mount Kilimanjaro, soda lakes pink with flamingos, the Rift Valley and the tribes in their traditional vibrant adornments. A lifetime could be spent exploring the region from the Selous, in southern Tanzania, to Lake Turkana, in north-west Kenya.

The astonishing sight of the wildebeest migration, whether in southern Tanzania in January, collectively giving birth, or running the gauntlet of the crocodiles at river crossings while heading for the succulent new grass of the Masai Mara in Kenya, is a rare and wonderful spectacle. Along with a multitude of bleating wildebeest on the move there is the graceful progress of giraffes across the plains; the elegant Maasai morans stride out, their red shukas billowing behind them; and there are forests of baobabs and the crystal-clear waters of Lake Tanganyika. These all form the images that visitors take home, generally finding that their safari far surpasses their expectations.

Known as the 'cradle of mankind', the Rift Valley of East Africa is the site of numerous significant fossil discoveries, which are of interest to many visitors, and here it is important to have a guide who enjoys visiting the archaeological sites along with traditional safari areas. If the cultural side of East Africa is of special interest, choose a guide with particular knowledge of tribal life.

Owing to its higher rainfall levels, Uganda has a tropical luxuriance rare in the rest of East Africa. Jungles and forests provide habitats for numerous primates. The chimpanzee, our closest relative, can be found here in Kibale Forest, as well as in Tanzania, along the shores of Lake Tanganyika. A visit to the habituated mountain gorillas in the Bwindi Impenetrable Forest National Park in south-west Uganda is a very special experience. There are others in the Virunga Mountains of neighbouring Rwanda. These magnificent and greatly endangered creatures (only some 700 remain in the wild) need all the help and support they can get from us to ensure their survival.

Western Uganda is the area that the great European explorers searched for the source of the Nile, which, as Burton and Speke discovered, is Lake Victoria. On a second expedition, Speke and Grant travelled further north, to where today the beautiful Murchison Falls National Park skirts the edge of Lake Albert. Here the water drains into the Albert Nile, travels through Sudan and then thousands of miles on to the Mediterranean. Nothing much has changed here. Fishermen still ply the waters in their dugout canoes; Ugandan kobs, and giraffes and elephants quench their thirst at the water's edge; and the Blue Mountains rise majestically beyond. This ancient landscape is just as it was when Speke and Grant finally arrived here in their quest for the source of the Nile. It makes you tingle at the thought!

Unfortunately, tragedy has struck this pristine area. In 2009, it was discovered that huge deposits of oil lie beneath the tranquil waters of Lake Albert.

The coastal areas of Kenya and Tanzania are among the loveliest in the world – deserted white sandy beaches, coral reefs for snorkelling and diving, or the exotic aromas of eastern spices and the colourful culture of Lamu or Stone Town, Zanzibar.

Whatever the images are that you want to retain, East Africa certainly lives up to its promise.

A SAFARI TO SOIT ORGOSS: LOLIONDO, NORTHERN TANZANIA

We left Ndutu Safari Lodge at dawn, taking a packed breakfast and lunch for the journey across the Serengeti into the north-western section of the Loliondo game-controlled area.

The immense undulating grasslands with their herds of gazelles and zebras melted into the distant horizon; well-fed hyenas waited by waterholes; stately giraffe ambled across the plain. It was a timeless scene, dry and dusty from the lack of rain, and there was no sign of the wildebeest migration. The year before, we had been among thousands upon thousands of them, grazing on lush green grass on these same plains.

It was the time of year for the migratory birds to gather together in preparation for their flight back to North Africa, Europe and Asia. In the early morning, we drove through great flocks of lesser kestrels stretching as far as the eye could see, flying or hovering over the grass, feeding and resting on the plains – a sight to remember when I see one hovering over a British motorway. A little later, swooping European swallows surrounded our vehicle, catching the butterflies disturbed by our passing. Dicing with death, they darted in front of the vehicle, always avoiding collision and never once missing the tasty morsels they were after.

We breakfasted at the foot of the Gol Mountains before meeting Nigel Perks's good friend, Parkipumy Kaisoi, a Maasai whose boma is in this vicinity and whom I had met the year before. He wanted us to visit his boma, meet his new wife and see the hut she had just completed. Nigel had told him three months ago that we would be there on 21 March and there he was, waiting for us by Nasera, a huge granite boulder rising out of the plain. He jumped into the car and on the way to his boma he related the story of a recent rain-making ceremony he had witnessed. The lack of rain was becoming critical. Ol Doinyo Lengai, the last remaining active volcano in northern Tanzania, and the Maasai God, required a sacrifice, so 272 naked women, one of them a wife of Parkipumy, had climbed to the top of the mountain taking with them 30 sheep. They slaughtered the sheep in an act of appeasement to Lengai, and remained up there for six days living off the meat of the sacrificed sheep. We all rather chuckled at the thought of this and asked him when the rain would come. He answered seriously: it would come on the 24th. And, amazingly, that was exactly what happened. We had massive storms that struck on the night of 23 March. When we drove back through the same area three days later, the grass was already turning green. Rain in Africa is always a welcome miracle.

After visiting his boma to admire his wife's newly built house and having bought a few trinkets, we set off to have lunch at the 'tree where man was born'. This huge ancient fig tree that stands alone with hardly another tree or shrub in sight naturally became a magnet for legends. The roots found a crack in the hard pan over 400 years ago and it just kept growing. There must have been other cracks in the pan, as it grows in a gully where there are wells that give fresh water all year round.

Travelling on, we followed a rough track northwards until the plains gave way to rolling, wooded hills interspersed with granite koppies. We knew then that we were entering the remote area of our destination. We turned off the road, leaving all signs of civilisation and tourist routes far behind. By mid-afternoon, we got our first glimpse of the jagged peaks of Soit Orgoss on the horizon.

Soit Orgoss (corridors of rock) is a secret, special place that is difficult to find on any map. Here the natural rhythm of the Maasai culture lives on in the traditional manner, untouched by mass tourism, and therefore the area is happily devoid of roadside begging. The downside for the visitor is that one may not photograph the people or their domestic animals. This takes considerable self-control, as there is nothing more appealing than the beautifully turned-out morans roaming the land or their delightful children tending newborn lambs and kids.

In 1989, Thad Peterson, one of three brothers born in Tanzania of American missionary parents, explored this area looking for new places to take his walking safaris. The Petersons' highly respected company, Dorobo Safaris, specialises in adventurous safaris in remote areas. Thad, who, like all great guides, radiates energy and charisma, persuaded the elders to allow him to use the area for his walking safaris, paying fees in return to the villagers. Having agreed to this, the villagers keep all their livestock out of Soit Orgoss during the season that Dorobo Safaris operates. Their cattle graze at Soit Orgoss only in the dry season, which is also the hunting season. In Tanzania the people own the land, but the government owns the animals and, in 1991, an Arab from Dubai paid the government for the hunting rights over this particular part of Loliondo. Luckily, Dorobo Safaris was already established in the area and although requested repeatedly by the Arab to do so, the villagers would not ask the safari company to leave. Being honourable people, they stuck to their word. Conflict is avoided, as the photographic safaris do not take place here during July and August, the hunting season.

A few years ago, Thad and the villagers discussed having one other operator, who would be able to use a vehicle combined with walking safaris in the area, to increase their income. Thad asked Gibb's Farm Safaris (the firm Nigel worked with) if they would like to be that company and, of course, they accepted.

Our campsite was set high up on a koppie with panoramic views, giving a sense of vastness and freedom. The koppies are made up of massive boulders, some as large as multistorey buildings; others balance precariously one on top of each other, resembling a natural Stonehenge. Due to water retention in the koppies, the plant life is luxuriant and diverse. Huge fig trees grow in the cracks and crevices, their fat white roots travelling down the rock to find the soil. Tall aloes, shrubs and exquisite tiny ferns tucked under the rocks all thrive happily together. The rocks are streaked with warm autumnal colours punctuated by swathes of silver or yellow lichen. Breathtaking in the first glow of sunlight at dawn, they beg to be explored. The koppies, which provide many secret hiding places for leopards, are also home to klipspringers flouting gravity as they prance from rock to rock on their tiptoes. Baboons scale the rocks to their safe roosts, where the playful youngsters pull one another down by their tails, then, finding a foothold or handhold, they scramble up again in a death-defying Spiderman act.

Flat-topped acacias dot the golden grass that sweeps between each string of koppies. Herds of sleek plains game graze on the nutritious grass: topis with their purple 'bruised' haunches, as well as hartebeest, Burchell's zebras, giraffes, dik-diks and impalas. The impala rams are exceptionally large here – apparently this is where trophy hunters came in the early 20th century when they needed a good specimen for their collections. There are buffaloes and elephants, and, of course, the cats also flourish here. However, all the animals are shy and skittish because of being hunted. One of the most astonishing sights was an enormous herd of eland. They rose out of a wooded gully in numbers to match the wildebeest migration. More and more kept appearing until the herd covered the hillside ahead of us before disappearing over the crest. They were difficult to count but must have numbered over 500.

Each morning we walked for three or four hours, after which we were met by the Land Rovers and offered coffee or tea and a lift back to camp. After our afternoon siesta, we usually went off to explore in the vehicles. Although there are plenty of animals in the area, this is not the ideal place for portrait photography, but perfect for viewing wildlife in its landscape. The prolific bird and animal life served merely to enhance the astounding vistas that opened up at each turn of our walks and drives. However, we had already spent three days at Ndutu before our visit to Soit, and everyone's need for close-up animal sightings had been satisfied. We had seen a lioness with tiny cubs, a very young baby elephant and its mother splashing near us in the water, two servals in a tree in the daylight (the reluctant female having been chased to the top by an ardent male), striped hyenas, and cheetahs and leopards.

We had witnessed plenty of interesting animal behaviour too. This is something one learns when travelling with a really good guide who takes the time to sit patiently and watch the scene unfold. Nigel had spotted a group of mongooses, which we observed as they ran, then grouped, stood up on their hind legs to survey their territory, and rushed off again in a most agitated manner. It had transpired that two jackals were trying to grab their babies, which they were protecting desperately while trying to get back to their den. In spite of their efforts, a jackal did manage to grab one of the babies before the whole group disappeared into the safety of their underground burrow. Nigel had recently spent two weeks with a crew filming mongooses, but they never saw anything like that.

A member of Dorobo Safaris always accompanies Nigel's safaris to Soit Orgoss; it is their area and they know it well. Our guide was a splendid Tanzanian named Pallangyo, who was larger than life, with crinkly grey hair, an infectious laugh and a great sense of humour that made him excellent company. We were well protected on our walks by Pallangyo with his rifle, and our Maasai tracker with his spear and bow and arrows.

The lions roared below our koppie all night and twice we heard the rasping sound of a leopard in the camp, so, on the second morning, Nigel decided we should find these noisy lions. Spotting two lionesses sitting on rocks high on the adjacent koppie, we crept round for a closer view while Nigel and our Maasai guide climbed a rock to find a route up to them. Needless to say, the lions vanished, but Nigel and the guide had spotted what they thought was an old disused Ildorobo hunter's shelter. Climbing the slope with excited anticipation, we looked up through the trees to see a man sitting high on a rock watching us. Wearing a worn brown coat over his shuka, he was an old Ildorobo who did not melt into the undergrowth when he saw us, but waited to greet us because he recognised Pallangyo, whom he knows and trusts. It was not a disused shelter after all, but his home, and he was sitting on the rock making new arrows that were like works of art. Smooth and straight, they had perfect grooves to fit the bowstring, reinforced with sinew and feathers meticulously cut and inserted into the ends, with only the metal arrowheads yet to be fixed.

The old man, with rheumy eyes, a grizzled beard and a gentle smile, invited us into his home. A great flat overhanging rock formed the roof and branches of dense thorn bush leaned against it, creating a protective wall around the dwelling. Bunches of vulture feathers used for the arrows were attached to a pole propped outside the narrow entrance. We stepped in past the smouldering fire and looked around. The ceiling was about two metres high; the room approximately six metres by four. On the left, two forked sticks supported a thin, straight branch on which hung curtains of buffalo meat. Bark and roots lay in heaps ready to be boiled and made into either medicine or poison for the arrowheads, and a pile of skins spread over a layer of straw served as the bed. His possessions were few: the clothes he was wearing, his bow and arrows, a small knife, a big metal pot, and his only concession to modern life, an old plastic water bottle. This was no dark and dingy cave but a light and airy place, cosy with the smoky aroma of burnt wood, and there were no bothersome flies. We would all have been happy to stay there.

On our last morning, while the camp was being packed up, he sat on a rock nearby, watching and bidding us farewell. It was a rare and special privilege to meet an Ildorobo still living the traditional life of his ancestors and seldom seen by outsiders. We had spent much time contemplating the origins of man, visiting Oldupai Gorge, trying to envisage life thousands of years ago. But we never dreamt that we would actually meet a hunter-gatherer.

NIGEL PERKS

I t is hard to imagine the cataclysmic explosion that must have taken place to create the vast bowl beneath us as we stand at the rim of the crater on a perfectly tranquil, cloudless morning. Nigel Perks is explaining how the Serengeti plains were formed. We are in northern Tanzania at the edge of the Ngorongoro Crater, which, at about 18 kilometres (11 miles) across and over 600 metres (2 000 feet) deep, is the biggest of the numerous volcanoes in this area, similar in size to Mount Kilimanjaro. The ash and dust created by its explosion were blown east by the prevailing wind, joining the ash and dust from earlier volcanoes and filling the valleys as far as the eye can see. This ash preserved all that lay beneath it and created a fertile paradise for the plains game that now feed there.

The road to the Serengeti winds down through a string of extinct volcanoes that fall away from the Ngorongoro Crater, so peaceful and green they give no intimation of the roaring infernos they once were. The ash from Mount Lemagrut, one of the older volcanoes on this route, was instrumental in preserving the rich fossil beds in the gullies and gorges here. The slopes are lightly wooded with flat-topped *Acacia tortilis*, and the ground is thickly carpeted with yellow and white flowers after the recent rains. Acacias are the favourite food of the giraffes that amble through the flowers as if in slow motion, nibbling at the tops of the trees.

This part of the world is Nigel's passion. He is a large man with a quick, infectious laugh and a gold tooth that glints in the sun. He is a New Zealander with the heart and soul of an African. He has the knack of making you feel that everything he sees is for the first time, creating a sense of discovery and wonder. He is such an excellent communicator that he sweeps up everyone in the drama of life and death on the Serengeti, both past and present.

As we explore the gorges with Nigel, we learn that the volcanic activity preserved a tremendous number of fossils, providing spectacular insight into life millions of years ago – not only human life but also the lives of the bizarre animals, long extinct, that once roamed these plains: *pelorovis*, a bovine-like creature twice the size of a buffalo with massive horns; a prehistoric elephant with tusks pointing to the sky; a giant hippopotamus and many others. Relics and images of these creatures can be seen at the museum situated at the visitors' centre at Oldupai Gorge, along with many other fossils unearthed in the gorge.

Oldupai Gorge has been investigated extensively over many years. It is near Laetoli, where paleoanthropologist Mary Leakey, whom Nigel knew, found the famous footprints (of which a cast may be seen in the museum) of the earliest known upright-walking hominid, *Australopithecus afarensis*. Mary Leakey's work is vital to our understanding and knowledge of human development, and the extraordinary animals that lived here millions of years ago.

Nigel was taking a group of us to stay at a tented camp at Ol Karien Gorge in the Gol Mountains so we could take a trip across the Salei Plains to view the volcano Ol Doinyo Lengai from the top of the escarpment. We were exploring an idea for a television programme, which would involve climbing this volcano before it next erupted. This could be quite soon, as the salt crust inside the bowl of the volcano had risen to the top – it was about 12 metres down 10 years ago, when Nigel last climbed it. Parkipumy was travelling with us, bubbling with excitement, as his boma is not in sight of Ol Doinyo Lengai and he seldom sees the mountain. When we all piled out of the cars at the first sight of the cone-shaped mountain on the horizon, Parkipumy stood on the rim of the valley gazing at it. This is a very holy place to the Maasai, and he spent a good 15 minutes standing facing the mountain and chanting his invocation, which carried loud and clear across the valley.

The Gol Mountains, in the Ngorongoro Conservation Area, right on the edge of the Rift Valley, are well populated with Maasai, but not with tourists. The fertile valleys and cool, high mountain slopes have been a favourite grazing area for their cattle probably since their arrival in East Africa, and Ol Karien Gorge and the Sanjan River are their traditional sources of water during the dry season.

Entering Ol Karien Gorge through a fissure in the echoing, overhanging cliffs is like walking into a secret world. The first narrow pathway opens up into rock pools rimmed with huge boulders and gnarled trees, then contracts again into a narrow passageway through more towering granite walls. The top of the gorge is a favourite nesting place for Ruppell's griffons, hundreds of which may be seen rising on the thermals and circling in the blue sky above. A trickle of water was running down the gorge, creating a little waterfall and splashing into a large bowl of transparent green quartz of startling beauty. The gorge is subject to flash floods after heavy rain in the mountains, when a wall of water roars through, carrying all before it. The Maasai lead their livestock deep into the gorge to drink at their ancient wells. The scene has a rather biblical flavour as the animals are herded up the narrow paths – boys whistling and shouting, the dust swirling around their red cloaks, cowbells tinkling, goats bleating and the women in blue robes bringing up the rear. The women collect the household water in containers that are loaded into straw panniers slung over the backs of donkeys.

The following day, we drove across the Salei Plains to the very edge of the escarpment. Wildebeest, zebras and giraffes ambled through the carpet of white flowers that had appeared after the recent rains. It was a glorious journey that took all morning and ended at the rim of the Great Rift Valley. Everyone gasped at the spectacle before us; we seemed to be standing on the very edge of the world! The land drops away steeply for thousands of feet into the valley, an inhospitable furnace surrounded by the escarpment and mountains. Towering above us to our right was Ol Doinyo Lengai, the rivers of white ash flowing from its crater clearly visible. Way below, Lake Natron shimmered in the haze. This huge soda lake is the only regular breeding area of the lesser flamingo in East Africa.

While we lunched in the shade of one of the few trees on the edge of the escarpment, Parkipumy was negotiating for us to visit a village perched on the edge, with Lengai as its backdrop. He returned with one of the village elders to collect us. Some of the morans stood in line at the entrance and greeted us very formally with handshakes. Foreign visitors in this part of the world are seldom seen and all the people of the village had dressed up for the occasion. The women wore beaded headdresses, large round beaded collars, necklaces, earrings and anklets. Their clothing was bright blue or red; nearly all of them had a baby on the hip or one on the way. The men cut imposing figures in their bright-red shukas with their hair pulled back in a band with tight ringlets. The women dress the men's hair with ringlets from strands of hair from wildebeest tails. It is then coloured with ochre and gathered in a loop at the back of the head. The men also wore colourful beaded necklaces and earrings.

They were laughing and singing, and the men gave us a display of their extraordinary athletic jumping. From a standing position they can jump as high as four feet in the air. The children were particularly excited, running around chattering away, many of them in English, as they attend a mission school and relished the opportunity to practise the language. They found it fun to look at themselves on the screen of a video camera.

Nigel's safaris are always full of surprises, and this visit, ostensibly to find porters for a climb up Ol Doinyo Lengai, had been a highlight for us. The conversation round the campfire that night was particularly animated.

From close up, the mountain looked daunting, and fitness preparation was planned before anyone felt they could come back to climb it.

Nigel is happiest on the Serengeti in the early part of each year when 1.5 million wildebeest gather to give birth to more than 200 000 calves in just a few weeks. But he is also drawn to the wilder, more remote areas of Tanzania.

As a young boy growing up in New Zealand, Nigel had a strong yearning to see the world. He spent hours poring over brochures lifted from the local travel agency, plotting and planning his future. He was passionate about wildlife television programmes, especially those from the BBC, and had read all David Attenborough's books. He would head up the river with a pair of binoculars, identifying birds and learning about the natural environment near his home. His father, a keen sportsman and marathon runner, instilled in his sons a love of the outdoors by taking them camping from an early age. Nigel has gone the nature route in his career and his brother, Craig, is the sportsman, a highly successful golfer on the American PGA circuit. He gained fame and fortune in August 2002 when he won the Players' Championship, known as the Fifth Major, which gave him three years entry into the Masters at Atlanta. (Nigel, at the time, had a fleeting fancy to drop everything and become his manager.)

Nigel was unsure of what direction he would take until his geography teacher spent a whole year teaching his class about Africa. From then on, he was hooked and the focus of his obsession became the Serengeti – he just could not wait to get there. Once he had finished studying zoology at university, he set off on his journey with $300 in his pocket. That got him to Australia, where he worked for six months to earn enough for the rest of the journey.

He and a friend travelled for 11 months overland from Asia to England via Thailand, Malaysia, Nepal, India, Pakistan, Iran, Turkey, Jordan, Syria and Greece. During this epic journey, he made a new friend – a chance meeting that was to confirm the direction of his life. In a bar he met a fellow traveller named Gary, who was driving a group of tourists to

Kathmandu in an overland truck for a British-based tour company. They bumped into each other at least seven or eight times again during their travels and became good friends. Gary had done several overland trips from London to Johannesburg and Nigel pumped him for information on Africa. The last meeting ended with Gary giving Nigel a cheerful invitation to look him up when he was next in England. Months later, Nigel arrived on Gary's doorstep, coincidentally just as Gary was about to depart for Tanzania. He was due to take a group of eight people in two Land Rovers but his fellow driver had let him down. To Nigel's great joy, he was offered the job – and grabbed it.

They spent more than 20 weeks travelling from London to Dar es Salaam on one of the most exciting journeys imaginable. It started with six weeks crossing the Sahara, climbing sand dunes, sleeping under the stars and learning how to survive in the heat and dust. Their journey first took them through Algeria, Morocco, Cameroon, Chad and then Zaire (DRC).

After two weeks' travelling up the Congo with the vehicles ferried by boat, they headed off through the jungle on rudimentary roads that sometimes just disappeared into mud holes. On one occasion, after heavy rains, it took 5 days to travel 20 kilometres on a muddy road bogged down with more than 100 other vehicles, also stuck in the mud. They all helped one another to get through, pushing and hauling vehicles and being bitten all day by flies and all night by mosquitoes.

The great reward for all this was a visit to the mountain gorillas at Jumba, a place that had only just been opened up to visitors and there were no restrictions. They could sit in small groups with the gorillas all day. In Rwanda, where the gorillas had been a tourist attraction for some time, only an hour was permitted with them, as is now the case there and in Uganda.

When they finally reached Tanzania, Nigel and Gary decided to stay and work together, driving visitors around Tanzania, Kenya and Uganda. Their clients were mainly young backpackers, mostly girls, who were looking for fun and adventure and who needed only to be driven around.

Nigel and Gary took turns to take the trips, which lasted three weeks. Each vehicle pulled a trailer with camping equipment and took four or five passengers, everyone helping with all aspects of camping. Somehow, they always managed to pack one too few tents, so someone had to share with the driver!

The group would roll across the plains singing and laughing, with the girls sunbathing topless on the roof of the vehicle. They did these trips for three years, following the wildebeest migration and visiting the gorillas in Zaire. Nigel returned to Jumba many times until civil unrest made the visits there too dangerous.

They explored the whole of East Africa with a freedom unknown today, and Nigel spent hours watching and learning about the animals and birds, and finding exciting new places. It was the best schooling any potential guide could have. He has never lost that first feeling of wonder he experienced at the vastness and eternal beauty of the Serengeti.

GIBB'S FARM

Nigel and Gary lived at the Kibo Hotel at the foot of Mount Kilimanjaro, from where they operated their safaris. Having British licence plates on their vehicles allowed them free access over the borders, but it took some time before the authorities caught up with their unlicensed safari activities. They were faced with two options: either pay the very large sum of money needed for foreigners to set up their own company, which they did not have, or operate through a local company. Around this time, they met Margaret Gibb, the owner of a coffee farm on the slopes of Ngorongoro, who wanted to set up a safari company based at Gibb's Farm, where she had built several guest rooms. She financed and supported their operation, which was able to run under her safari licence. In 1991, however, Gary split away from the partnership to set up on his own. Nigel remained loyal to Margaret, and with immense hard work and dedication they turned Gibb's Farm Safaris into one of the most successful and respected companies in Tanzania.

Margaret, who was born in Tanzania, had met her English husband, Jim Gibb, when he travelled overland to Africa after World War II. He was headed for South Africa to start a new life, but at the bar in the New Stanley Hotel, Nairobi, he learnt that a coffee farm was for sale in Tanzania. He bought the badly neglected farm, revived it and married Margaret in 1959, and together they made a success of the coffee farm. Their house stood in an exquisite garden started by Margaret in 1960, overlooking the coffee plantation spread out in the valley below.

When the price of coffee collapsed in the 1970s, they decided to turn the farm into a guest lodge from where the tourists could visit the surrounding areas, like Lake Manyara and the Ngorongoro Crater. They built guest rooms in the gardens overlooking the plantations, which have been renovated in 21st century style.

Jim died in 1977, but Margaret, who later remarried, stayed on through Tanzania's socialist era, when foreigners were leaving in droves and land was being nationalised. She and her farm survived and today it remains a place of tranquillity and beauty. The rich soil produces an abundance of fruit and vegetables that supply the lodge and the safaris' catering needs. Producing such a great quantity of food in an eight-acre garden has its problems. The area has to be kept very secure from animals, but there is nothing that will stop hungry elephants that have a penchant for strawberries! Guards have to be on duty all night banging on tin cans to keep the elephants away from the newly ripened berries.

Margaret also has an interest in Ndutu Safari Lodge, which is on the edge of the Serengeti. The co-owner is her good friend Aadje Geertsema, who also has an interest in Gibb's Farm. When she was very young, Aadje had travelled from Holland to Tanzania with her father, a friend and adviser to Prince Bernhard of the Netherlands, who was a keen hunter and conservationist, and the first president of the World Wildlife Fund. Africa did its familiar act of digging itself under Aadje's skin, causing her to return. She spent a large part of her life in Tanzania. She started by working for George Dove, owner of Ndutu, a tented camp that George had set up as a tourist venue. There she first met Margaret Gibb, a friend of George and frequent visitor to the camp. Aadje's role was that of general assistant, but whenever she had some spare time she took out one of the Land Rovers that belonged to the lodge and explored the bush.

During this time she made a short film about servals with a Super-8 movie camera, which she set to the music of Pink Floyd. It was a great hit and got her funding to do the first research on the serval. It took her four years, during which she lived alone in the Ngorongoro Crater. The cats were so shy and elusive that it took six months to record her first data, but eventually she had some well-habituated servals and plenty of information on them. Her data was published in the *Netherlands Journal of Zoology* in 1985, after which she went on a lecture tour in the Netherlands, raising money for the Save the Rhino Foundation, before returning to Tanzania. Her heart has always been in Ndutu and when she learnt that it was for sale she decided to buy it, together with Margaret, and run it herself.

Aadje and Margaret, both early starters in the modern tourist industry of Tanzania, were Nigel's mentors. They gave a tremendous start to this enthusiast, and he soaked up their knowledge. They were familiar with every nook and cranny of northern Tanzania, and willingly passed on all their knowledge of the whereabouts of little-known places. However, they didn't make it too easy; they would describe a place, for example Ol Karien Gorge, and, with a few vague clues, send him off alone to find it. The gorge is a most secret place. From the outside, you would never know it was there with its narrow, twisting passages through the mountains and the ancient Maasai wells, though the circling vultures might give it away if one knew they nested on the high granite walls.

Nigel ran the mobile tented safaris from Gibb's Farm. The safari staff were trained at Gibb's Farm where its kitchens, restaurant, bar and guest rooms provide the perfect opportunity for on-site training. They had the great advantage of the farm supplying delicious home-grown produce – meat, fruit and vegetables – for both the lodge guests and the mobile safaris. It was a very convenient base and a lovely place for the clients to begin their stay in Tanzania.

Early on in Nigel's involvement with Gibb's Farm one of his wildest dreams came true – he met and drove David Attenborough into the Serengeti when the BBC was filming *The Trials of Life* series. Gibb's Farm often played host to film-makers and writers because of its reputation for excellence in terms of both the setting and the quality of the guiding.

Margaret was also a great friend of Mary Leakey, who, after she had given up her camp at Oldupai Gorge when she returned to live in Nairobi, frequently stayed at Gibb's Farm on her visits to Tanzania. When Nigel started working there, Mary was quite an old lady but still full of life. He often took her out on safaris and tells the story of her last visit when he had the unique privilege of being with her when she uncovered the hominid footprints she had previously discovered for the very last time:

'I had the pleasure of knowing Mary and taking her on a couple of memorable safaris before she passed away a few years back. She was in her late 70s and early 80s when I knew her, and was always incredibly energetic and enthusiastic, and loved coming back to Tanzania. Each year we endeavoured to get her out to the Serengeti. Mary would often drive herself down from Nairobi to Gibb's Farm (an eight-hour drive), arriving like the living dead, but soon revived after a couple of large whiskies and a cigar, thrilled to be back and raring to go!

'A few months before Mary died, she joined an expedition to Laetoli to uncover and preserve the famous 3.6-million-year-old hominid footprints that she had first discovered back in the 1970s. The footprints had been formed when three hominids walked through damp ash. They were then naturally preserved by continuous ash falls from the local volcanoes.

'It was probably the most significant archaeological discovery ever made – a huge responsibility for Mary and her crew, who documented them. When discovered, the footprints had survived 3.6 million years, but any further interference could destroy this most important site. Mary and her team recovered the footprints so they would be protected from erosion and human interference.

'Imagine how she must have felt when they were first uncovered again? Had they sieved the returned soil enough to remove seeds, so plant roots wouldn't

crack the footprint trail? Had they left it as it was for future generations? Had anyone vandalised the site because she had made the world aware of it? Over a whisky the night before, we sat and talked about these issues.

'With a great deal of apprehension, we visited the site the next day. To her obvious relief, everything was in perfect condition, as we all knew it would be, because of the painstaking effort Mary and her crew had put in all those years ago. It was an incredible honour for me to be standing at this site with Mary Leakey and seeing the footprints for the first and last time. The footprints have been scientifically buried and there is no plan to ever open them to human eyes again!

'Mary died knowing that she had not only made some of the most momentous archaeological discoveries, but had also given the world an insight into our past.

'Her funeral was exactly as she had planned. Her coffin was placed on a huge bonfire overlooking the Rift Valley where she was cremated with all her family and close friends attending. She had requested that they finish off her whisky and cigars, which they did, throwing the butts into the fire in her honour.'

Nigel spent years exploring and learning about the Serengeti and the surrounding areas, getting to know the people and becoming thoroughly familiar with this vast and beautiful land. He waited 15 years to witness his first leopard kill in the daytime. It came down from a tree and made use of the presence of the vehicle to help stalk a wildebeest, then killed it in front of them in broad daylight.

Another very exciting moment was the first time cheetahs used one of his vehicles as a vantage point. Nigel had very slowly approached a couple of cheetahs on the plains, and stopped about 20 metres from them. One cheetah stood up, walked towards them, creating great excitement in the car, as it was the first time his two American clients had seen a cheetah. The next moment it jumped up on the vehicle and they lay on the floor taking photographs while it sat on the roof with its tail hanging down into the car.

On a previous safari, he had been observing a cheetah with three little cubs for a couple of days when he saw the mother take on a Grant's gazelle. The gazelle turned on the cheetah, flipped her over and stabbed her with his horns, killing her. Over the next few days, they watched the cubs die. It was sad, but, as he says, 'it is survival of the fittest and the best genes. She should not have taken on a Grant's, but gone for a Thomson's gazelle with no horns.'

One of his most startling moments was while he was driving in the Ruaha National Park in the early morning. What looked like a stick lying across the road suddenly reared up and hit the windscreen at eye level, just a few inches from the open roof. It was a black mamba. It had been surprisingly fast, as it was a cold morning and snakes don't usually move fast in the cold. Then, after dropping his guests off at the airstrip, he returned to camp, where one of the staff told him there was a little snake in one of the store tents. He had seen it going in. Nigel lay down at the entrance to see if he could find it and was immediately confronted by a six-foot cobra sitting up waving in the air and ready to spit. The man had seen only the cobra's retreating tail and thought it was a small specimen. Nigel told him that he must take care of his 'little' snake himself. Two snakes in one day were enough!

He has journeyed all over Tanzania. Katavi and Ruaha are both very large but little-visited reserves of great beauty and huge stocks of animals. Katavi has buffalo herds of more than a thousand on open plains reminiscent of the Serengeti. Ruaha, in southern Tanzania, has a rugged, rocky landscape with forests of baobabs and a beautiful river. Walking is permitted in both parks. In Ruaha it is possible to look down on an eagle's nest from the top of a koppie. The Mahale Mountain National Park, which borders Lake Tanganyika, combines white sandy beaches and snorkelling in the crystal-clear lake with trekking in a forest where you can observe chimpanzees going about their daily lives.

Nigel has driven right across Tanzania. Near Lake Rukwa, along part of the old slave route, he came across long lines of mango trees that had grown from the pips of the fruit given to the slaves to eat a century ago.

Sleeping under the stars, washing in clear, unmapped streams, following a compass and not knowing what would be over the hill or where he would be that night, was truly a safari into the unknown.

As so often happens, visitors become attached to a particular guide, and want him to accompany them on safari in other parts of Africa. This has been the case for Nigel. He loves to take his clients to new areas, as it gives him the opportunity to meet other guides with expert knowledge of their areas, and to study animal behaviour elsewhere. Nigel's observations on animal behaviour are fascinating and the differences in geographical ecologies have become one of his major interests.

UNUSUAL ANIMAL BEHAVIOUR

Nigel has observed examples of animal behaviour that are far from the supposed norm. He has three stories that illustrate these observations. The first involves cheetah behaviour in Ruaha National Park:

'The Serengeti is unique. The animals are so easy to see and study here that the behaviour observed and studied on animals in the Serengeti is treated as normal everywhere and seldom questioned. Cheetahs are plentiful there and we all know about and have seen wonderful films showing their speed and expertise when hunting. The cheetah is known as the fastest animal on earth. However, in Ruaha National Park, there are many cheetahs too, but they are seldom seen because the bush is thick and the grass long. Here, they stalk their prey as secretively as leopards and without having to unleash the lightning sprint we are familiar with, they get up close to their prey and pounce on it, just as leopards do. This is very different behaviour from the studies done in the Serengeti.'

His second story concerns wild dogs, which provide another good example of different behaviour in particular habitats. Although no longer seen in the Serengeti, the wild dogs would pursue their prey until it fell from exhaustion. On the open plains wild dogs could chase a wildebeest for over an hour. In more heavily wooded habitats, such as Botswana, the hunts are over in a few minutes as they swiftly chase impalas through the trees. In the late 1980s, before the wild dogs were wiped out by distemper and rabies caught from the Maasai dogs, Nigel had some of his best game viewing. The packs were large, comprising 12 to 15 adults and up to 20 pups. They were magnificent to watch. Once he spent five days with a group of guests, morning and evening, observing one pack:

'We would be on the plains in the evening watching this pack take off, and they would go after big animals – wildebeest or zebra. The lead dog would work out the strategy. He would pick an animal, causing chaos. There would be wildebeest running in every direction, dust whirling up, red in the evening sun. I would see the way it was going and race about 5 kilometres across the plain in order to get the action coming straight at us. The lead dog would race behind the beast for about ten minutes, the rest of the pack trotting along behind in a straight line. When he was tired, he backed off and another dog took up the chase, and so on until the animal dropped and the kill took place. It was fantastically well-organised teamwork.'

His third story is about the perilous lives of lion cubs:

'One stunning evening at Ndutu's big marsh, in the glorious last light, we were lucky enough to be sitting watching and photographing two lionesses with three young cubs. It was a wonderful scene, with very playful cubs jumping on each other, tumbling, play-fighting and generally being complete poseurs to my Land Rover full of very keen photographers.

'We left after a classic Serengeti sunset and decided to return in the morning to spend more time with this happy family! We arrived at the marsh the next morning at first light to a very different scenario, however. What had been a perfectly relaxed, happy family the night before had turned into a very tense situation.

'Two unknown male lions were with the lionesses. One of the females had a fresh bite wound and one cub was missing. It did not look good for the remaining cubs as we assumed that these new males were in the process of taking over the pride, which generally means certain death to young cubs.

Infanticide is something that occurs commonly with lions, but very few people ever witness it – and even fewer have photographed it.

'We sat there in morbid anticipation. No one wanted to watch cubs being killed, but observing infanticide is scientifically important.

'The lioness with the missing cub was flirting constantly with one of the new males and eventually we watched as they mated every fifteen minutes for the next two hours. It's bizarre to watch such behaviour, but it makes genetic sense as the male obviously wants to father his own offspring and by killing another male's cubs he brings the females back into oestrus. For the female, she hopefully will then be raising his genetically superior cubs.

'The other lioness that was still with her two cubs had moved away from the mating pair, but was incredibly nervous and never took her eyes off the other intruding male. He would edge towards her and she would move the cubs away. This went on for hours until it looked as if the lioness had given up and walked her cubs over to the male. Then it happened; we witnessed the infanticide – the male picked up the cubs one by one and killed them with fatal bites to the head. It was shocking to watch as it had such an inevitability about it. The male then proceeded to eat the cubs.

'The strange thing about what we had observed was that these two male lions were not huge, black-maned specimens, but young blond nomads – maybe four years old – that had literally just wandered into another pride's territory and taken up with the females. It was the middle of the wildebeest migration and there was such a huge abundance of food around that the pride was well spread out and the males of the pride were not spending any time with the females. This led to a totally opportunistic situation where the young male lions were successful.

'Over the next few weeks, we returned to the marsh to observe the progress, expecting to see the original pride males back with the pride and the blonds expelled. But, amazingly, for two weeks we watched the two infanticide males mating constantly with the lionesses; bonding was occurring.

'It was an unforgettable experience and something we all found fascinating, but we were astonished by the females' acceptance of the new *males after the killing of their cubs – although it all makes sense in the natural order of things.'*

RUAHA NATIONAL PARK

Nigel spent many months in Ruaha National Park, where he established a tented camp for six weeks each year. It is a vast, wonderfully remote park, rarely visited by people, but frequently by elephants. He tells the story of an elephant that visited the camp several times:

'Having a camp in Ruaha National Park was quite an expedition. Organising supplies was difficult, as Gibb's Farm, with its vegetable garden, is a three-day drive away. The camping equipment and dry supplies can be trucked in, but fresh vegetables and meat have to be brought on the charter flights with our guests.

'Our camp was on the bank of the Ruaha River with a stunning amount of wildlife around day and night. Some of the highlights included a pack of wild dogs killing an impala 50 metres from the camp in front of one of our guests' tents, leopard hunts, watching sable and roan antelope drinking, lions roaring and endless elephant activity. Elephants would even drink from our shower buckets!

'Our first group had arrived and with them came baskets full of wonderful vegetables and fruit to last us the next five days. We had a delicious dinner and went off to our tents, anticipating our first night in camp.

'At about two o'clock in the morning I was awoken to the sounds of elephant wandering through camp; I rolled over and went back to sleep thinking how wonderful it was to be back in Ruaha. A few moments later, I awoke again to excited screaming from the kitchen tent. I raced over to see what all the commotion was about and witnessed one of the funniest things I'd seen. An elephant had broken into our store tent and was hoovering up all our valued vegetables. Silas, one of our cooks, was unimpressed and was tugging at one end of the tent as the elephant pulled at the other. A couple of our crew were using tent poles to try to persuade the elephant to move on. The elephant (later named Fred) had no intention of moving off and it

took us several minutes of abuse to get him on his way. During this entire hullabaloo, Fred had managed to trample most of our supplies and eat 20 avocados.

'Nothing further happened that night, and in the morning we surveyed the vegetable damage and sent the crew off to Iringa (our closest market) to scrounge supplies so we could eat for the rest of the trip. The whole encounter was very odd, as no one camps in the spot we use, so there is no rubbish left around and over all the years we had been visiting Ruaha we had never had animals in camp looking for food.

'I spoke to the rangers about Fred and they told me that there was a young male that had be raiding the lodge's rubbish pit and had got very used to the taste of camp food – but surely this wasn't the same standard as our camp food? The rangers' description sounded very like our Fred.

'The crew arrived back with fresh supplies and we decided that it made a lot of sense to keep everything locked up in the back of our truck. That night, Fred arrived again and this time broke a window to get at the supplies in our truck. Again, our cooks yelled and screamed to try and scatter him. Eventually Fred disappeared leaving us a nice pile of dung full of avocado stones!

'By now, the park rangers had decided that Fred was a problem and thought the best solution was to scare him off by firing gunshots over his head. Not really what I wanted in camp – but there was nothing we could do. I warned my clients that they might hear a gunshot in the night. On the third night, Fred was back. But this time he was in for a surprise at the kitchen tent! Off went the shot and we were awoken to Fred charging off through the camp. I thought that would be the last of Fred, as Ruaha elephants were severely poached in the 80s and always moved well away from guns. So, night four came and at three o'clock the gun went off again. I rushed out expecting to see Fred, but it was a herd of elephants charging through the camp! I yelled at the ranger and asked what he thought he was doing. "Oh," he said, "I thought you did not want any elephants in camp."

'The whole thing was getting out of hand, so I asked the ranger to leave. He replied, "This is not possible – I am here for your clients' safety."

'Night five came and again a gunshot! I hurried out of my tent to see a leopard charging through camp. It was wonderful, all these nocturnal sightings, but I had not had any sleep for five nights, so when the ranger explained that he thought we did not want any animals in camp I sent him packing.

'Finally we got some sleep. Fred eventually came back, but was very well behaved and never attacked the camp again apart from once pushing over a small tree onto the kitchen tent.'

Nigel, like all guides, worked hard to build a good business and an excellent reputation for himself, but there were not many companions of his own age. Most of the guests were a lot older, so it was with great excitement that he set off one day to collect three clients from Kilimanjaro Airport – mother, father and daughter. At last, he thought, someone of his own age to chat to. The daughter turned out to be 63, the mother 84 and the father 90!

Light appeared at the end of the tunnel, however, when Margaret Gibb asked him to pick up a friend's daughter, who was coming out to work at Ndutu Safari Lodge. She was called Fiona Denton, and she was taking six months out from intensive-care nursing in London. At that time, Nigel tells me, there were about 20 white men to every white girl in Arusha, and he was thrilled to be the first to meet her. Fiona was sent straight to Ndutu to work, as it was the busy season. Nigel regularly visited Ndutu with his clients, so he got to know her and when things quietened down they took a couple of safaris together.

Over the next four years, Fiona would come and work at Ndutu in the busy season, and go back to London to nurse when it was quiet. Slowly, she grew to adore the bush … and Nigel. But he put her through many initiations, including climbing Nasera Rock and Ol Doinyo Lengai. Her first visit to a campsite was during the BBC filming of *The Trials of Life*, where she met David Attenborough. Looking after a film crew is hard work; Nigel was up in the dark at 5 am and with the crew all day. The plan at the end of one day was to film the moon coming up with zebras in front of it. It was the second day of the full moon, so it should have appeared just after sunset, but was nowhere to be seen. They waited until 9 pm before someone realised there was an eclipse. Nigel and Fiona were sleeping in a small A-frame tent with broken zips. At about 11 pm, a lion started to roar right next to the tent. Fiona sat bolt upright and tried to wake Nigel, who grunted, turned over and said, 'Go back to sleep, it's only a lion.'

For someone who lives in London, a lion roaring outside your bedroom is something particularly alien. She sat up all night, terrified, while the lions wandered around the camp. Eventually she got her own back on Nigel, though. While on a marketing trip in America, they stayed in a flat at the back of a tour operator's office in New Orleans. One night, at about midnight, there was a loud racket in the street below them. Looking out of the window, they saw a gang smashing windows and going on the rampage. This time, it was Nigel's turn to be terrified. Being an urban girl, Fiona went straight back to sleep, and didn't worry about it at all. Nigel took a couple of Maasai spears off the office wall and stood by the door for the rest of the night, just in case.

Nigel and Fiona spent many hours in the bush together, camping, photographing and learning about wildlife – and each other. He felt he had met the perfect soulmate. They got married in 1993 and set up home at Gibb's Farm. Their children, Jake and Jessica, were born there, but Nigel and Fiona eventually decided to live in New Zealand.

In 2001, Nigel set up his own company, Nigel Perks Discovery, and the Gibb's Farm safari company was turned into Amazing Tanzania (ATZ), as it was clear that Margaret was hoping to sell Gibbs Farm in the near future. Everything was moved onto a three-acre coffee plantation that Margaret and her husband owned. The compound consisted of the garage/workshops, offices, staff quarters, manager's house and a guesthouse. The new companies were well established when Gibb's Farm was sold in 2004. His Serengeti safaris continue to be based at Ndutu Lodge in the lower Serengeti.

In 2001, the Perks family moved, but, despite the move, Nigel could not give up safaris. This is his passion, and life is always somehow filled with compromises. So, now he has one of the world's longest commutes – Auckland to Arusha. Lots of people say to Nigel how lucky he has been. He acknowledges that it's true: 'I have been lucky. But you also have to get out there and make your own luck.'

When Nigel settled in New Zealand, he decided to establish a new division of his safari company. He had many friends around the world who had been on safari with him, particularly in America which is not as far from New Zealand as Europe is, so he designed some magnificent holidays in his homeland, and still 'commuted' to take safaris in Africa – a blessing for us all!

Nigel is a little greyer these days, but his passion for life is stronger than ever, and his enthusiasm for New Zealand is as staunch as it is for Africa. He scoured the whole country for the greatest scenic drives. He swam with dolphins and watched the whales; he experienced adrenalin-fuelled activities, including bungee jumping, heli-skiing, white-water rafting; he found the very best small inns and B&Bs and the most beautiful beaches, and learnt where to find an incredible diversity of bird and plant life, which has evolved in an extraordinary way due to the islands being isolated for millions of years. Self-drive holidays are easy in New Zealand but Nigel guides when required – usually for the first few days to get the guests going and he also has excellent local guides for areas of special interest.

Nigel's love for Africa never wanes; he continues to find new things to marvel at, and still has access to the magnificent Salei Plains. He no longer has his own tented camps but instead uses the facilities of Colin and Laura, friends of his who now own Amazing Tanzania, and who have the sole concession for a tented camp in the Maasai land overlooking Ol Doinyo Lengai. The wonderful safaris at Soit Orgoss are no longer available, as the Arabs who have the hunting concession in Loliondo have forbidden access to safari operators. Depending on the time of year, he will camp at Moru Kopjes, in the west of the Serengeti, climb the Mahale Mountains by Lake Tanganyika to spend time with the chimpanzees, watch the wildebeest crossing the Mara River at Kogatende, in the northern Serengeti, while staying at the lovely Camp Lamai, owned by nomads, or check out the animal activity along the palm-fringed banks of the lakes and Rufiji River, in the Selous Game Reserve.

Nigel has many unusual safaris up his sleeve – perhaps an overland journey through Katavi and Lake Rukwa into Ruaha, or perhaps a butterfly- and bird-watching visit to the floral paradise on the Kitulo Plateau, known to the locals as the Garden of God. No matter how many times you may go on safari with Nigel, each time it is as fresh and as thrilling as the first.

Nigel's children continue to flourish in New Zealand, but his marriage to Fiona did not last. He now has a new wife, Ashley Frechette, an American whom he met in Tanzania, and they have two daughters, Zinnia and Wren.

RON BEATON

In a darkened cinema the audience sat on the edge of their seats holding their breath, watching in horror as a small boy walked across the lawn towards his house, tenderly carrying a tiny lion cub. Behind him, the lioness, having discovered her missing cub, was accelerating through the bush towards the blissfully ignorant child.

This was one of the heart-stopping moments in the film *Where No Vultures Fly*, released in 1953 and shot in Kenya with the help of Ron Beaton's father, then warden of Nairobi National Park. The incident, though considerably dramatised for the screen, was based on a real story. Ron had done just that at the age of five. A lioness was keeping her small cubs not far from his house. While she went hunting Ron picked up one of the lion cubs, and took it home to his mother, who nearly fainted when he walked into the kitchen with the little creature in his arms. After a sound beating from his father, they took the cub out and placed it on the road. The lioness heard it mewing as she walked up the road with the other three cubs. She sniffed it, licked it and, miraculously, took it back.

The lioness used in the film was a pet called Iola, a beautiful animal that was eventually shot by a farmer who mistook her for a cattle killer. Quite a lot of people in Kenya brought up orphaned lions at that time.

Ron's family had three lionesses as pets, and they ended up in a zoo when, quite frankly, they would have been better off being eaten by hyenas when they were cubs. Ron was never quite sure why he took the cub, maybe it was because lions had killed his Staffordshire terrier on the lawn outside their house and this was retaliation of a kind. He was, after all, only five.

Ron Beaton is a large man, with an easy, relaxed manner, generous smile and twinkling eyes. He has never lost his curiosity or ceased to marvel at the magnificent country in which he has been so fortunate to live. This, along with his many years of experience, makes him a cosy and fascinating companion. For many years he owned and operated a delightful, small bush lodge called Rekero, just outside the Masai Mara National Park in Kenya. The lodge, together with a small but luxurious tented camp he owned on the Talek River in the Mara, plus his expeditions to Lake Turkana in northern Kenya and the Omo River in Ethiopia, provided his safari guests with a unique and very exclusive range of wildlife experiences. These were made all the more interesting by Ron's extensive experience, gleaned from a lifetime in the bush, along with his sense of fun and adventure.

Soon after the lion-cub incident in the Nairobi National Park, Ron's parents separated. His mother married Tuffy Marshall, who worked for the Kenya Wildlife Department, while his father, Ken Beaton, set off to make a new life for himself in Uganda. Growing up with both parents being involved in parks and wildlife management gave Ron an understanding of life in the bush. He spent every school holiday in Tsavo or with his father in Uganda, until his father died in 1954. Ron's mother and stepfather, Tuffy, lived in Tsavo, where his stepfather was the head of Tsavo National Park. His *ayah* (nurse/maid) was not a woman but a man, a former poacher named Nduma. He had been caught poaching by Tuffy and given two choices: prison or looking after his son! Ron adored Nduma, who had him completely wrapped around his little finger, and Ron would do anything for the old rogue, even steal Tuffy's cigars for him. Nduma instilled in Ron a true empathy for wildlife and bush lore.

Sadly, Ron was still quite young, but at boarding school when Nduma died of malaria.

Children travel a long way to school in Africa and Ron was no exception. He was six when he started boarding school, and for years, at the beginning of each term, he boarded the Mombasa–Nairobi train at Mtito Andei in Tsavo to attend a Catholic boys' school in the capital.

During World War II, Ron's father had served in the King's African Rifles and fought in Abyssinia (Ethiopia). He returned to Kenya with Italian prisoners of war and bullion by a circuitous route down the Omo River to avoid the shifta (Somali bandits), who infested the country. They were merciless. In fact, at the final capitulation of Gondar, the town had to be surrounded by British troops in order save the Italians from being slaughtered.

When the war ended, Ken, after many years spent working for Kenya Parks and Wildlife, was sent to Uganda as the first director of Uganda's national parks. He was a great hero to Ron, who adored those visits to Uganda. His father's brief from the governor was to set up two new designated parks, the Queen Elizabeth National Park and the Murchison Falls National Park, without upsetting the local people – not an easy feat, as there was plenty of opposition to their relocation by the locals. Uganda was a protectorate, not a colony and therefore the local Bagandan people in Kampala decided all civil issues in the civil courts. Ken had to deal with these anti-British people, so he started by identifying the chief opponents and asking them to let him show them what he wanted to do. They all piled into a DC-3 to look at the area from the air. None had ever flown before; flying was a novelty for Englishmen in those days, let alone Ugandans, and the excitement was tremendous. Plied with food and drink, they were flown over the magnificent landscape and shown the proposed boundaries of what was to become the Queen Elizabeth Park. Their resistance melted away and the park plan was then passed quickly through Parliament and gazetted.

Murchison Falls National Park, in the north, was much easier to set up, as it was remote and sparsely populated. The big draw is the Murchison

Falls, where the Victoria Nile squeezes through a narrow opening in the rocks, creating an incredibly powerful spectacle. The journey up the Nile to see the falls is a spectacle in itself, as you glide past a multitude of wildlife and wonderful birds.

Ron had come on a particular visit when his father was launching a brand-new boat on the Nile to take visitors to view the falls, and accompanied him on the trial cruise. Ken Beaton had been given the job of escorting Princess Elizabeth and the Duke of Edinburgh on safari during their visit to Uganda. This was the trip that ended so sadly for her with the death of her father, King George VI, while they were on a visit to Treetops in the Aberdare Mountains in Kenya after their Ugandan safari. They were to be the first visitors on the river cruise.

Standing on the deck one morning with his recently arrived assistant, Frank Poppleton, Ken pointed to the shore, and said, 'Do you see all those crocodiles, son?' Ron could see nothing but the rocky shore, but on closer inspection, it became clear that the whole shore was carpeted with crocodiles. Frank, a real daredevil, decided he wanted to do something completely crazy to impress Ken. With no warning, he suddenly leapt overboard, splashing and kicking, and making a tremendous racket. As one, the monsters rose and plunged into the river. Frank swam swiftly through them all, and climbed out onto the riverbank to the sound of incredulous cheers from the boat. He believed – quite rightly, as it turned out – that, because of the noise and sudden confusion, he would be perfectly safe, but it was a heart-stopping moment for all on board. Frank eventually went on to become head of the Parks Department in Uganda.

Sadly, Ron's time with his father was limited. After Ken's early death, Ron's stepfather took over the paternal role, but Ron has enduring memories of the happy times spent during his early years with his father.

In Tsavo, where Ron spent most of his holidays, Tuffy was opening up the park, which included road building in Tsavo and the Chyulu Hills. At this time, Tsavo had an abundance of black rhinos and elephants but very little plains game, as thick bush is not their true habitat. The elephant population was estimated at 43 000.

Hanging around the park headquarters was not very exciting for young Ron, but some activities held great appeal – anti-poaching sorties, for one. David Sheldrick, who lived at Voi, coordinated all anti-poaching units in Tsavo. Simon Trevor, now a film producer, had recently arrived from Zambia, where he had been involved in game control, to be assistant warden to Tuffy. Simon would go out on anti-poaching patrols with the rangers and take his camera equipment. Ron remembers well how he was always filming something or other and that although filming was meant to be his hobby, it was really his main interest in life.

Ron decided to go on some of these trips, which horrified his mother, as they were potentially dangerous, but that, of course, only intensified the pleasure. On one of the trips he awoke to find that hyenas had eaten his only pair of shoes in the night and for the rest of the trip he was barefoot, in the thorny *commiphora* scrub. The rangers, who were Borana and Somalis, were excellent, fine-tuned Bushmen. After independence these men were disarmed and their jobs given to men from the ruling Kikuyu tribe. Unfortunately, the Kikuyu at that time were not true Bushmen and no match for the Borana and Somalis, who, having lost their livelihood, now turned to poaching, their intimate knowledge of the bush making them perfect at this. These men were one of the main reasons behind the success of poaching in Kenya, and the new anti-poaching units were no match for these professionals. However, coups linger at the back of the minds of African leaders and to have an armed tribe that was not under their control must have seemed inadvisable.

Ron thoroughly enjoyed school, especially sports and although he did not see his own parents from one holiday to the next, the parents of the boys who lived in and around Nairobi were very kind to the country boys, and invited them for 'outing Sundays' and half-terms with their own sons. On one occasion, Ron was supposed to go home for the day with a friend called Christopher, but for some reason, now forgotten, in the end he went with another friend instead. When they returned to school that evening, they found everyone in a dreadful state because Christopher had been kidnapped, killed and used in a Mau Mau earth-taking ceremony.

These were terrifying times for everyone. The Mau Mau rebellion was run on superstition and threats, and even the most loyal employee could be dragged into it, and once the oath was sworn there was no turning back. White children were prime targets for some of their ceremonies. In this case, one of Christopher's parents' gardeners had taken the oath and had grabbed the child that afternoon when he wandered out on his own with his catapult.

Security at the school was tightened considerably after that. Barbed wire was placed around the perimeter of the school grounds, with machine-gun towers at intervals. The rules became extremely strict: no one was allowed out of bounds at all, and if a boy was caught out of bounds he was expelled immediately.

Ron and his friends were growing up and resented the prison-like environment, so the urge to escape was very strong. He tells of one illicit journey into town:

'A senior boy in the Young Farmers' Association had a 650-cc Thunderbird Tiger 110 motorbike, which I, along with my friend Martin Schofield (later to become Chief Conservator of Natal Parks Board in South Africa), decided to borrow to go into town to see if there was any action! On the way back at about ten o'clock, we broke down next to the graveyard, which made us feel decidedly creepy! Knowing how exceptionally wicked it was to sneak out of school, was this an omen?

'A few minutes after we had started pushing the motorbike back to school, headlights appeared in the distance. We rushed off the road, hiding the bike behind a bush that only had room for myself and the bike. Martin jumped into the storm drain beside the road, crouching low, trying to keep hidden. The old Austin A40 that ground to a halt right across the road was full of our teachers, Catholic priests and brothers who having been to a party in town were all as drunk as skunks. As they tumbled out of the car, the sound of their voices was clearly heard on the night air singing, "... But for all that I found there I might as well be, Where the mountains of Mourne sweep down to the sea."

'Only one alighted on the side of the car facing us, it was Father Paddy Noonan, our boxing coach. He wandered over to the culvert, where Martin was hiding, picked up his cassock and peed on Martin, who was crouching dead still in the dark. The teachers, having relieved themselves by the side of the road, climbed back in the car and took off down the road, still singing The Mountains of Mourne.

'Martin jumped up shaking himself like a dog and said, "Christ that was close! Did you see what happened?" I was doubled over laughing so hard I couldn't reply. We pushed the bike back to school, climbed in through the windows, and no one was the wiser – we thought. Three days later we were in the sparring ring together and Schofield had a bad habit of hitting with the inside of the gloves, which caught the attention of the coach. Father Paddy Noonan climbed in through the ropes and said in his Irish brogue: "Schofield, ye're rabbit punchin' again. And, Schofield, by the way, have ye had a warm shower lately?" This was an old-fashioned, tough school where the boys only had daily cold showers; he just wanted us to know that he knew Schofield had been in the ditch.'

When Ron left school, his stepfather encouraged him away from safaris and hunting. He could see the writing on the wall for hunting and he was right, as it was soon to be banned in Kenya. Tuffy felt the future was in farming and sent him to England to study at Cirencester Agricultural College. He came back and very nearly went straight into hunting as he was offered a job as an apprentice hunter with Ker and Downey in Botswana. He was swayed from the offer, however, because at the same time he was offered something else: a job buying and transporting cattle to a cattle station on the coast. He and a man called Johnny Antoni were employed to go up to the northern frontier to buy cattle from the Somalis and then walk them to the cattle station. Here they would be fattened up on the lush coastal grass before being sold.

The lure for Ron was the coast. As a teenager, he had been passionate about diving and spear fishing, at times spending six or seven hours in the water. He longed to get back to it and the job of looking after cattle for six months on the coast was too good to turn down. On their first journey a group of Somali shifta armed with stolen British Bren guns attacked them and stole all the cattle. He and Johnny had only one .375 rifle and seven rounds of ammunition, so they prudently abandoned the cattle but, as luck would have it, they got them back again within 48 hours. Ron reported the loss to the Stock Theft Unit and found that one of their officers was on holiday in Malindi with his plane. The officer searched for the cattle by air, found them and got them back, killing one of the Somalis and recovering the Bren guns (which had been stolen from the Stock Theft Unit) in the process.

While waiting for the cattle to fatten up, Ron was able to indulge in his passion for diving. The Mnarani Club asked him to lay a line for yachts to moor on, which needed to be secured on the seabed with weights. Diving was fairly unheard-of in the mid-1960s – there were no diving centres; Ron was self-taught. On one of his dives he came up too quickly, and was stricken with the bends (nitrogen narcosis). There were no decompression chambers, and the nitrogen bubbles, which settled in rugby bruises on his body, caused excruciating pain. He had done three journeys north buying and transporting the cattle, luckily with no more trouble from the shifta. But after his bad diving experience he took the decision to move on.

Next, he accepted a job opening a chemical plant, a job offer that got him into Tanzania, but it did not last long. Then he met up with an old chap called Ben Pretorius, a professional hunter of Afrikaner descent, and decided to join him. In spite of Tuffy's warnings, this was really the life he wished to pursue at that time. Ben's father, Major General Pretorius, had been a dashing hero in World War I. He had boarded the German cruiser *Königsberg* dressed as an Arab labourer to help the British remove the guns and scuttle the ship, which they succeeded in doing. His story is alleged to have been the inspiration for a similar story told in Wilbur Smith's *Shout at the Devil*, although there is a firm disclaimer at the beginning of the book.

Ron and Ben were based at Moshi, near Kilimanjaro, and together they hunted all over Tanzania, but especially in South Maasailand and down the Pangani River, where Ron bought a beach house:

'There was at that time an odd social thing about hunters in East Africa. There were the hunters of British origin, who had the finesse, charm and sophistication to entertain the rich clients who flocked out to Kenya, but many of them knew very little about hunting, had difficulty even tracking an elephant and relied on local trackers to help them out. And then there were people like Ben, who had no etiquette at all, but was a truly fantastic hunter. He had a sixth sense in locating the game and predicting their movements. He understood the habitats and how to use them to the hunters' best advantage. Ben's sister, Elsie, who hunted barefoot, was one of only two women on the continent who had a hunter's licence.'

Their happiness and success ended very abruptly when the Tanzanian economy came to a standstill and everything was nationalised by President Julius Nyerere. Tanzania became a very unpleasant place to live. Ron had many friends, one of whom was the head of Shell Oil, who were sent to prison or concentration camps on very flimsy political grounds. Bands of TANU (Tanganyika African National Union) youths loyal to the government would walk the streets looking for women wearing trousers and imprisoning any they found. Ron was nearly put in gaol himself for wearing shorts in the streets, which was perceived as colonial. Ron suggested they take them off him, as he would be happy to walk through the streets naked but was afraid it might shock the Muslim women! Ron's house on the beach at Pangani was taken from him by the state. One morning a number was painted on it and that was that.

The Tanzanian government decided one day that the borders were to be closed that very day. The parks were full of safari operators from Kenya, who lost everything they owned. They were allowed to return to Kenya with their guests, but all their equipment – tents, vehicles and aeroplanes – had to remain behind. It was in this climate that Ron returned to Kenya with his first wife, Sally, and their baby.

They travelled with another man Ron had hunted with, also of Afrikaans descent, named Robin Ulyate, with whom he formed a farming partnership. Robin married Janet Woods, the daughter of Sir Michael Woods, founder of the Flying Doctor Service in East Africa. Their farm, which grew mainly wheat, was about an hour's drive north of Rekero.

The land was leased from the Maasai and involved bush clearance. In the days before electric fencing, this meant culling a large number of buffaloes and elephants – crop farming and large wildlife just don't mix. This was very detrimental to the wildlife, cutting off their ancient migration corridors and reducing their living areas. In 1974, when Ron first started farming, the wildlife was so prolific that this was never seen as a problem and the Masai Mara was a very different place. There were few camps or visitors. Governor's Camp had four tents and a manager who spent his time writing pornographic poetry, which had to be well hidden from his wife, but was shown to those he considered the right guests. It was another 10 years before the park began to receive the massive influx of tourists and large number of lodges that define it today.

Once the farm was up and running, it became apparent that two managers could not run it. In 1981, Ron married for the second time. He and his wife, Pauline, went into tourism and photographic safaris on the edge of the Masai Mara Reserve, but remained partners in the farm with the Ulyates.

Their tourism career began in an old farmhouse on a different site from the one they would use later. This wasn't a very satisfactory place because it could get cut off during the rains, and occasionally they had to swim their clients across to the house.

After a year they decided to move to another location and built Rekero Guest House specifically for tourists. It began as a bit of fun and a hobby, though the timing was superb, coming soon after the release of the film *Out of Africa*, which stimulated a huge popular desire to go on safari in Kenya. He and Pauline did their own marketing and, through friends and guests, they acquired excellent contacts all over the world.

Even so, some of the early years were challenging and they took in film crews to make ends meet. Four different productions have been filmed from there, including parts of David Attenborough's *The Private Life of Plants*. The BBC's *Big Cat Diaries* also did some of their filming from Rekero, especially when leopards were being filmed, as there are plenty in that area. As the general public had no access to the lodge, it was easier for the film crews to operate there.

Eventually, Ron and the Craig family, who own wildlife conservancy Lewa Downs, decided to join forces to make their lives a bit easier. Will Craig, Chris Flatt and Ron were the instigators of this concept, which they called Bush Homes, comprising a collection of houses and lodges around Kenya – the only criterion being that the owners live there and personally host their guests. Each is independent of the others but all come under one umbrella for marketing and bookings, which Chris continues to run from Nairobi. They seem to have the formula just right, as the business has been a great success.

Ron's camps became so popular that very few film crews could be accommodated. The Rekero cottages and tented camp were filled with safari guests. The tented camp especially, being situated on the Talek River near its confluence with the Mara, and very close to the main crossing point of the wildebeest migrations, is a real hot spot for game viewing.

Ron continued his adventurous safaris in northern Kenya and into Ethiopia for a few more years. This was an arid but spectacular area, where naked Turkana tribesmen still fished the jade waters of Lake Turkana with their cone-shaped nets. His original motivation for going up the Omo River in Ethiopia was to trace his father's footsteps taken all those years ago with his Italian prisoners of war.

Ron timed his expeditions into Ethiopia to coincide with some of the traditional ceremonies still practised by the tribes in this remote part of Africa, in particular that of bull jumping, a rite in which youths pass into manhood by jumping and running across the backs of eight bulls.

Ron took his last safari to Ethiopia in 2005. Up until then, the Omo River was a wild and remote place where his guests could get a glimpse of the old Africa with its deep-rooted customs and traditional tribal ceremonies. This all began to change with the commercialisation of the tourist industry and the arrival of missionaries who put up windmills along the riverbanks. This all rather spoilt it for the tourist, as it no longer had the same appeal that it used to have for intrepid travellers, although it was, of course, a great benefit to the people living there to have fresh water and electricity. Today the river has been dammed, so it is no longer navigable in the dry season and it is cluttered with drilling rigs, as there are almost certainly deposits of oil there.

KOIYAKI GUIDING SCHOOL

For some time, Ron trained Maasai as safari guides. Having lived there so long, he knows them well and felt passionately that they should be more involved in all aspects of running the Masai Mara. He was a prime mover in the creation of the guide school on the Koiyaki Group ranch adjoining the northern boundary of the reserve. Ron was instrumental in securing funding and using his expertise to make this initiative come about. Three hundred applicants came forward for 23 places in the first intake! The idea was to train and employ young Maasai men and women to guide at all the lodges in the Mara. This is especially important because visitors always want to know about the lives and customs of this colourful tribe. The guide school's students learn about all aspects of guiding, and are taught good English to equip them with the vital communication skills required for social interaction with Westerners. The students already have a deep understanding of animal behaviour and tracking before they enrol. Their teachers are highly respected guides from various countries who have reached the top of their profession, and I expect Garth Thompson's book, *The Guide's Guide to Guiding*, will be on the shelves. The trainee guides obtain practical experience with guests at the in-house lodge by participating in walks and game drives with them.

In order to concentrate on running Rekero Expeditions and setting up the guide school, Ron sold his share of the business to his son,

Gerard, a fourth-generation Kenyan, and his wife, Rainee, a talented and successful artist, who ran Rekero Tented Camp (the cottages have been closed down) with Jackson Saigilu Ole Looseyia, his Maasai partner and one of the guides featured in this book. The Koiyaki Guiding School is often visited by the Rekero guests.

In March 2005, Gerard and Rainee's first child was born – Charlie – the fifth generation of Beatons in Kenya.

Rekero Camp was sold to Asilia in 2009. Both Gerard and Jackson had three-year contracts to continue to work there. Gerard has signed on for another three years, but Jackson and Rainee have set up their own safari business called Nomad Encounters (which you can read more about in the chapter on Jackson).

After he stopped guiding, Ron became involved with setting up the Koiyaki Guiding School and continued to steer its course and help with funding until it was handed over to the Maasai, who now run the project themselves. Ron told me about Lex Hes's hugely helpful contribution to the school and other centres that needed training support.

Ron was also instrumental in creating the Olare Orok Conservancy Trust. The following quote, taken from the Olare Orok website, explains how the conservancy works:

> *In May 2006 a landmark agreement was reached with Maasai landowners for the formation of Olare Orok Conservancy bordering the Masai Mara Game Reserve.*
>
> *The deal brokered with the 154 Maasai landowners is now the template for the Mara community wildlife conservancies and is set to become the outline for the sustainability of the greater Masai Mara ecological unit.*
>
> *Olare Orok Conservancy is a fascinating new conservation conception on land-use. Prior to 2006 the Olare Orok and Motoroki Conservancies, 35 000 acres of prime grasslands, riverine forests and Acacia woodlands, were populated by rural homesteads and grazed in an uncontrolled manner by large herds of cattle, sheep and goats.*

The Maasai landowners own Olare Orok Conservancy and this community directly benefits from 100% of the rents being paid by tourism partners with bush camps within the conservancy. These landowners have facilitated the core area, completely free of settlement. In times of low tourism, management directs a strict rotational grazing regime, which is beneficial to the grasslands with parts of the conservancy intensively grazed during the long rains season and other areas left naturally grazed with wildlife habitat.

This policy benefits the landowners' livestock and ensures diversity of wildlife species through these different grazing regimes. In times of intense drought parts of the conservancy are made available as a dry weather grass bank to ensure landowner livestock survive these droughts. Olare Orok Trust has facilitated capacity building to the community through the Koiyaki Guiding School and the Olare Orok outreach program.

The conservancy is very well managed and the Maasai get a good annual income. Olare Orok is one of a number of conservancies that act as buffers for the Masai Mara – an excellent way of protecting the animals and enriching the local people whose land it is. Ron believes that the best blueprint for the conservancies is Ol Pejeta, in Laikipia. Ol Pejeta combines community projects, agriculture and livestock along with wildlife tourism. The internally generated revenues are combined with donor funds that help run this highly successful organisation. I hope that eventually it will be able to run without funding, as self-sufficiency must be the ultimate wish of all conservancies.

Ron and Pauline live in a beautiful house on Olare Orok in a lightly wooded landscape that drifts down to the Masai Mara boundary. Lines of wildebeest stream past the house along with many other animals that wander in and out of the trees, and nearby the most successful pride of lions in the whole area rest up in a cattle-free part of the conservancy. It is truly a mini-paradise.

As Ron no longer has any involvement in the Koiyaki Guiding School or in the Olare Orok Trust, he and Pauline plan to take a year out, travelling the world and enjoying themselves. He has been approached with requests to help with other new conservancies in Kenya, particularly around Tsavo, which for him would be going back to his roots, but this is something he will only consider after his travels.

JACKSON SAIGILU OLE LOOSEYIA

S aigilu Ole Looseyia, known as Jackson, has become one of the best-known and most highly respected guides in Kenya. He crosses the divide between traditional tribal life and the Western world effortlessly. Many articles have been written about him in newspapers and magazines, including the *Sunday Times* and *Sunday Telegraph* in the United Kingdom, the *Boston Globe*, *Travel and Leisure*, and several South African publications.

Jackson is a tall, well-built man with an easy, graceful manner, natural charm and well-honed communication skills. Like all the top guides, he has clients returning again and again to enjoy yet another safari with him. Not only do they have a very exciting and successful game-viewing experience, but they are also captivated by Jackson's tales of the cultural life of his people, which adds a wonderfully unusual dimension to their safaris. As a partner and shareholder in Rekero with Gerard Beaton, Ron Beaton's son, he has travelled on marketing trips in South Africa, the United Kingdom and the United States.

Jackson's whole being is infused with his love of the bush and wildlife. As we sat discussing his life story on a still, warm afternoon by the Talek River, the stillness was broken by a flurry of bird chatter.

'Listen,' he said. 'They are having roll call: "Is everyone all right? I haven't seen Jane. Where's Mary?"'

The twittering continued for a few minutes and then they were gone. Many species apparently gather like this a few times every day just to check that all is well.

His attention was then taken by a small herd of elephants grazing on the long, sweet grass so abundant in February. Elephants, he told me, are 80 per cent grazers and only 20 per cent browsers (leaf-eaters). Every single one of his senses was trained on his surroundings as he wove the story of his childhood, his life and dreams for the future. He remembers vividly the annual arrival of the wildebeest migration when he was at school. The migration was always a spectacle, even though the area was more heavily forested then and not as large as it is today. The wildebeest came right past his school, creating clouds of dust that could be seen for miles and causing the excited children to abandon their work to watch.

Jackson was born in the Masai Mara, he and his sister the sole survivors of five children born to an Ildorobo hunter-gatherer and a Maasai woman. His father, Selel Ole Looseyia had been married before, but his wife had been unable to bear children, a harsh and sad thing for any woman, but particularly for Maasai women, as not only do they need to be cared for in their old age but their whole social structure revolves around childbearing. So she was allowed to return to her own family, where her brother gave her one of his daughters to bring up as her own. Her family assumed the responsibility for the care and dowry of this little girl. Selel then married Jackson's mother and she remained his only wife for life, although culture permitted him to have more than one.

Before the 1930s, a large population of Maasai lived in the north of Kenya with the Samburu people, on the Laikipia Plateau and around Nairobi. However, owing to pressure by the colonists, who wanted this fertile land for dairy and sheep farming, the Maasai were persuaded to move. The *Ol oiboni* (an adviser with powers of divination and prophesy, commonly known as the medicine man) approved the move and they came south with their cattle in their own great migration. The men who walked to the Mara are now all dead, including Jackson's great-grandfather, who died in 2001, aged about a hundred. The men who were babies on their mother's backs are still alive. Although some Maasai already lived in this area, it was mostly inhabited by Ildorobo hunter-gatherers. The word 'Ildorobo', occasionally with slight variations of spelling, means 'tsetse fly' or 'poor man who has no cattle'. It can also mean 'a village where bees live'.

The Mara was thickly forested and each Ildorobo family marked out its own territory for its bees, but the hunting was communal and could be done all over the land. The Ildorobo were incomparable beekeepers, and kept their hives in hollowed-out branches placed in trees near to the abundant blossoms required for the honey. They knew which trees to use and when they would flower, and moved the hives accordingly. They were naturally very shy people, hiding in the forests and trying to continue to live as they had always lived, in spite of the arrival of the Maasai. They wore skins, even after the Maasai had switched to cloth shukas. Nomadic people, they hunted with bows and arrows.

The rolling hills and thick forests of the Mara are very different from the terrain at Loliondo, in Tanzania, where we came upon the Ildorobo house under a granite overhang. Here, the women would hollow out a large termite mound and light a fire inside to turn the earth brick-hard. It was warm, cosy and watertight. The beauty of these functional shelters is that there is always another home waiting to be quickly made or reinhabited in the next place. They knew the forests so well that when the first white traders came into the area looking for ivory, the Ildorobo knew where to find ivory where the dead elephants lay. This was the beginning of trade for them, as they took a few goats for each tusk.

With many new Maasai moving into the area and burning the forests to create pasture for their cattle, it was inevitable that the culture of the hunter-gatherers would begin to disappear and that the tribes would intermix.

In the late 1940s, the Masai Mara Game Reserve was gazetted and hunting within its boundaries made illegal, although this was not the sort of news to reach a hunter-gatherer tribesman. Licensed hunting safaris took place along with the game control area outside the reserve, but Selel continued to hunt in his traditional grounds, which were now out of bounds. He was caught and sent to prison for three years. Prison for a freewheeling soul like Selel, used to roaming at will, was extremely difficult. It was a culture alien beyond imagination. Having learnt this lesson, however, he did not heed it, but continued to hunt, was caught and spent another three years in prison. When the head warden of the area found him a third time, and he didn't run away, he asked Selel, 'Why don't you run? Are you not afraid of me and another term in jail?'

He answered, 'No, I hunt to live. It is all I know, the only way I can feed my family. What else can I do?'

The man who caught Selel hunting illegally the third time was the colonial game warden of South Maasailand, Lyn Temple Boreham, who wisely decided to employ Selel rather than imprison him yet again. Known as Temple by the Maasai, this rather eccentric man was educated in the United Kingdom and Russia, his father having been in the diplomatic service. He was an imposing character, over two metres tall, physically powerful and popular with the Maasai. He managed to persuade them to set land aside for the Masai Mara Reserve and hence one of the very few Caucasians to be given land by the Maasai. Jackson mentions his name with great reverence to this day.

Selel was now employed as a game ranger. Temple took away his bow and arrows, replaced the skins he wore with a shirt, shorts and long boots, which he found most uncomfortable, gave him a gun and taught him how to shoot. Selel took to shooting with ease: anyone who can kill a buffalo with a bow and arrow has little problem learning how to use a gun. He was thrilled, as he could now feed his family legally. Being a ranger meant being involved with game control, and game control meant culling animals outside the park that interfered with farming and villages, which included many elephants and lions. Considering how aggressively this policy was carried out, it is quite amazing that so many animals still live outside the parks. Temple never regretted his decision, as Selel was a superb tracker – so good, in fact, that he was also employed to track Mau Mau fighters in the 1950s.

Jackson was brought up strictly in the traditional manner of his people. Maasai children learn at an early age to be responsible for their animals, so Jackson tended the goats and the sheep as a small boy and the cattle when a little older. The elders know every single animal they own by name. Even if there are hundreds of sheep, they will know which one is missing, which have had lambs and which are not well. In times of plenty, the herds stay close to home, but, when drought persists, the animals are taken far away to better grazing near the water in the established Maasai wells. When this happens, layonis (young uncircumcised Maasai boys) are sent along with the morans to help care for the animals and to act as runners to come home and report how they are doing. About once a month, an elder might come out and inspect the animals, but with enough trustworthy sons this is usually unnecessary. They live on maize-meal porridge and the occasional goat or sheep, usually one that has succumbed to illness or old age. However, they are allowed to slaughter a goat if all their maize meal is finished. It is always a joyful moment when the message comes that the rains have arrived and they can go home to their families.

Jackson attended the local mission school, but continued to be responsible for the goats and sheep, tending them each evening. In the flock was a pair of twin male goats that had been castrated; they had a close bond and never parted. One evening, on returning from school, he noticed that one of the twins was wandering around alone; there was no sign of the other. He sought out the small boys who had been herding them during the day and asked where it was; they vaguely muttered something about a leopard. Jackson noticed guilt written all over the face of one of the boys and asked to see his knife. It smelt of meat.

The boy insisted they had killed a gazelle and eaten it, but there was no evidence of any extra meat for the family so this was patently untrue. 'I smell goat on your knife,' he said.

The boy was defiant but obviously scared. Having tried to probe for the truth, he now decided it was time to seek his father's advice on how to proceed. After careful contemplation, Selel decided to speak to the boy's father, but as they approached the man's hut it was apparent that they were walking into a family dispute. The boy's older brother was cowering in the back of the hut, begging for mercy and asking forgiveness. He had killed the goat and sworn the boy to silence. Such action necessitates retribution and the fine was very heavy – two goats and eight calves had to be paid to Jackson's family. His detective work had truly paid off, though, sadly, not for the remaining lonely twin goat.

Maasai do not traditionally grow crops. Surrounded by cattle and goats, their natural diet is mostly meat, which is hung in strips on fences to dry out, making it portable protein.

It is stewed and roasted, and soup is made with the bones, but the greatest delicacy is the buffalo tongue. In Jackson's time, so prized was this portion that the custom of one of the tribes, who hunted with dogs and spears, was to cut out the tongue, and present it to the first man who had speared the animal. The Ildorobo were very careful killers; mothers and young were never touched, as conservation of the herds was paramount. An old buffalo bull was popular. Although the flesh would be tough, there was a lot of it, along with large amounts of marrow in the bones and a lot of fat around the kidneys – excellent for soup. One of their greatest annual treats was Jackson's mother's specialty – buffalo hooves. These she split and stored on the ceiling of her hut, where they rotted, dried and were smoked for about two months. She then boiled them for a day and a half, by which time they were so tender they could suck the meat out of the bones.

All the rituals of a young man growing up in the Maasai culture were observed. Jackson had to experience the ennobling passage to warrior status by submitting courageously to having his two lower front teeth removed (cut out by his grandfather) and to the rite of circumcision. For Selel, the old traditions lingered on and he made sure that his son learnt self-sufficiency in the bush, and the art of hunting with a bow and arrow. Western culture was encroaching rapidly upon them, however, and Selel's plan was for his son to be a good warrior and join the army, as he felt that this would be an excellent career. Jackson reluctantly acquiesced, but he never really wanted to be a warrior or a soldier.

Young Maasai boys are aware of what will be expected of them as time goes on, and Jackson and his friends were no exception. As little boys knowing there was so much to learn, they started teaching themselves about the traditional poisons. First, they would poison ticks to see how long they took to die, then mice and other small creatures, as it was essential to understand how the poison worked. They then practised with little bows and arrows dipped in poison, and shot lizards, birds and porcupines, until, one day, they were able to shoot their first large mammal, a Thomson's gazelle.

Selel decided the time had come to take his son, now in his teens, out into the bush with a bow and arrow to teach him how to stalk and kill successfully. To kill a giraffe, he learnt how he had to creep up on it very slowly, getting close enough to shoot the poisoned arrow into the animal at the first try. When Jackson's arrow hit, the startled animal jumped and looked around but, seeing nothing, continued browsing. The poison took about half an hour to work. Jackson lay still in the grass, keeping an eye on the giraffe until it moved off to browse a little further away. He then climbed a tree where he waited and watched. Once the animal fell, he had to get to it very quickly and cover it completely with branches to hide it from vultures until it could be butchered. Giraffe meat remains his favourite to this day.

Jackson's other tasks were to kill a buffalo, a lion and an impala. The buffalo was dispatched without too much trouble, but he was very insecure about stalking and killing a lion. The prospect filled him with terror, and he hoped his father would not realise just how afraid he was. They spent most of the day together stalking a lion until finally they got within sight of it. Once again, it called for shooting from close quarters. His father stayed back and made him approach quietly and carefully upwind, so as not to alert the lion and to get a clean shot. Armed with only his bow and arrow, he was aware of 'chills in his legs' and a thumping heart as he crept closer and closer. Just as he felt sure his end had come, the wind direction shifted suddenly, the lion got a whiff of him and Selel, and streaked away as fast as it could, to Jackson's great relief!

However, the most prestigious animal to learn to kill was the impala. Impalas are so nervous and acutely sensitive to all that goes on around them that they are about the most difficult animal to stalk – it is said that even their hairs have eyes. If you hunt them successfully, you are considered a great hunter. Jackson managed this feat, so, even though the lion got away, he gained the respect he sought.

Ron Beaton, who was at his nearby lodge, Rekero, around this time, had a group of clients who wished to visit a Maasai village and Ron asked if Temple could recommend anywhere. Temple suggested Selel's village and, because Jackson had a smattering of English, he was asked to show the guests around. The visitors were to learn this was a place of mixed cultures. Their tour took them through one of the village houses before they went to see how the bees were cared for and how the cows were milked. Full-blooded Maasai never keep bees or grow crops, but in Jackson's village they had a small vegetable patch.

Selel took Ron to show him his hives and the disturbance caused some angry bees to sting poor Ron – but not Selel. Apparently, because they knew Selel they never stung him! The bees were usually docile but became aggressive at mating time, when the hives were full of larvae. Then the drones fly from the hives in a swarm, high up into the air, trying to mate with the queen, then down in a tight ball, nearly hitting the ground before bursting like a skyrocket, dispersing up into the air, only to form again. At this time, everyone, even Selel, stayed well clear until the bees had settled down into their family units once more.

During this visit to the village, Ron had been extremely impressed by Jackson's expertise when he was showing the group around and felt he had great potential as a guide. So he invited Jackson to stay at Rekero to perfect his English and to learn the Latin and English names of the trees and plants he knew so well. This marked the beginning of Jackson's training as a guide. As a young man he had watched the safari industry burgeon, observing the guides and trackers, and he longing to be one himself. However, he knew no one who could help and was told he would have to go to Nairobi, where the travel companies had their offices, to find work. But he had no intention of going there, as he had heard chilling tales of what happens to you in the big city, so he stayed and continued living his traditional life in the village. His meeting with Ron was a dream come true.

Over the years Jackson perfected all the skills required to be a top safari guide – perfect English, Westernised table manners, the ability to make polite conversation as well as the practical skills of being able to drive and repair vehicles. His love of the bush was there from boyhood and, having tracked and hunted, he already had great bush skills. He and Gerard Beaton became firm friends and one feels that he is truly a part of the Beaton family.

Tribal tradition was such that Jackson was expected to marry young and quickly produce sons to help with the cattle. Over the years, his mother had chosen no fewer than 11 suitable girls from Maasai families, but none was right for him. He didn't want to marry young. His plan was to work in the safari industry and to have time to keep learning his trade. A few years later, while he was working for Ron, he met the girl who was to become his wife.

They met at a social event at Jackson's church, always merry occasions, filled with enthusiastic discussions and plenty of singing. He spotted two attractive girls and introduced himself. One of the girls – who were housemates – was full of fun and always game for a party; the other, though charming, was more reserved and shy. The quiet girl, who worked as a clerk in a small local company, watched Jackson having fun with her friend, all the while knowing in her heart that it was her he would marry. Eventually her friend took off with an older man and moved away. Jackson continued his friendship with the quiet girl, their relationship blossomed and he was elated when she agreed to marry him.

This story is a clear indication of how quickly the Maasai living in multiracial areas had adopted Western values and customs – the fact that he could choose his own wife and follow a career of his choice was a great leap forward in personal freedom.

As his bride had not been betrothed to him at birth, the first thing that had to be done was a formal introduction to each other's families. Once this has gone well and the dowry decided, it is customary for the church elders to have a talk with the couple and only with their approval can the engagement be announced. Jackson's life and experiences had moved so far away from his tribal upbringing that it was essential that he and his future wife should carefully discuss how their life would evolve. He was in one way moving away from the traditional Maasai life, although still living ostensibly as a traditional Maasai in his home. His education had opened his eyes to knowledge denied his ancestors and some of his contemporaries. Managing a life between the two cultures calls for a very fine balancing act. For example, he has learnt that circumcision for girls serves absolutely no purpose at all (it was believed that uncircumcised girls were infertile, in spite of the fact that they regularly became pregnant). His daughters will not have to suffer this cruel procedure, his main concern being that his daughters make friends with similarly educated children and don't get swayed by other girls whose parents are not as enlightened as their own.

His son, on the other hand, will have to go through the agony and suffering that all Maasai boys have to go through, including having two of his teeth cut out. This, Jackson believes, will make a man of him. Nothing that life throws at him will ever be quite as difficult as it would have been had he not courageously faced the traditional initiation into manhood. Jackson will have only one wife; although Maasai culture still allows him more than one, he does not want more. He is very strict about Maasai inheritance laws; his son is his sole heir, as he was his father's sole heir.

Jackson has been managing and guiding at the Rekero Tented Camp, on the Talek River, right in the path of the annual migration. His future plans include running a camp in the Shaba National Reserve along with

Gerard Beaton. So far this has not come to fruition but they still hope it will, as this is a beautiful and underused park.

He will also assist in the Koiyaki Guiding School. He plans to take as many of his guests as possible to the visitors' lodge to experience walking in a wilderness area. The students there, already know the land, the river crossings, the secret places and the traditional cultures: they just have to learn how to communicate them to visitors and how to make their brief visit to their land one of joy, knowledge and understanding. A Maasai guide can bring a whole new meaning to a discussion on local culture by being able to say 'we' instead of 'they'. It is Ron and Jackson's plan for every tourist vehicle in the Mara to have a Maasai guide, either driving or accompanying the driver.

Jackson has been very busy since I first met him. In 2008, the BBC's *Big Cat Diary* became *Big Cat Live* and Jackson was included as a presenter for the second series. They spent three weeks watching the cats, culminating in live broadcasts from the Masai Mara each night for a week. Although working in television was new to him, he did extremely well. As one of Africa's great safari guides and with his natural gift of communication, he came across brilliantly, a true professional. In my perhaps biased opinion, he far outshone all the resident professionals. He has also worked on other television programmes, including *Planet Earth Live* with Richard Hammond of *Top Gear* fame, and the Disney film *African Cats*.

'I was lucky to be chosen to speak on camera as a presenter on BBC Big Cat Live, I had never spoken on live television before and the best thing was that I never saw myself on live television – to me it was just life in the Mara, my office as normal. I thought I was just speaking to the two people in front of me during my live shows. I didn't understand I was speaking to millions of people at that minute. It was a terrifying thought.

'The most difficult part was dealing with the television people and trying to understand what they were talking about, what they wanted me to say and how they wanted me to say it. The creative mind of producers was something I struggled with but after a few months I started to understand what they were talking about. I had to go back and forwards repeating again and again – this angle and that light. It was frustrating and sometimes I just said what I know and not what I was asked to do. The easy part was sitting and waiting for the wildlife action. I loved every minute of that and wished I were there forever and ever. The big cats' life, the movements, behaviour, encounters, caring and hunting skills, etc., was the very best part of my filming experience.

'Disney was much easier to work with because they wanted to know what I think of the wildlife in the Mara and of the Maasai people. Therefore, that was just perfect for me. When every now and then they lost the main characters that they were filming I had to help the spotters identify them and keep their eyes on them during the filming.

'Many people wrote to me by email and letters, and phoned. It was a little difficult realising that I had to cope with the new life that was born after TV. But the good news was that our business at Rekero boomed. Lots of people learned about Rekero and wanted to come and visit me in my office. The other good thing was being with the wildlife and I knew some of the big cats before the filming but now I had people with great passion wanting to spend time with lions and leopards, and understanding they are wild animals not pets.'

As mentioned, in 2009 Rekero was sold. Gerard Beaton and Jackson, who were partners in the business, were contracted to work at Rekero for three years. When the time was up, Gerard remained with Rekero. Jackson, however, who was used to being his own boss, decided to leave and set up his own company along with Rainee, Gerard's wife. Together, they have created Nomadic Encounters. They have three new houses and a mobile camp. Two of the newly built houses, Mara House and Acacia House, are situated on the original site where Ron and Pauline Beaton set up their safaris many years ago. The third, Topi House, is not far from where Ron and Pauline now live in the Olare Orok Conservancy. Each of the houses, known as Mara Bush Homes, are single storey with three bedrooms. The mobile Nomadic Camp started in 2012 and is proving a great success.

This is a private camp that takes from 4 to 12 people. Jackson has chosen Maasai guides of the highest quality, but if guests want Jackson to guide, they have to book well in advance, as he now has a very busy diary. He still takes walking safaris but it is becoming increasingly difficult to do traditional walks, as the new conservancies are not set up for this. He has personally selected excellent sites for his mobile camp and I am sure this will continue to be a safari in the time-honoured way. So far their dream of having a camp in Shaba has not yet come to fruition but, one day, Nomadic Encounters may expand to other areas.

Life often moves in circles. From 2013, Asilia, the South African company that bought Rekero, leased two of Nomad Encounters' bush homes, and Gerard, Rainee and Jackson are now all shareholders in Asilia. Gerard is the country manager and Rainee oversees quality control. Jackson remains a freelance guide, mostly for the Nomadic Camp, but he also guides or consults for Asilia, Jonathon Scott, James Robertson, Simon King and Keith Scholey and others – as well as doing his own private guiding. They are all very happy with the set-up, as it has allowed them to live normal family lives with the understanding that they have support from the Nairobi operations, finance and marketing team.

Jackson is not only a phenomenal safari guide, but is also well travelled and fully aware of the changes that the 21st century is making. The Maasai are no longer isolated rural people – they are part of modern Kenya, and Jackson is aware that they have to pull together with all the tribes for the good of the country. Jackson spends a good deal of time talking to the communities, about many things, especially education and changing traditions. He points out to them that Kenya has a soaring population, which can only be addressed by good education. The knowledge of science and the world around them will enlighten their people, but will also change their traditions, and one of the traditions he would like to see stopped is female genital mutilation.

Jackson now has five children. His eldest daughter, Damaris, is at university studying accountancy; the others, two daughters and a son, have dreams of their own far away from safaris. Silvia would like to be a computer engineer; Morris wants to be a scientist; and Pauline plans to be a lawyer but has a dream to study in the United States, which terrifies Jackson. The baby is four and still at home with Mum.

BETTY NAYIANDI MAITAI

Betty is an excellent safari guide at Richard's Camp in the eastern Mara Koiyaki Conservancy. She has also worked at Ol Seki Lodge, and is a graduate of the first intake of the Koiyaki Guiding School. As a little girl, she would wave to the smiling tourists passing her home on their way to the Mara and yearned to be part of whatever it was they were going to do.

She luckily had parents who respected girls' rights to education, so she went on to complete high school. During a school visit to Seronera Lodge, in the Masai Mara, she met some of the tourists. One lady took a particular interest in Betty, and asked her many questions about Maasai women and encouraged her to aim for a position in the tourist industry – for which she was clearly cut out. Unfortunately, as her parents could not afford the fees for the tourism school in Nairobi's Utalii College, she applied to the army for military training and was accepted. On completion of the training course, which was by all accounts gruelling, including 12-hour walks with heavy backpacks, she heard that there was to be a school built for Maasai people to learn to be safari guides and that they were taking women. This was far preferable in her eyes to life in the army.

She was the first to apply to Koiyaki Guiding School and was accepted, one of 3 girls and 20 boys. The experience for her was all she had ever wished for. Everything the boys did, the girls did too – she learnt to drive a four-wheel-drive vehicle, how to strip and put together an engine, first aid, the botanical and English names of birds, bugs and beasts, how to lay tables and make up rooms. There was no aspect of a guide's life that was left out.

She knows what a lucky break she had that the school was founded at just the right time for her. She is an inspiration to all the girls in her village, encouraging them to stay at school, and not to be circumcised and married at 13. She tells them it is their right to say 'No': 'Why shouldn't girls get educated? They do not look after the cows – the boys do that and educating girls helps to make the whole country better educated.'

Betty is content and working hard. She believes that God has made her greatest dream come true. She loves her job and hasn't had a moments regret in her choice of profession.

CALVIN COTTAR

W hile sinking into a hot canvas bathtub, I can't help but marvel at the scene before me. A scattering of flat-topped acacia trees on a grassy slope that melts into riverine forest, beyond which the vast plains of the Masai Mara stretch to the distant purple hills where vultures gracefully circle. As I take in this timeless scene, I wonder if the late Queen Elizabeth, the Queen Mother, then Duchess of York, had enjoyed the same view from her canvas tub in 1924, when on safari with Bud Cottar, son of Chas. In those days, everyone on a luxury safari had the opportunity to indulge in a hot bath – bucket-showers were not introduced until much later. Now, Calvin Cottar, Chas Cottar's great-grandson, born two weeks after Kenya's independence, has come full circle and reintroduced this blissful treat in his own safari business: Cottar's Classic Safaris.

Calvin is tall and handsome, and in his battered brown safari hat resembles a character that has stepped out of a Western. He is quietly spoken and has a calm sense of authority in the bush, and is very aware of his family heritage. His beautiful camp is situated on a rise overlooking the Masai Mara and styled to evoke the camps used by his great-grandfather in the 1920s. From there and from his father's bush home, Bushtops, he takes walking safaris for those with an adventurous spirit. Both are soul-restoring experiences.

Teddy Roosevelt wrote a book in 1909 called *African Game Trails*, which is about his safari the year before. When Chas Cottar read this book at home in Oklahoma, his imagination was so fired up that he went off to Africa to see if all that the president had said was true. It certainly was. He spent three months there, fell in love with the place and went back to America to gather up his wife, six daughters and three sons – Mike, Bud and Ted – and returned to East Africa in 1912. He spent the rest of his life there, becoming one of the top safari guides in Africa. Together with his sons, he mainly hunted but also took photographic safaris, which he made available as early as the 1920s. His was also the first safari outfitters to use vehicles on safari and the first to film the animals. He made a colour feature film called *Africa Speaks* in 1928. Chas was an adventurer and a risk taker, whose action-packed life ended abruptly while filming a charging rhinoceros!

Calvin's father, Glen, was unlike his own father, in that he was not a showman in the mould of his father, uncles and grandfather. However, he was similar, in that he was an explorer and a serious hunter who was very popular because of the care and expertise he displayed. His clients knew that, with him, while they would not shoot a lot of game, what they did shoot would be the best quality. He spent hours picking out the best animal; he would not choose the best out of only a hundred buffaloes, but more like three thousand.

Glen's explorations took him far afield. He opened up Katavi and hunted in Rukwa with Jack Bousfield, and the tracks they made in those remote areas are the ones still in use today. He was in the first group of East African hunters to go to Botswana. This was virgin territory; southern Africa did not have the same hunting ethos that East Africa had, and the area was ripe for the picking. In the 1950s and early 1960s, tourism had not yet reached the Okavango Delta, so these East African hunters had a field day. Glen was one of the first people to venture into areas that are all so familiar to tourists today. He discovered the Selinda

Spillway, which was overflowing with water and teeming with game. He told of huge herds of animals that stood looking at them fearlessly. In those times the game was indeed fearless, as they had never seen vehicles or people, rather like penguins in the Antarctic.

Photographic safaris really only started in earnest in the 1970s, around the time the hunting areas came under strict control. Some of the hunters stayed to hunt while others started photographic safaris, as this was a place of breathtaking beauty, which, once the secret was out, they knew everyone would want to see for themselves. Glen, however, returned to East Africa, as he was first and foremost a Kenyan. Back home he continued to hunt, but started to combine hunting trips with photographic safaris, as he was quick to see the potential of the latter. In 1964, he built the very first dedicated tourist camp in Tsavo. At the time, Tsavo had 40 000 elephants and 10 000 black rhinos. By 1975, only 11 years later, most of the big game in Tsavo had disappeared as a result of drought and poaching. Deciding it was time to move, Glen sold his camp and built another just outside the Masai Mara at Siana Springs. By the time all hunting in Kenya was banned in 1977, he was well set up to service the tourist industry.

Calvin was born in Nairobi where his mother, Pat, was what was known as a 'safari widow', living in Nairobi with her daughter and son and she kept the logistics of the safaris going. The family would visit the Tsavo Camp from time to time and one of Calvin's earliest memories is of a rhino chasing and whacking their car.

When Calvin was 13 he went to stay in a hunting camp with his father, who felt he was then old enough to stay in the camp and help the staff. His father taught him how to drive and use a rifle, but his father's trackers and gun bearers taught him about everything else – the bush, animal behaviour and tracking. One of Glen's hunting campsites was not far from where Calvin has his camp today – a lovely place with big trees and a sparkling stream called Oloibor Miotoni (the River of the Martial Eagles). This is where Glen taught Calvin to shoot with a large-calibre rifle. He was a natural shot: after one afternoon of target practice into a tree, he bagged his first antelope the following morning.

Calvin spent most of his teenage years at the Mara camp. By the time he was 15, he was taking guests out on game drives, which gave him a very early introduction to guiding. At 18, having finished school, he set off to find out what the outside world was like. He went to America to explore his Cottar roots, though there are no more Cottars in America. The last one, Tom Cottar, was sheriff of Red Bluff, in northern California. The Cottars are related to the Waltons, an extensive American family that boasts several thousand at its reunions. Calvin met up with his sister in Colorado, where they had both been offered a job in a restaurant belonging to a family friend. His last two months in America were spent skiing and, once he had blown all his money on skiing, and especially the après-ski part, he left for home. He had gone to see if the grass was greener, and found it wasn't.

At the time when Calvin returned from America, Glen was running Cottar's Camp at Siana Springs. It was a large camp with 20 rooms, about to be increased to 30. They didn't see eye to eye over this. Glen was keen for Calvin to take over Cottar's Camp, but Calvin's heart was set on running a small, exclusive camp, with no more than six tents. Glen believed that only big camps made money and stubbornly refused to change his plan. Calvin, equally stubborn, left to join Robin Hurt to hunt in Tanzania. Calvin did not have a close relationship with his father, who had been away for long periods while he was a child. This, combined with the fact that Glen's own father had died when Glen was a child, leaving him with no paternal role model, left little room for understanding between father and son.

At about the same time (1985) a Maasai friend of Glen came to tell him that a Kikuyu man wanted to farm in a beautiful valley, very close to the Mara, and the only place Glen had ever seen roan antelope on that side of the Mara. He felt it would be dreadful to have a farm so close to the park and decided to take over the area himself. He paid the Maasai more than the Kikuyu farmer had offered and built Bushtops, the Cottar family bush home, taking apart an old house he had had at his original camp and rebuilding it on the new site. It remains a special place for the family. Glen always loved it and his ashes are scattered there.

The years spent working for Robin Hurt were some of Calvin's happiest. Hunting is a young man's adventure; he had no responsibilities, was fearless, and thoroughly enjoyed shooting and exploring. Hunting is in his blood; it's what his family has always done, although he no longer hunts. Like many young men, he grew out of it. He also became disillusioned with the way hunting was run in Tanzania, so he began to look for an alternative life in the bush. Back in Kenya he became involved in wildlife management. He worked as a consultant for the Kenya Wildlife Service in a programme devised to help farmers manage wildlife, but it was not very successful or satisfactory. At that point, encouraged by his father, Calvin went back into the safari business. Being in wild, remote areas, he realised – waking each day with a feeling of excited anticipation as to what the day might bring and how he would open its splendours to visitors – was the only life he wanted to live.

The lessons he had learnt during his hunting days were very useful for the many walking safaris he takes, but one, in particular, has been invaluable, as he relates in the following story about a wounded buffalo:

'One of my most frightening moments was on a hunting safari with a client who had come to shoot a buffalo. We found the one we wanted, a very big old guy, in a thicket ahead of us. When shooting a buffalo, the gun rests on a tripod of sticks held with a rubber band. I had slung my gun over my shoulder in order to use both hands to secure the sticks, telling my client to be ready to shoot it in the heart when it smelled us, which should take about ten seconds. As I was lowering the gun from my shoulder, and with absolutely no warning, the buffalo charged straight for us, wild with explosive anger. The client pointed his gun at this advancing juggernaut, which was moving like a bullet from hell, and shot it between the eyes ten metres from where we stood. The massive creature collapsed, its nose scraping the ground, eyes bloodshot and bulging, and lay dead five metres

from us. It was an incredible shot; if he had hit it anywhere else it would not have died, as he only had a .375, which is a small gun.

'I think I would have been able to shoot it but I will never be certain, and it taught me one of the biggest lessons of my life. You can only assume so much of wild animals. Normally, a buffalo will stop, look and sniff the air, before running away. But they are like people: their behaviour is not always predictable. Whether it is lion, elephant or buffalo, ninety-nine times out of a hundred you can guess what they will do, but it is that one time that they will get you.

'The reason that this buffalo had been so charged up was because he had a stump stuck in his hoof, between his toes, causing a painful, suppurating sore. His leg was very swollen and he was in agony. He would have killed someone, whether it was a honey hunter or a game warden just checking the area – he was going to strike at someone, who most likely would have been completely defenceless. We were glad we had killed him.

'Now when I walk, particularly in bush country, where you can't see, I always carry a loaded gun. It is far more reliable, as you don't let up on safety. You are constantly aware of where the gun is pointed and what support there might be from the bush and trees around you. I realised that the time it takes to load the gun and be ready to shoot could cost a life.'

The Cottar family count among their friends many well-known people who have been on safari with them. One in particular is Peter Beard, an American photographer, artist and author. He was on safari with Calvin when an elephant attacked him. The following is Calvin's account of that incident. But this time, having his gun ready would not have helped:

'Peter, an old family friend, had been staying at my camp with me for three days' filming. On the fourth day we planned, that fateful morning, to drive to the waterfall. On the way we saw a nice herd of elephants and decided to stop and film them. They were about 40 metres away from us on the top of a slope, at the bottom of which is a large termite mound. Peter and I stood on the mound while being filmed. When the cameraman had finished, we started to walk back to the car. The cameramen were ahead of us.

'I said, "Peter, those elephants are so calm – let's stay and watch and walk a bit with them." Peter was in a bit of a dream world that morning, not really into the elephants, more in tune with his own feelings, but went along with it nevertheless.

'By now the elephants were at the top of the slope, about 150 metres from us, moving slowly away. The wind was coming from them to us and we were walking parallel with them.

'Suddenly, from the back of the herd an elephant gave a mock charge. We immediately started to walk away from them, not running but stepping up our pace. She was a young cow, probably in her first pregnancy. The size of the wound Peter was to receive, as seen later, indicated the size of her tusks and her age. All of a sudden she lost the plot. Her ears went back and she charged down upon us. We ran for our lives, a very long distance, but you can never outrun an elephant. I turned and looked at her, she was practically on top of me. Peter suddenly veered off to the left. He is an amazing man; although 60 years old, he was terrifically strong! The elephant saw a quicker and easier target than me – and went for Peter. I turned and saw him on the ground with the elephant about to pierce him with her tusk.

'I tore to the car. The driver was in a state of paralysed fear with his hand stuck on the horn. I pulled him out and drove to Peter, who was now surrounded by six or seven cows that had come down to see what was happening. They were walking around him in a circle and I was sure he lay dead in the middle of them. The car scared them all away. As I jumped out of the car, up popped Peter's head, "Shit, Curly," he said. "It looks like my screwin' days are all over, man!"

'Notorious for his womanising, these were the first words out of his mouth. The tusk had pierced his thigh, missing both the artery and the bone. But the broad part of the elephant's head, at the top of her trunk, had crushed his pelvis. And it was certainly crushed: when we moved him, we could hear the shattered bones crunching. From the radio we always carry I called AMREF [the East African flying-doctor service – one of the finest in the world] and got him into the vehicle while he bellowed with pain, cracking jokes in between the bellows. It took an hour to get to

Keekorok, the nearest lodge and airstrip, as we were deep in the bush and the roads were quite rough. At Keekorok we were able to get some morphine for him. The plane arrived half an hour later and we left for Nairobi. On the stretcher going into the hospital his heart stopped. They revived it with electric charges and kept him in the hospital for about seven weeks until he was stable enough to fly to New York. Once in New York, his broken bones were replaced with titanium to hold up his pelvis. When I last visited him, there were two gorgeous Russian models with him, one on each knee! He is an incredible guy. Ever commercial, he used the story and the publicity to sell more pictures at even greater prices.'

Accidents like that are very rare in the bush, but, as we know, wild animals can be unpredictable. Experiencing the adrenalin rush in close encounters with these animals in the wild, especially when walking, is probably the reason that many people find Africa so exciting. However, Peter Beard has told Calvin his African days are over.

During the time Glen and Calvin were discussing Calvin's future, Glen became terminally ill with cancer. There was no longer a camp for Calvin to run, as Cottar's Camp at Siana Springs had been sold. So, together they planned to operate mobile safaris in the style of the safaris run by Chas Cottar and, later, his sons in the 1920s. Father and son became much closer with the excitement of creating this new and unusual form of retro mobile safari. In the 1920s and 1930s, the safari tents were white, big and elegantly furnished; the camp staff dressed in long, white robes with red fezzes and sashes, and many little luxuries were provided. After Glen died in 1996, Calvin went to work on recreating the safari style of the 1920s and went into business running mobile safaris.

I went on one of those early safaris with a group of friends and witnessed at first hand just what was involved. The safari was superb and we were looked after like royalty. I had never slept in such comfort in a tent. It went very smoothly and professionally. The staff were immaculate and friendly, the food excellent and the drink flowed. We dined on fine china, drank from crystal glasses and were surrounded by well-researched memorabilia that decorated the sleeping and mess tents.

The day we moved camp I watched as all this opulence was packed into wooden crates to travel on two large trucks 600 kilometres over some of the worst roads in the world. We spent two days at Bushtops while the transportation took place, before flying to Shaba National Reserve, which was to be the next campsite. On our arrival, a vintage, wooden-bodied car was at the airstrip to pick us up and take us to the campsite, which had been the last home of Joy Adamson, author of *Born Free*.

The scene was magical – lunch and a view to die for, set up and ready for us under magnificent spreading acacia trees. It seemed flawless and everyone had one of the best safaris they could have had – fantastic game viewing, excellent guiding and the most luxurious camps imaginable.

Before his father died, Calvin had met and married an Australian girl of exceptional beauty, an ex-Miss Australia. They had a son, Danni, but the marriage was not successful. Meanwhile, Calvin was starting up his new mobile-safari business, buying the equipment and marketing the concept. It was a very ambitious undertaking and his wife made an excellent contribution by designing the tent interiors, but Calvin's personal life was distracting and causing him to feel great anxiety.

The mobile safaris went very well; guests were happy and satisfied. However, behind the scenes all was not well and the next two years proved to be more difficult than he could ever have imagined. Every journey they made between camps saw more and more of their precious items being broken, and replacing them was a drain on the finances. Meanwhile, Calvin's marriage was breaking down and that was taking its toll. A brief reconciliation, which had not been successful, produced a second son, Jasper. Calvin's manager was plagued with personal problems too, so no one was keeping an eye on the ball.

ENTER LOUISE

It was around this time that Calvin met Louise Seaman through mutual friends in Nairobi. Louise was later to become his wife. She was running the United Nations (UN) World Food Programme in Mogadishu, Somalia, and was having a short, well-deserved rest in Kenya. This was at a time when Calvin was at his lowest ebb; in Louise, he found a sympathetic and intelligent ear. She is young and lovely, and with her no-nonsense, forthright attitude she was Calvin's lifesaver.

She worked in Somalia for four years organising the distribution of famine relief to the refugee camps in the country. This was a very frustrating task, as by the time the trucks arrived at the camps the food was already badly depleted. The food was transported in UN trucks, which were highly visible targets for Somali rebels to hijack. The UN staff had no mandate to shoot and wholesale theft was taking place. The lorries would be hijacked and the drivers had to stand by helplessly as people – mainly children – swarmed all over, taking whatever they wanted. The Somali warlords orchestrated the thieving and the food was sold on. It was a situation that was deeply worrying for the people running the programme.

Louise gave this a lot of thought and came up with an idea that she took to the directors of the programme, who occupied offices in Nairobi far away from the operations on the ground. They rejected her idea, thinking it might backfire if the press got hold of it, but she continued to exert pressure on them until, finally, they gave her the go-ahead, but they would not take responsibility for it.

The following is Louise's explanation of her plan to protect the food and make sure it reached the refugee camps. It was an audacious strategy and it worked:

'Seeing that Somali traders were importing their own high-value food items, such as sugar, without loss from theft, I developed a system whereby the Somali importers provided to the UN a bond equal to the value of the UN food and the cost of transport. These importers would arrive in my office

with the cash – sometimes as much as a quarter of a million US dollars. The dollar bills would tumble onto my desk, out of pockets, from up their sleeves and down their trousers. The importers would then collect the food from ports such as Mombasa, ship it in and transport it by road to the destinations required by the World Food Programme. The food travelled from the port in their vehicles with their own tough Somali guards. If it arrived and I could see and verify that it was distributed without loss, the importers would be reimbursed their bond and given a margin on top. Such was the success of this method of transportation of food that it is now being used in several other insecure countries.'

The only white woman on the World Food Programme, Louise showed remarkable courage to work in Somalia. She had to be present at the docks and at the point of distribution, as the high-value food cargoes were particularly at risk from criminal gangs in a lawless country. She was shot at and only just avoided being kidnapped – they couldn't find her and took her colleague instead. Louise is a strong and clever woman. Once she and Calvin decided to pursue a life together, she invested in and became part of his business. She first examined the company accounts and was shocked at the rate at which the company was losing money.

Hard reality had to be faced. Staff were trimmed and economies made; marketing was increased. It was clear that the company could not continue to operate mobile safaris, as the running costs were too high. They terminated the mobile safaris and decided to build instead a permanent camp. Retaining the 1920s format, they built a camp at Olentoroto, on the edge of the Masai Mara. The new camp has flush loos and showers (canvas bathtubs on request); it has old-style white tents, four-poster beds and comfortable sofas, but there is greater space. The added luxury of a massage during the siesta is much appreciated by guests.

It has been incredibly hard work, but is a great success story and their happiness is clearly evident.

CALVIN'S PLANS FOR THE FUTURE

The Cottars have initiated the Maasai Development and Wildlife Conservation Trust, whose objective is 'to ensure the continued co-existence of the wildlife and people of the eastern Mara area in the long-term through the development of a sustainable system for land use and management'.

Calvin's camp is in the eastern part of the Mara, close to the Tanzanian border. It is an area in which the family has operated safaris for many years, making them well known to the local Maasai community. The area, called the Olderikesi Group Ranch, is 800 square kilometres in size and has a population of about 4 000 Maasai.

It is an area Calvin knows well and many of the local Maasai are friends. It is his fervent wish to maintain this pristine wilderness area by working with the community and improving their standard of living and providing revenue. Taking a leaf out of Botswana's philosophy of high-cost, low-density tourism, he wants this area to operate in a similar manner. Much of the Masai Mara is swamped with vehicles and large tourist lodges, but the eastern part, where he operates, has far fewer tourist facilities. Calvin's 1920s-style camp along with one other upmarket mobile-tented safari company, which has the use of a campsite in the area, are the only operators here at this time. He is passionate about keeping it this way and his plans have the full approval of the park warden.

Instead of building yet another large lodge, he has located two sites and plans to build three houses on one site and two on the other. These will produce revenue for the community in the form of fees and jobs, and benefit them in many ways, including healthcare, education and animal husbandry. Dams will be built in areas where the cattle usually graze when water is present in areas away from the wildlife tourist areas, to lessen their impact on the park during the dry season.

His idea of providing bush homes for those who prefer to holiday in the bush rather than at the beach is unusual. He would oversee first the building and then the maintenance and care of the houses, providing staff and guides. A guide school is part of the overall plan, thereby increasing the involvement of the local community in tourism.

To own a house overlooking the Masai Mara, one of the most beautiful and abundant landscapes in the world, must appeal to anyone who aspires to 'have a farm in Africa', but without the hassle.

Calvin and Louise completed their own beautiful family bush home in 2012 near their 1920s camp, commanding a magnificent view across the plains. Jessica's portrait of Calvin hangs in the house. Cottar's Camp is thriving, and Calvin has a group of exceptionally well-trained Maasai safari guides looking after the guests. He does less guiding himself these days but occasionally goes out with old friends.

Calvin is busy setting up a conservancy trust. Once this is completed, the cattle, sheep and goats will move away to other areas of their land and the tourist area will become a wildlife sanctuary for the camp's guests. Visits into the Masai Mara Park will then seldom be necessary.

Calvin has permission to build five houses that will be sold as bush homes on this land. The Ol Derikesi elders signed up in January 2013 to the conservancy trust he has created. When each house is built and sold, the new buyers will own the house, but the land on which the house stands will remain the property of the Maasai landowners and the conservancy. His plan is to use the houses to underwrite the conservancy when it is set up. Once sold, the owner of each house will have to produce $50 000 a year for the conservancy trust. The money will come from the owner and guests' conservancy fees, but if there have not been enough guests to produce the amount required, it will be up to the owner of the house to top it up. Once this deal is in place it will be a totally secure piece of land, as the whole community owns it. One of the reasons it took so long for Calvin to complete the deal is that it is difficult for everyone in the community to agree. In many other conservancies it has been easier to set up a trust, as the land has been divided into small plots with individual owners. Each has been able to sell his own plot and join the trust. However, what happened in one conservancy, where there are individual owners, is that a Russian casino owner persuaded a Maasai owner to sell his land at a vastly inflated price so the Russian could build his own camp there, in spite of the fact that that owner had signed up to the trust. At Ol Derikesi, the entire community own the land, so they can only sell to one another, and not to outsiders. The owners of the new houses will be part of that community. Calvin's original dream is still there but has taken a new direction.

Establishing conservancy trusts may sound complicated, but they are vital for the continuation of wildlife. Calvin speaks for all the conservancies that are being set up around National Parks:

'The main thing I would like to convey is that conservation has to be financed, and it's all about land. Tourism can only reach a limited area, and this fractional idea is just a way of getting longer-term commitments from people who want to help conservation and want to experience the best of safari as well. The feeling of ownership is important in this. But as for the bigger picture, you can say that we are looking for any new ways to get land leased for wildlife, and in this regard we are interested in REDD+ [reducing emissions from deforestation and forest degradation]*, which is a value put on carbon and biodiversity. It's really a lease programme for land to remain natural … It's exactly what I have been saying for years actually!'*

Calvin and Louise live in Nairobi with their two daughters, Charlie and Ella, who are still at school and take frequent family holidays in their house at Olentoroto. Calvin's son Danni is studying art and Jasper finishes his A levels in 2014.

HOWARD SAUNDERS

Howard Saunders is an Australian who visited East Africa at the age of 17 on a safari with his parents. Completely enthralled by all he saw, he went home vowing that he would make his life Africa.

Born in Sydney in 1972, Howard grew up with his time divided between the city and his parent's farm. All their holidays were geared to outdoor activities and these, together with the time he spent on the farm, engendered his love of the bush. He would catch snakes with his father, learn the names of the birds and sleep out under the stars. His parents knew he would enjoy Africa when they took him on safari. And how right they were. On his return, he taught himself to speak fluent Swahili and read everything he could on East Africa. At university he did a business course that included international relations, specifically with regard to developing countries, and returned to Kenya the moment he finished university in 1994, at the age of 21. In Nairobi he found his Swahili was too pure to be understood in Kenya. It would have been fine in Tanzania, but the Kenyans use a slightly different version, which he quickly picked up.

Soon after his arrival in Kenya, he was offered an apprenticeship with a company called Natural Selection owned by a New Zealander, who probably felt kinship with a fellow antipodean. They focused on mountain gorillas, taking four-wheel-drive safaris through northern Tanzania to Lake Victoria and into Uganda's south-western corner, home of the mountain gorillas. He learnt about the management of mobile tented safaris and started to take them himself. Later he acquired his own vehicle and freelanced until 1999, when he was invited to join Ker and Downey, an old and respected safari company. A year and half after joining, he became the first Australian to be invited to be a full partner in the firm. Ker and Downey have a mentorship programme whereby new young guides are attached to older, experienced ones. Howard's mentor was Alan Earnshaw, the chairman of the company. With Alan as his mentor, he learnt how the company liked safaris to be run, how to do the marketing and about the vital aspects of conservation.

Being on safari and in remote wilderness areas are the moments when Howard is at his happiest. He also takes conservation very seriously. He is a member of the Kenya Professional Safari Guides Association and a director of Campfire Conservation in Kenya. He is involved in educating the Maasai elders who run the Masai Mara, helping them to think ahead and understand the importance of the community being economically independent, vital for the benefit of the whole community, and not just a few individuals. Many Maasai see farming as an alternative source of revenue and, up to now, they have had few benefits from tourism – a situation that has to change. The revenue from the Masai Mara National Park is worth approximately $8 million a year – a very substantial sum of money, and this should deter them from mechanised farming. The collection and distribution of the money, along with independent management of the money, is the subject of an ongoing project in which Howard is involved.

He also helps Ron Beaton and Jackson Looseyia with the Koiyaki Guiding School. He is pleased that Ker and Downey have a partnership in Namunyak and takes many guests to visit the Namunyak Wildlife Conservancy. Everyone realises the importance of involvement in community projects that protect wilderness areas for safari visitors.

However, some of his most exciting moments have been in Uganda. Ugandans welcome people to their country in their efforts to expand their budding safari industry. Howard is currently working on a programme to train Ugandan safari guides and takes as many safaris to that country as he can. It is not only about gorillas and chimpanzees, however. There are numerous exciting places to visit and sights to see in this beautiful country, as I discovered while travelling with Howard on a visit to Uganda and Rwanda.

Howard's wife, Steffie Dloniak, is an American scientist who has spent the last three years studying hyenas in Kenya and is about to embark on an ambitious project to study the lion population in the Masai Mara. Their joint contribution to the wildlife experience is exceptional.

Howard is thrilled that his dream has come true, that he is working and living in East Africa, as he dreamt he would when he was 17. He puts his heart and soul into all he does, and feels a special responsibility for the future:

'To be involved in securing a future for the great charismatic creatures of the East African wilderness is surely to conserve far more than just the animals themselves. It will enable future generations to experience those sights, which have been part of the human heritage since our ancestors first strode across the Cradle of Mankind. East Africa is the home of much of the story of how humans evolved, from the great apes of the rainforests to those evocative savannahs lined with flat-topped acacia trees. Conserving this environment should be a matter of pride and deep importance to all those who have ever visited. Having been moved to follow a life out here in this wilderness, I believe it is crucial that we, the younger generation of professional safari guides, become the ambassadors for this unique resource. It is up to us to pass on the treasures of Africa to others around the world in a way that inspires them to see the value of what we have here.'

I believe that Howard speaks for all the young professional guides in both East and southern Africa. Together, they give us faith that there is goodness, strength and the will to battle against the odds to do the right thing to the best of their ability.

Howard has continued to take safaris all over East Africa, using lodges, and Ker and Downey camping equipment. Ker and Downey was started as a hunting company in 1946 by Donald Ker and Syd Downey but switched to photographic safaris in 1977, when Kenya banned hunting. The company has always had excellent guides and Howard has become one of the very best. He loves to weave in unusual and interesting experiences, such as a visit to the mountain gorillas, the chimpanzees or the Great Lakes of the Rift Valley. A treat that Howard provides in Uganda is a private tented camp set up for your own group in the Murchison National Park, on the shore of Lake Albert, where the Blue Mountains of the Congo soar above the water. The water that flows out of the end of the lake on its way through Sudan to Egypt and the Mediterranean is the Nile. It is an unimaginable privilege to be able to stay there.

Perhaps the true meaning of luxury on a safari in this day and age is to stay in exclusive areas where there are no other tourists – just your own group in a mobile tented camp with the uninterrupted views and calls of the wild. Howard loves using the selected campsites that Ker and Downey lease in the Kenyan parks but, to my mind, the 30 000 hectares adjacent to Amboseli and the Tanzanian border must be one of the most spectacular places: it is an elephant paradise with a backdrop of Kilimanjaro all to yourselves. The local Maasai tribespeople who live in this area see few tourists and, as these people are not commercialised, interaction with them is a truly interesting experience.

Howard lives in Nairobi with Steffie and their two children. Steffie has heightened Howard's concern for conservation. In 2007, Howard and some of his guiding friends created their own wildlife trust, which helps young guides with education and sponsorship, and is involved specifically with the carnivore projects in the Masai Mara, Shaba, Samburu and with the Lion Guradian project in Amboseli. Carnivores are becoming extremely endangered, especially lions and cheetahs. They need all the help they can get. Asian communities who believe that the bones of tigers are medicinal have more or less killed off all their tigers and are now going after Africa's lions for their bones. This horrifies Howard.

During each of his safaris, Howard invites one of the many graduate researchers who are doing vital work in Kenya, to come to the camp to give a short lecture to his guests, so they have a deeper understanding of the work that is going on in Kenya's national parks. Recently on his last trip he called the researchers in to tranquilise a snared hyena and remove the rope from its neck. It was a great experience for everyone involved. This has been a great success and occasionally inspires individuals to do more than just listen:

'In 2006 I took a family from California on safari. They had with them their fifteen-year-old daughter, Tracy, who was deeply intrigued by all that she learned during this journey. A few years later, the family returned with their daughter, and visited Tanzania and Rwanda. Tracy was completely inspired by all she saw, and in 2011 she came to Kenya and joined the Masai Mara hyena programme as an assistant to the researchers. In 2013 she came to do her PhD on carnivores and was based here for some time. Tracy will be one of the researchers that I invite to lecture to my safari guests, eight years on from her first visit to Africa. This shows that safaris can truly be life-changing.'

SHACKLETON AND SELOUS SOCIETY

Over the last few years, Howard has been mulling over an idea to link together some of the top guides around the world and finally it has become a reality.

The Shackleton and Selous Society is Howard's brainchild. The organisation is named after British polar explorer Sir Ernest Shackleton, and African explorer and conservationist Frederick Selous. Those reading this book will by now understand the merits of having the best safari guides. Howard, along with Michael Lorentz, Peter Silvester and Sandor Carter, four excellent guides, created this exceptional plan to link together the very best guides around the world, not just in Africa, who specialise in adventure, exploration and travel off the beaten track. The purpose of the society is to enable people to find the best person to take them to the destination of their dreams.

Twenty men and women have been invited to become fellows of the society, which was launched in Australia in April 2013 and in New York in June 2013, in conjunction with The Leading Hotels of the World consortium. These specialist guides are based around the world in 32 countries – destinations that range from their deeply captivating cultures to their wild and remote environments. It offers 'an unrivalled portfolio of top-flight adventures, including all the Arctic territories, Antarctica, Alaska, eastern, central and southern Africa, Australia and New Zealand, Turkey, Mongolia, Myanmar, Bhutan, Nepal, Patagonia and the Galapagos Islands'.

NAMIBIA'S PRIMEVAL LANDSCAPES AND RADIANT LIGHT

Namibia has a landscape as old as time: a spectacular desert of dusty-brown, rocky mountains streaked with hues of purple, pink and gold, surrounded by shifting sand dunes ranging from white to rusty red.

I t is as if the forests and the grasslands have been peeled away to expose the bare bones of Africa, making the great upheavals that took place when the earth was formed look as fresh and clear as if they happened yesterday. The Namib Desert stretches the entire length of the coastal area from the South African border, in the south, to Angola, in the north, and inland for about 150 kilometres. This is the most beautiful and interesting part of Namibia; the names themselves evoke a sense of mystery: Damaraland, Kaokoveld, Sossusvlei, the Omaruru, Khumib and Hoanib rivers and, of course, the Skeleton Coast.

Once called the Kaokoveld Coast, the Skeleton Coast, as it is now known, gets its name from the numerous shipwrecks and bones, animal and human, that were found strewn on the shore. The treacherous, icy sea thunders onto the beaches, which are extensions of the desert and home to thousands of Cape fur seals. Each night the cold air above the Atlantic Ocean (kept this way by the Benguela Current from the Antarctic) meets the hot inland air, creating a fog that creeps over the land, sometimes as far as 50 kilometres inland, bringing life-giving moisture for the desert creatures.

The fact that such a variety of wildlife lives in this arid area is extraordinary and makes the Namib Desert unique, as no other desert of this size supports anything like the number of animals that survive here. There are desert-adapted elephants, which never destroy their source of food, oryx, springboks, ostriches, black-backed jackals, spotted hyenas, lions and giraffes. These are found only in very small numbers outside the Etosha National Park, but with only two perennial rivers in Namibia, situated at either end of the country, it is remarkable that they manage to find enough to eat and drink at all, especially considering how much water animals, especially elephants, need. Hidden in nooks and crannies are a surprising number of little oases formed from freshwater springs, and some of the rivers retain water from rainstorms for quite a long time. Nevertheless, the elephants have had to learn to adapt to less water here.

The solitude and sense of peace one feels in this landscape are beyond compare. The breathtaking beauty of the colours and sculptured shapes of the sand dunes never cease to please or surprise. If you scoop a little sand from a pink-flushed dune and look at it through a magnifying glass (or binoculars the wrong way round) you will think you are holding a cluster of diamonds and rubies rather than particles of garnet and quartz. It is my theory that the extraordinary glowing quality of the light is caused by the reflection from the myriad particles of sand, allowing even the novice photographer to produce spectacular pictures. The sharply outlined red dunes and rocky mountains against cobalt-blue skies, and the spectacular vistas punctuated occasionally by a pair of finely etched oryx against the golden sand also help.

It all looks untouched, with no sign of human interference, and the care that is taken to keep parts of the Namib Desert in pristine condition is admirable. There are large, well-managed national parks with programmes for reintroducing black rhinos, heavily depleted by poaching, into their old Kaokoveld habitat. Etosha, the best known of Namibia's parks, has permanent waterholes, ensuring a greater abundance of animals. A whole day spent at one of them will, without a doubt, give anyone exceptionally rewarding game viewing.

The guides in this part of Africa have extended their knowledge to include geology and desert habitats. Some are real experts who raise the experience their guests have of this magnificent country to the highest level, such as Jan and Susie van de Reep, at Huab Lodge, Chris Bakkes, with Wilderness Safaris, whom I have not met, and the Schoeman family whom I know well.

BERTUS & ANDRÉ SCHOEMAN

S itting on the bank of the Kunene River, which marks the border
between Namibia and Angola, we picked garnets out of the rocks
with our fingernails as we listened, enthralled, to André Schoeman's tale
of the coastal elephants. A small herd had lived peacefully by the edge of
the sea before the Angolan Civil War, when they disappeared.

André's plan to return elephants to the mouth of the Kunene was
to fly them to the coast suspended from a specially constructed mega-
microlight. The Schoeman family has operated in Namibia for 25 years
and they are highly respected for their innovative ideas regarding the
care and protection of this splendid region known as the Kaokoveld.

This was the last morning of our fascinating journey with André that
had begun four days earlier with a dawn flight from Windhoek to the
legendary orange dunes of Sossusvlei. As we flew south, the scattered
farmsteads near the town were soon left behind and the seemingly empty
land rolled away into the distant haze. One of the most unexpected
aspects of Namibia is the kaleidoscope of earth colours: beneath us the
straw-coloured grass growing on silver sand turned, as if by the stroke
of a paintbrush, to pale ochre on deep-red earth as a series of hills came

into view. The landscape was dotted with clumps of dark-green trees and 'fairy circles' – large, perfectly round areas of bare earth, rimmed with thick tufts of grass.

We climbed the dunes of Sossusvlei before flying over them for nearly an hour – a rolling sea of rusty-red/orange dunes that give way to the newer, creamy dunes of the coast, where we landed on firm ground next to a sandy beach for our picnic lunch. The ruin of an abandoned prospector's house stood in the sand nearby. What must once have been a shed had disintegrated, leaving the rusty chassis of a 1920s truck proudly facing the elements having been abandoned many decades ago.

The sculpture-like backbone of a whale lay among lesser bones of seals scattered on the beach. A little family of jackals, which had made their den in the foundations of the old house, were very startled by our arrival.

We walked on many beaches along the Namibian coast next to the icy, roaring sea, watching the Cape fur seals surf and dive through the waves with grace and ease. This Skeleton Coast shoreline is littered with not only a variety of bones but also the flotsam and jetsam of countless shipwrecks, victims of the treacherous Benguela Current. For centuries, the strong cross-currents, high winds, fog and shifting sandbanks have been a nightmare for the navigators of sailing ships, and, once grounded, they had little chance of survival in the barren dunes and blistering heat.

How merciful it would have been for shipwrecked sailors if they had had André or Bertus to guide them to freshwater springs not far inland. The Schoemans know of these springs, ancient sources of water that create tiny pools hidden in folds of granite that were once used by the Strandlopers or San people. When the Schoemans find a pool, they explore the area nearby to collect more information on the San. Their explorations have led them to hidden caves, some with rock paintings. The Schoemans have been gathering geological and historical information about the region for many years, and it makes a wonderful learning experience for guests who travel with them.

At first glance, what seems like a barren desert in reality hums with life. Every morning the fog rolls off the icy sea onto the hot, dry land bringing life-giving moisture to the lizards, geckos, gerbils and snakes that inhabit it. One could spend days just studying the differences in desert creatures' methods of drinking. Sidewinder adders lick the droplets off their bodies, while little tenebrionid beetles obtain moisture by standing on their heads, allowing the condensation to run down their legs and bodies into their mouths.

Under the expert guidance of André or Bertus, eyes are opened onto an undreamt-of world. Their knowledge fires the imagination and fills one with awe. There are rocks here that are so ancient that they formed the landscape of Gondwanaland, well before South America split from Africa. Unimaginable geological upheavals caused what was once the muddy bed of a lake to stand up vertically, stretching hundreds of feet up into the air, the ripples still clearly visible on the surface. Our flight over the Ugab River Valley revealed the incredible rock formations on the summits – mile upon mile of furrows undulating neatly into the distance as if formed by bulldozers. We stopped in far-flung places where only God and the Schoemans can see a landing strip, exploring wild coastal areas or remote rocky valleys. A timescale of 2 000 million years is hard to grasp, but it was an astounding geography lesson. As Bertus brought the formation of the earth to life, the layers of time became clearly visible and especially exciting.

We saw animals that manage to eke out a living by finding nourishment in dry grasses and detritus known as 'desert muesli', which is blown in on the east wind and caught on scrub and dry twigs. Gemsboks (oryx), springbok and ostriches all manage on very little water, but most extraordinary are the desert elephants, picking and choosing branches of trees along a dry riverbed. They have learnt to preserve their food source, and never push the trees over, as they do in other parts of Africa where trees are abundant.

During our safari, André had to intervene in an incident in Purros that concerned the local community's involvement in conservation. The Himba people, a traditionally nomadic group, are gradually becoming settled in certain areas for extended periods. Their children, by law, have to go to school. That, and the influx of tourism, has changed some of the Himba's customs. They still live and dress traditionally, but their diet has changed. They now eat maize meal sold to them by traders, along with sugar and other modern delights such as Coca-Cola. Money, unknown in the past, has therefore become a requirement. The week before we arrived, two male lions living in the vicinity of Purros, on the edge of the Skeleton Coast National Park, had killed the Himba's only bull (having already killed seven cows), so the community was understandably irate. The natural inclination of the Himba was to track down and kill the lions.

André was due at a meeting a few days later when this issue was to be discussed. Our group had visited the Himba settlement that morning and had spent money on some of their craft items, such as baskets, beads, carved palm nuts and other things they make. Although we had not spent very much money in our terms, it was nevertheless enough for them to buy at least two more bulls if they wished. André was there to discuss this point with them: if the wildlife is killed off, then what incentive would the overseas visitors have to come to the area? The community is being encouraged to protect and understand the value of their wildlife, but old habits die hard. The animals along the Skeleton Coast have been greatly depleted. Twenty-five years ago, lion tracks were commonplace on the beaches. The final outcome to this crisis was that André replaced the bull with one from his farm and made an agreement with the tribe that they graze their cattle away from the lions' territory.

Our journey had brought us to the Kunene River, a wide, green expanse of water flowing swiftly to the Atlantic Ocean between rocky banks and the desert beyond, a marvellous sight in this thirsty land.

The Himba people on both sides of the river water their cattle here. Baboons scamper on the rocky cliff faces and some of the largest crocodiles on earth bask in the sun or lie in the shallow waters by the bank. Quenching our thirst with fruit juice and looking for garnets, we sat listening to André make plans for the future. We were all very sad that in an hour or two we would be flying home.

The Schoeman family has had some rough times, but their stoicism and hard work have seen them through. Bertus, André, Leon, Marie and Henk Schoeman are all involved in the operation of Skeleton Coast Safaris, the company their father, Louw, started in 1977. André and Bertus are the two brothers I know. Henk has obtained a commercial pilot's licence and joins his brothers on some of the safaris. Their beautiful sister, Marie, was until recently in charge of the marketing and Bertus's wife, Helga, a pilot and guide, accompanies her husband on many of his safaris, and has been influential in their development.

When I first visited Namibia, I had very little or no interest in geology, probably in common with many others. However, after a four-day trip on a fly-in safari with Bertus or André in north-west Namibia, you will come away electrified by the splendour of the creation of our planet. For it is here you can really see the bones of the earth, untouched by humanity. Due to the stable weather pattern and lack of water in a large portion of this country, the crops, settlements and forests that conceal these bare bones across most of the rest of the earth's surface have been unable to grow in Namibia.

The Skeleton Coast National Park was created in 1971; Louw Schoeman had been instrumental in establishing it. In 1977, safari companies were asked to apply for a licence to operate in the park; only one was to be granted the concession.

Only one person applied – Louw Schoeman. Louw was a lawyer whose clients were prospectors, and as he had explored the area intensively as a young man he understood the miners' needs. He also saw the potential the area had to thrill and fascinate. His competitors were surprised at his application for the safari licence, thinking he must be crazy. They were mistaken: Louw gave his clients undreamt-of excitement and adventure in a new and pristine environment for 16 years. On safari with Louw, grown men whooped with joy as they slid down the roaring dunes, marvelling at the white prehistoric 'castles' in a narrow canyon at Hoarusib (some 10 000 years old, these castles are towering structures of solidified sand that look as if they have been poured from a giant's tablespoon). They rode on the roofs of the Land Rovers sweeping up and down the steep dunes; they collected agates and tried to get to grips with the age of the *Welwitshchia mirabilis* (prehistoric, low-growing plants that look like aloes but are related to the pine tree, and some of them are over 1 000 years old). And in the evening they settled under an omumborumbonga tree with a cool beer, watching a tame genet scamper along the branches while peering down at the visitors with great curiosity. Louw would tell them the omumborumbonga is a leadwood tree, sacred to the Herero tribe, who believe it is their ancestor – one of many snippets of information in Louw's desert treasure chest.

The world soon realised that Louw had access to an area that was unique, and human nature being as it is, Louw's concession became coveted by others. Every five years he had to reapply for the concession. Other operators held off for a time out of respect for what he was doing, but after 15 years the government decided to alter the way the concession was handled. While the ministers were planning their new strategy, he was granted the concession for just one year. The following year it was granted for 10 years (1993 to 2003) to the only other applicant, Olympia Reizen, a German company with no known track record of tourist activities in Namibia. It broke Louw's heart. The German company had not complied with the requirement that the applicant should have extensive knowledge of the Namib Desert, the park and the adjoining areas. He felt it would cease to be managed in the careful manner that is required for such a fragile and delicate environment. He decided to take the case to court, but, unfortunately, he died of a heart attack before the case was heard. In the end, the Namibian Cabinet granted the concession to Olympia Reizen. Skeleton Coast Safaris' application to operate in other parts of the park was turned down. This is well documented in Amy Schoeman's book, *Skeleton Coast*.

It was a very sad ending for a man who had a unique vision to put Namibia on the world tourist map.

Once Olympia Reizen had the concession, unfounded rumours flew around as to what they were going to do. One such rumour was that the company was going to build an enormous hotel; another that they were going to use it for the disposal of nuclear waste. In the end, nothing happened and the area was virtually unvisited, generating little revenue for the Namibian government. Needing to find another source of income from the park, the state then allowed Wilderness Safaris to operate under the Olympia Reizen licence. Wilderness Safaris is a company with a strong ethical and ecological culture, and they established a beautiful camp, successfully making the park's wonders accessible to many visitors.

Louw's sons took up the challenge to keep their operation going. Although they no longer had access to some of the more unusual sites inside the Skeleton Coast National Park, the places they visit are all spectacular and deeply interesting. One of their prime areas is Purros, where they have, as Louw had before them, worked very closely with the community. Olympia Reizen had tried to get that concession too, with generous proposals to the local community. The community held a three-day indaba (meeting) over the issue. Their conclusion was that they considered Louw to be their father; now that he had died, the boys were orphans and it was not in their culture to abandon their children. Today, the Schoemans work in a successful partnership with the local community in Purros.

André and Bertus are able to reveal the beauty and secrets of the Namib Desert to us so skilfully because they have lived with it all their lives. Their knowledge and expertise go back to the time they played as toddlers on the remote, desolate beaches of the Kaokoveld Coast. Their father had prospected the area long before any tourist had ever heard of it. Louw started out as an attorney and one of his clients had mineral rights in the desert. He became a director of his client's company and finally left law to prospect and seek his fortune in Namibia's mineral-rich ground, looking for precious and semi-precious stones. While prospecting along the coast, he marvelled at the mystical beauty of the land and gradually altered his focus of interest. A couple working for Louw's company lived in a hut at Cape Frio doing research. They took their leave for a month in December and Louw decided to move his family into their hut for their Christmas break. Bertus, the eldest, remembers his first plane ride at the age of six, when they went to inspect the hut and meet the researchers.

The family spent every Christmas holiday after that in the researchers' hut until the centre closed down when Bertus was 15. The research station was originally based at Cape Frio but later moved to Möwe Bay. While Louw explored this empty and wild environment, the children played. Wearing their cowboy outfits, they played cowboys and crooks in the dunes. They pretended to be submarine crew in the boiler of the *Dunedin Star* wreck when it washed up on the beach resembling a submarine. They played cricket and rounders with palm nuts and wreckage debris; and the old derelict mine and its equipment were perfect for *Star Wars*-type enactments. Their favourite game of all, though, was aquaplaning behind the Land Rover. A long rope was attached from the car to a piece of wreckage, and the children took it in turns to hold onto the wreckage and skim over the waves while being pulled behind the Land Rover as it raced around the bay.

Most of the wreckage on the beach was the remains of a wooden-hulled sailing ship and while digging around they came across broken pieces of blue-and-white china. This was identified as European porcelain, an imitation of Chinese porcelain used on sailing ships in the 17th century. Later on, as the boys grew older, they helped their father with his work.

Marie's early memories are of endlessly cleaning fish at Rocky Point and going on expeditions to collect drinking water at Orupembe, a day's drive there and back from Cape Frio. Their mother was passionate about collecting interesting stones and Marie recalls helping her find exquisite examples for her collection.

Maureen, Louw's first wife and mother to all five children, died in 1979 and is buried close to the old Sarusas Camp in the Skeleton Coast Park. Louw married Amy Cosburn a year later and she was instrumental in helping Louw set up his business. Amy is extremely knowledgeable about the area and, as I have already mentioned, wrote a definitive book on the Skeleton Coast and illustrated it with her own excellent photographs.

The children, naturally instilled with deep knowledge of this special area, never really wanted to go away from it, but higher education was calling. Before leaving for university, Bertus spent a year helping his father, who had become more interested in showing people the Namib Desert and exploring the possibility of building a travel business within the Skeleton Coast Park than in prospecting. He had created a camp in the abandoned Sarusas Mine buildings, which is where Bertus lived while waiting for his father to fly in with guests. Bertus had not yet obtained his pilot's licence, but he could drive, as all the Schoeman children had been driving since they could reach the pedals. When the first group of guests – eight women from South Africa – arrived, Louw took four of them in one Land Rover and the teenage Bertus took the others. So began a most impressive career.

Bertus and André went to Stellenbosch University. Bertus read geology and André did a degree in business administration and marketing. André's entrance to university was postponed for seven years while he flew for the South African Air Force. He started out in jet fighters, but later transferred to helicopters, and became involved in search-and-rescue operations in Angola during the Namibian War of Independence. Bertus says he had excellent teachers. Those teachers were equally lucky in their pupil, not just for his eagerness to learn but also because he was able to provide access to some of the most interesting geological features in the world. The whole class visited the Skeleton Coast for one of their field trips.

Louw established his first campsite, inland on the Khumib River near the Sarusas Fountain, a freshwater spring. The Khumib is a mostly dry riverbed, but occasionally it floods dramatically when heavy rains occur inland. This is where the omumborumbonga tree is situated. It is not a large tree by most standards, but is impressive to find one in a desert and with its spreading, gnarled branches it made a perfect spot for Louw to set up his bar.

Finding that the drive between Khumib Camp and Cape Frio made for a very long day, Louw set up a beautiful beach camp so guests could experience the coast, the wrecks and the seals. The beds were in snug little wooden huts nestling in the dunes. On the beach, facing the sea, there was a striped mess tent, from which one could watch the sun setting over the crashing waves. Dinner entertainment included little ginger gerbils, residents of the dunes, hopping about on the floor looking for crumbs. The camp had a dreamlike quality. Being lulled to sleep, warm and cosy in a wooden hut by the roaring ocean, it was easy to picture those early sailing ships dipping and rolling as they struggled in the swirling spray.

The Schoemans set up a third camp in the park and, lastly, a camp outside the park, on the Kunene River, bordering Angola. With these four camps, they had the perfect format for showing their guests the intricate ecology of this intriguing area. Although their camps are no longer within the park boundaries, they are all in appealing places. However, very little time is spent in camp, as everyone is far too busy exploring the surroundings. Sometimes it is an effort to get people back into the planes in time to make the next camp before dark.

Each morning brings excited anticipation of what wonders will unfold that day as you are greeted with a smiling Bertus or André calling 'knock, knock' outside your tent with a hot cup of tea or coffee. Few people are as knowledgeable as these two guides. Their enthusiasm for the surroundings and sense of adventure are infectious and even addictive. Bertus and André both give their guests memorable safaris, but they are different in character. André is jolly and easy-going with a quick smile, rosy cheeks and twinkling eyes above his bushy moustache. He instantly sweeps you up in the magnitude of the landscape with his great energy and enthusiasm. He is married and has a bevy of children, and he farms in his spare time.

Bertus is a quieter, more reticent man; he is never ruffled – though one can sense his passion for the area, and he has the greater geological knowledge of the two. The more his guests show interest, the more he opens up to reveal his fascinating insights. Bertus married later than André. His wife, Helga, is now part of the team. An extrovert, she sparkles with fun and laughter as her enthusiastic comments fill the airwaves making her a perfect balance to Bertus on larger safaris where two planes are required. They clearly adore each other.

In fact, flying with the Schoemans is one of the most exhilarating parts of the safari. When they fly very low, sometimes between towering granite walls, you feel you can almost touch the tufts of grass beneath you as you watch a startled springbok darting off. A Boeing 747 pilot once remarked to them that they were flying at the height he normally sat at when taxiing down the runway.

At other times they fly higher so their guests can appreciate the immensity of this ancient landscape with its intricate network of craters, mountains and dunes spread out beneath. They are both superb pilots. André became the South African champion for precision and rally flying while at university, and was sent to England for an international competition at Sywell, Northamptonshire, where he came fourth out of 150 competitors.

Being on a Skeleton Coast safari is an exhilarating experience for the whole family, including children. Sliding down dunes, exploring caves, examining skeletal remains of whales and seals, hoping to find a human bone here and there, and picking up semi-precious stones are experiences beyond the wildest dreams of most children. But the greatest thrill is when the children get a chance to sit up front in the plane, and are shown how it flies and can hold the dual controls for a moment to get an understanding of how it works. Even adults can have a go. Flying from the coast to Etosha, I sat in the cockpit next to Bertus, who showed me how to hold the plane steady at quite a high altitude. Watching the horizon and the wings was very exciting, but best of all, he helped me to bring it down to circle the lodge near the strip where we were to land and disembark. Concentrating with all my might, I thought I was doing quite well, when he quietly said, 'Susie, if you don't pull back on the controls we will hit the ground!' I abruptly yanked back the control column and in doing so discovered why so many people love to fly. The plane banked steeply, my stomach and soul soaring. It was one of the most unexpectedly rapturous feelings I have ever had. Bertus then took over (no doubt he had been in control all the time) and with my hands on the dual controls the plane landed and, frankly, it took about 24 hours for me to come back to earth. However, I am sure the two ashen-faced Belgians in the seats behind us were very relieved to see the back of me.

The Schoemans' fame has now spread worldwide and their visitors' book must read like a who's who of the Western world. But, in the early days, their holidays were not always very well sold, probably because most travel agents hadn't done their research and had no idea how it all worked. André remembers their first group of Italian guests. Neither spoke a word of each other's language and the visitors did not quite understand how the day would unfold:

'At breakfast, I watched bemused as all the food on the table disappeared into little rucksacks that they donned before stepping into the vehicles. Obviously worried as to when the next meal would come, they were taking precautions against hunger. The first time I stopped to show them something they all alighted and immediately took off in different directions, returning after about an hour. Oh well, I thought, if this is what they want to do, I will just have to let them. The same thing happened the next time that I stopped the vehicle. This time, they skidded down the steep banks of a ravine and as I sat on the top watching them, I could see a large gemsbok coming round the bend, clearly on a mission to get through the ravine. He caught sight of the group of humans and stopped. He must have been escaping a predator, for he certainly did not want to go back. As he circled uncertainly, the Italians suddenly saw him, and for a few seconds they stood looking at one another. Then the antelope lowered his head, shaking his massive horns from side to side in a threatening manner and walked forward. Startled, they shinned up the rocky cliff as fast as their legs could carry them, never again leaving the vehicle on their own. They settled down after that and having devised a method of communication, started to learn about the interesting features of the area and ended up having an extremely happy safari.'

Leon, who has an uncanny likeness to Louw, takes care of the multitude of vintage Land Rovers that they use, building and rebuilding these wonderful workhorses. The new computerised variety would not last five minutes in this environment, nor could they be rebuilt on the spot. Astonishingly, they just leave these vehicles dotted about the desert, standing next to an almost invisible airstrip, keys in the ignition, ready for the next arrivals. However, it is so empty and remote, there is no one there to steal anything.

Bertus enjoys nothing more than exploring unknown places, where no man has trodden before. His excited anticipation as to what he might find is contagious and the thrill his guests get out of going where no one else has ever been spurs him on.

André still longs to get elephants back on the beach at the mouth of the Kunene. The 12 elephants that once frequented the area often crossed the river into Angola and, while patrolling the border during the war, he would herd them back with his helicopter, afraid they might get caught in crossfire. In 1992, these elephants disappeared completely. One cow and her calf joined the Hoarusib elephants near Purros and one died of wounds inflicted by AK-47 bullets. The other nine went missing. Louw and millionaire John Aspinall, who ran a private zoo in England and used the profits from his casinos to protect wild animals, had often speculated on how to relocate elephants back into the area once stability returned. Aspinall was a good friend of the Schoemans and had been involved in the protection of the desert elephants, and he designed the mega-microlight aircraft that would have the capabilities to transport an elephant. He and Louw both felt it would be feasible if the elephant was sedated and flown in at night. That support sadly ended after Aspinall's death. André would still dearly love to see the reintroduction of elephants, and maybe one day his wish will come true. He and his youngest brother, Henk, recently went on a trip to Angola, where he spotted elephant dung and tracks from the air in Angola's Iona Park, which links with the Skeleton Coast Park. They are planning to get samples for DNA testing to see if by any chance they are the original Kunene elephants.

André takes one or two riding safaris each year, sleeping under the stars and exploring dry riverbeds that run down to the sea. These safaris provide access to hidden places that can be reached in no other way. It is also possible to travel with André or Bertus for 10 days or more, discovering Namibia from the South African border all the way to the Iona National Park in Angola. There they explore marine fossil beds, a hidden oasis behind a huge rock arch, which is home to flamingos and a multitude of exotic birds. A visit to the Baia dos Tigres (Bay of Tigers) reveals dune cliffs the colour of tiger stripes and inland grow *Welwitschia mirabilis* twice the size of those in Namibia.

In 2009, the Schoemans decided to close down their Purros Camp, as the area had become rather busy, and to build a new one in a more secluded place along the Hoarusib Canyon. They have named the new camp Leylandsdrift, after a British Leyland truck that Louw Schoeman had that became stuck in a bend of the Hoarusib River while transporting goods to his camps. This new camp is on the edge of a high cliff above the river with views down Hoarusib Canyon. Occasionally, guests get a glimpse of the desert elephants strolling along the river. It's a magnificent view and the drive down the riverbed to Purros gently winds through rocky canyons and dry gravel shores, with grass and trees along the way. It is a very picturesque experience, with pools of water attracting a variety of birds along with gemsbok and elephants, and any other thirsty animals; there might even be a shy lion. The Himba village is still situated at Purros and the women are always happy to demonstrate their art-and-craft skills to the visitors.

For many years with only two brothers running the safaris, they had to hire a pilot when they had large groups. Now that Henk Schoeman has become a pilot guide he has joined his brothers, Bertus and André, permanently, and Henk is particularly good with children. André's daughter, Cindel, is also working in the Skeleton Coast office, so it remains a family affair.

Their original camps have been fitted with solar lights and comfortable mattresses. A five-night trip includes visiting Luderitz and the NamibRand Nature Reserve, and is a very rewarding extension to the Skelton Coast, both for the natural- and human-history elements.

A fly-in safari with the Schoeman brothers is still one of Africa's juiciest cherries. There have been a few changes but the heart and soul of their safaris are deeply embedded. If you have not been to Namibia with the Schoemans, I truly recommend you try the experience. The brothers continue to explore new areas, adding fresh excitement to their safaris. No two are ever the same – a compelling reason to return again and again.

INTO THE FUTURE

What began many years ago as a wild and daring adventure has become a serious tourist profession with a deep understanding of its responsibility for the protection of the environment. Its professionalism and understanding must go on if there is to be a future for safaris and wildlife in Africa.

I write here of my own personal hopes and wishes for the timeless beauty of the African bush, its animals and its people. My feelings and thoughts come simply from observation and chats over the years around many campfires.

Safari guides are anything but 'devil-may-care' people, but they do have a tremendous sense of fun and adventure that liberates their guests, dispels their inhibitions and induces joy from the world around them. They cannot reproduce a magnificent wildlife television programme, but what they do give has far greater personal value – the excitement of observing animal behaviour in the wild, learning to recognise a leopard's grunt in the night or identify a bird the second time you hear it. Overcoming fear, shedding material worries, thinking laterally about the universe and creation: all these things can be a life-changing experience. The guides achieve this with their expert knowledge, courage, excellent organisational skills, strong sense of theatre and a controlled temperament. In the course of interviewing the guides I have included in this book, the future of safaris and the Africa we all know and love often crops up in discussions. Most of the guides are optimistic, especially the younger and more recently trained guides, but a nagging worry lingers for the future of the wildlife and wilderness areas that have given many people so much pleasure.

The word is spreading that specialist guides give their guests a remarkable experience. They create a market of return clients unparalleled in most other long-haul holiday destinations. A safari can open a multitude of windows on the world, with intriguing views never dreamt of. But the visitor needs to be led in the right direction. There is plenty of fun to be had, along with drama and pathos, tenderness and terror unfolding in the wild every day, if only one can take the time to sit still and observe with an expert.

There is a worldwide realisation that something must be done to protect and preserve these precious spaces. The people who are optimistic about the future are those on the ground in Africa trying to do something about it. In my experience, those who shrug their shoulders and say 'Africa is doomed' are most likely to be sitting around a dinner table somewhere in the developed world. Perhaps one day they too will change their attitude. Often we seem to be on a path of destruction, but this has been noticed, and there are some very dedicated people trying to help. Isn't it imperative to make an effort for future generations?

These days many more young men and women are training to become guides, and guides are important. It is heartening to note the huge increase in interest shown by the indigenous people of the popular safari destinations in becoming guides. This is of paramount importance, not only because their livelihood is so often intermingled with game reserves and conservation areas, but also because they are the people to whom their governments will listen when they put forward the case for the protection of their natural heritage. It can be difficult for white guides, regardless of how many generations of their families have been in Africa, to gain the same attention. I firmly believe, however, that there should always be a place for good guides. Whatever their nationality or colour, passion and knowledge should be the priority.

BUFFALO THORN

I once had an experience that graphically illustrates the need for local culture to be explained by the people who know it best. I arrived at a lodge in South Africa in time for the evening game drive. There were five of us – a couple who had already spent two nights at the lodge and two other tour operators, who had arrived with me. Our guide, a jolly Zulu called Zacharias, had been looking after the couple and it was their last evening. They had not seen any elephants during their visit and were desperate to do so. Zacharias set out determined to find them. After about an hour, his radio crackled and another guide contacted him to say he had located a small family of elephants, resulting in the two of them talking a great deal on their radios. It was dark by the time we caught up with the second car and the herd had disappeared into a thicket. The second vehicle was positioned behind the thicket on the other side of the elephants, and between them they tried moving the elephants out of the thicket, flashing their spotlights on the animals who were frightened and trumpeting angrily. It was appalling behaviour, but at least the guide managed to allow his guests to get a glimpse of elephants before their departure.

The following morning the three of us set off on our game drive with little confidence; but we had a surprise in store. We had driven with Zacharias for about an hour, birding and enjoying the early morning light, when he stopped by a buffalo thorn tree (*Ziziphus mucronata*). This tree has supernatural qualities, both religious and medicinal, and has vicious double thorns that hook inwards and outwards, causing great difficulty if you happen to get caught on them. We settled ourselves under the thorn tree, our backs warmed by the rising sun, gazing on the green hills fading to purple in the distant haze. Zacharias spoke of the importance of the buffalo thorn, illustrating it with the story of his father's death and his mother's grief.

His father, who had been working on the mines outside Johannesburg for some time, had got into trouble over money. This led to a drunken brawl outside a bar, a knife was pulled and his father fell in the street, fatally wounded. When this sad news came back to the family, his mother was inconsolable, heartbroken that she had been unable to bury him in his homeland. Zacharias had never visited Johannesburg, but decided he would take the train and go there to help his mother in her misery. Before leaving, he broke a branch off a buffalo thorn, wrapped it in a sturdy cloth and set off for the nearest station. With the branch cradled on his lap, he sat up all night on a wooden bench in a crowded third-class carriage. On arrival in Johannesburg, he faced another long journey, this time in a bus, to the mine. From the records of his father's death, he managed to find the bar and the exact spot where his father had died. It was here that Zacharias unwrapped his buffalo thorn branch and carefully laid it on the ground, saying a prayer to his ancestors. In this way his father's restless spirit was caught on the thorns, which he rewrapped and carried back on the train to his home. His mother, overjoyed, buried the branch that held the spirit of her husband next to her house, where he now rests in peace.

The Zulu people are great storytellers. They spin their stories out with colourful embellishments. This was no exception and we were all enchanted, as it was so gently and beautifully told. I wouldn't for all the world have missed that morning, gaining an understanding of Zulu beliefs and customs told with such sensitivity by a man who had shown such scant sensitivity towards the elephants the night before. Better training on game drives is all that is required to instil respect for the wildlife.

Rural people and animals are traditionally linked together in the wilderness, where they have lived in harmony for thousands of years. Today, with the dramatic increase in human population, the conflict is all too obvious. The pressure on land is relentless and unless they benefit from another source of income, those dazzling plains might be teeming, not with wild animals, but with combine harvesters. Can we not find a way to empower the people most affected to protect their heritage and simultaneously gain from it?

Guides are of great importance in the grand scheme of things. The better trained and more widespread they are, the more enlightened the world will become. Many intelligent, forward-thinking safari guides all over East and southern Africa are working towards this goal. A safari is an excellent medium of contact between the wilderness and visitors from the outside world. A safari opens their eyes to the splendours of the wild and makes them conscious of the need for conservation.

WHAT ARE THE ANSWERS?

It is vital that wilderness areas throughout the world, and especially in Africa, are not destroyed, as they have been in so many other parts of the world, by greed and ignorance. There is most definitely an increased awareness of conservation worldwide. Ten years ago Chicago would not have dimmed its lights for migrating birds in the spring and autumn. Today it does. Before the Chicago skyscrapers participated in this programme, birds migrating at night navigating by the stars and the moon would become disoriented by the lights of the tall buildings, and die in their hundreds as they flew into the plate-glass windows. This is only one example of many acts of public awareness and concern for the natural rhythms of nature.

Huge areas of contiguous land are required to preserve the wilderness. The larger the area, the less 'management' is required: nature manages far more efficiently than man ever has. Man tends to blunder in and destroy the very thing he thinks he is preserving. I think the most sinister idea that has crept into environmental management in recent years is the concept of 'sustainable utilisation of land', or, in other words, in order to survive, it must make money. This often means meddling with nature and, most assuredly, killing.

Elephants are a prime example. Map Ives has noted in his monitoring of the Chobe elephant population that they have a key role in natural environmental management. Their particular brand of 'farming' is clear in Botswana, where elephants systematically crop the mopane forests. Acres of trees are broken down to about two metres in height, while clumps of tall seed-bearing trees are left standing, as the seed pods are a gourmet delight for elephants, and this assures regeneration. In the dry season, these stark black stumps look forlorn in the dusty grey landscape. But, come the first rains, when they burst into leaf, the baby elephants that have been suckling during the dry months reach the fresh green leaves with ease. In an ever-changing landscape, they share this nourishing crop with browsing antelopes, thus opening up areas to other species that have been hard-pressed to survive in them in the past.

There is a move afoot to cull elephants in Botswana. If this happens, it could mean a serious setback for tourism in a country whose second-most important industry is tourism. I can't see how the plan can possibly help the elephants, although what do you do if there are 'too many elephants'? But, then again, how would you know? I fear it could mean reaping profit from a natural resource: skin, meat and ivory. Elephant culling is often promoted by those with their own agenda and with little understanding of the immense contribution the elephants make to the bush. Elephants have a complex social structure, which has already been discussed in this book, and one of the most important factors for elephants is their matriarchal memory. The drought in Botswana in 2003 was devastating in Savuti and Chobe, an area that is an habitual range for elephants. There was such a shortage of water that some elephant families were walking to the Okavango Delta to drink. Travelling through the night when it was cool and resting during the heat of the day, it took them three days to get to the water. Even though the weak and vulnerable were dying, the families that knew where to go were the ones with matriarchal memory from the last drought. Some of the babies from the families on that journey will in time become matriarchs themselves. Their memories will lead their families to the water during a future drought. It may be 40 years on, but the memory will never fade. Culling could shatter this eternal gift. The plan is to wipe out whole families – a difficult and cruel process.

Map Ives and Michael Lorentz have both spent many years observing the structure and pattern of elephant families, and their dependence on the animals and environment in which they live. Their knowledge is considerable and it is a subject on which both could speak for many hours. The following is their combined view:

'As Africa's human population expands, its natural habitat and biodiversity become ever more pressured, with human conflict the inevitable result. As this habitat shrinks, many "keynote species" such as elephant, which function naturally as ecological engineers, are deemed the villains and not the victims of habitat destruction. The result is a heating up of the culling debate once again.

'In addition to the purely ecological argument, it is also necessary to take heed of the social and emotional impact that culling has on the elephant population. Elephants are highly complex, sentient beings with a lifespan similar to our own. Their society is structured around a tightly knit family unit with the accumulated wisdom of the matriarch and her sisterhood of elders being the fabric that weaves the lives of the herd together. They are animals who, like the great apes, whales and dolphins, share a high degree

of emotional intelligence with us. All of those who have worked closely with elephants will testify to this deep intelligence and family bonding. It is obvious that mass slaughter of members of this society will have an enormous and traumatic effect on the population as a whole.

'With the jury still out on the environmental imperative to cull, and in light of the unacceptable social and emotional impact, would it be anything less than morally irresponsible to advocate culling?'

Sadly, by 2013, the horrendous levels of poaching have now made us think how on earth we can actually save the elephants.

HAND IN HAND

Ultimately, the animal numbers must be allowed to recover after the devastation inflicted on them by our ancestors over the last century and a half. There was no respect for the animals: they were either vermin or sport. Trophy hunting is still common throughout Africa, but there is hope that it will one day be banned completely. Botswana has one of the most responsible wildlife policies in Africa and, for a while, banned elephant hunting. Later the government banned lion hunting due to lack of control, a depleted gene pool and an increase in levels of bribery and corruption. Unfortunately, however, powerful foreign politicians and hunters – who should know better – try to put pressure on the Botswanan government to lift the ban. On the other hand, Botswana ended its moratorium on elephant hunting, and regular visitors to Botswana will have noticed that the gentle giants they used to see are often now aggressive and nervous. This was clearly the impact of renewed hunting pressure. In January 2014, Botswana banned all hunting except on private ranches. What does that mean? Are the animals fenced in on private ranches? And what about the Bushmen who hunt antelopes with bows and arrows to feed their families? How will they manage? With luck, trophy hunting will die out with the older generation. Perhaps intelligent younger people will not appear to have quite the same macho need to kill for fun. And if enough land is reserved for the animals and the Peace Parks work, that should be a solution for 'too many elephants'.

Like so much in this day and age of fast food and instant gratification, old-fashioned hunting ethics are hard to find. There are of course a notable handful of ethical professional hunters, who still strive to hunt in such a way as to cause minimum impact and who reinvest the proceeds in conservation. However, there are few hunters today who want to stalk their quarry for three or four weeks, as they used to. Minimum effort, maximum impact and back on a flight home with the trophy to follow is more the norm these days.

As an example, in 2002 in Tanzania, 20 000 hunting licences were issued to residents alone. Each licence represents one animal, to which many more would have been illegally added. A lot of extra killing is done under the 'legal' banner. It is not uncommon for a licensee to kill one leopard in a particular area and then to use the same licence in other areas to kill many more. In addition there are the licences issued to foreign hunters. How long can the animals survive?

The counter-argument in Tanzania is that vast tracts of land have been saved from farming development because of hunting, though most likely the tsetse fly alone (ironically, Africa's saviour) would remain a deterrent to human habitation. One day, I am sure, Tanzania will open up these areas for photographic safaris, benefiting local communities with jobs in the tourism industry, with the income being used to finance schools and clinics. Hunting often means wealth beyond belief for a tiny minority, but non-consuming tourism means a richer life for all.

Of course, local people have traditionally killed animals for food, but with expanding populations, this too has more of an impact. I once visited Richard Peek's farm in the Matobo Hills of Zimbabwe. He farmed eland commercially. Elands are large, heavy antelopes that produce excellent meat and, being natural to the African habitat, unlike cattle, they do not destroy the land. His farm was a paradise of lush pastures, unlike the surrounding areas of dongas (arid ditches) and thorn scrub caused by overgrazing of cattle and goats. Would it not be possible for innovative farmers all over Africa to copy this idea?

Although nature provides significant climatic changes, bad land management can accelerate the damage. For example, the Romans' 500-year occupation of North Africa significantly helped wipe out the fertile land that existed before their empire spread from Europe. Things moved more slowly in the ancient world, and unless something is done, and quickly, it will take far less than 500 years to destroy the remaining wilderness areas today. The true value to our planet is to allow large tracts of land to remain unmolested by humans for the generations to come – they should not have to justify themselves financially. Our forefathers did not truly understand this, but we do, and it is up to all of us to protect our planet and halt the mindless destruction that is so prevalent. Are we capable of doing this?

PARTNERSHIPS

Plans for private concessions in Kenya are being set up with increased momentum. Ian Craig of Lewa Downs has initiated extremely successful community projects on the Laikipia Plateau, on which tourist lodges are built, owned and run by the Laikipia Maasai. Ian and the Maasai elders have put in safeguards to make sure the funds are correctly managed, something that was lacking in an earlier experiment. Il Ngwesi was the first of the new projects and winner of many awards, including the Equator Initiative Award from the United Nations Development Fund. Tassia, the newest lodge, in the Lekurruki Conservancy, is part of the Il Ngwesi group ranch.

The Namunyak Wildlife Conservation Trust, a project run by Samburus in an equally beautiful area, near the Matthews Range north of Lewa, has been Ian's mission since the early 1990s. With funding from his Norwegian friend Halvor Alstrup, he employed anti-poaching personnel and, once the poaching was under control, the trust was set up, the lodge built and vehicles provided. Ian, along with Piers Bastard, Ker and Downey's senior guide, have forged a partnership that will give security to the project. Ker and Downey have made a 15-year commitment to bring their guests to the lodge in exchange for the exclusive right to do so. These large regions known as group ranches have ensured a substantial amount of land for the regeneration of wildlife, sorely needed after decades of poaching. Ian estimates that, with the animals' normal birth rate, and sound management of cattle and finances, it will take about 20 years to complete.

The Honourable Francis Ole Kaparo, Speaker of the Kenya National Assembly, has been closely involved throughout the development of the community initiatives, working alongside Tusk Trust, which has been instrumental in providing much of the funding.

Since 2004, Ian Craig's projects have grown dramatically. The community conservancies have joined together and have now become the Northern Rangelands Trust, an area of 25 000 square kilometres hosting 20 communities, an initiative that is run by the elders of the tribes involved. Many more people have become involved; there are new communities and beautiful new lodges, particularly, Saruni Samburu. An American-based charity, The Nature Conservancy, became involved in 2006 to help the continued success of the trust, and in 2011 the Craig family sold the farm they inherited to The Nature Conservancy to ensure its future along with the continuation and growth of the trust. Lewa is the heart and soul, and administrative centre, for the Northern Rangelands Trust, which is a massive and dynamic project with beautiful safari lodges surrounded by breathtaking scenery, helping to create income for the benefit of the communities involved. All aspects of conservation are tackled, with security and poaching being the priorities. But, at the end of the day, these safari venues must make money in order to be truly successful. The spectacular dry panoramas, the tribal people and the wild animals that roam in this landscape are an incredibly interesting contrast to the lush green Masai Mara, and they blend well together. Travel agents – take note!

Partnerships with local people are on the increase, a vital condition for the continuation of safari businesses. Countless intelligent and forward-thinking people are beginning to realise how quickly the wilderness is disappearing and how precarious are many of the most beautiful and seemingly timeless environments. They create or join conservation projects, often helping with isolated pockets of wildlife or wilderness areas where there is a particular problem. Of course, every little bit helps, but the noblest vision of all is the Peace Parks Foundation, started in South Africa by businessman and conservationist Anton Rupert.

TRANSFRONTIER PARKS (PEACE PARKS)

Although fraught with political obstacles, the idea behind Transfrontier Parks is to link national parks across international borders through as much of Africa as possible, in what will be known as Transfrontier Conservation Areas, or, more commonly, Peace Parks. Ancient corridors will be reopened, along which animals will be safe to migrate, breed and thrive with no encroachment from farming or hunting. It's a grand and ambitious idea, which needs to be supported by all conservation groups and governments. And it need not just be national parks, but could include private concessions, such as the group ranches in Kenya, which could surely link up without losing their own identity and personal incomes.

The first and most successful project was establishing the Kgalakgadi Transfrontier Park, which straddles the borders of South Africa and Botswana, and opened in May 2000.

The second is the removal of the fencing along the Mozambican border of the Kruger National Park. In a country such as Mozambique, which has been ravaged by war, this involves far more than just removing fences. Not only do many species need to be reintroduced into the areas where poaching by soldiers decimated the wildlife, but rangers must also be trained to care for the park and, most importantly, the local people must be taught the benefits of protecting the animals. The Peace Parks Foundation will be in charge of the difficult job of administering these requirements.

Thirdly, work is being done on a very ambitious project called the Four Corners Park. This is the area where four countries converge at Kazungula on the Chobe River – Namibia, Botswana, Zambia and Zimbabwe. The land under review encompasses Hwange National Park, the Victoria Falls National Park, the Kazuma Pan National Park and Matetsi Safari Area in Zimbabwe; the Kafue National Park in Zambia; the land from Chobe to the Okavango Delta in northern Botswana; and, eventually, the Khaudum National Park in Namibia, on Botswana's western border and the creation of a new park in the eastern Caprivi. The plan is also to include south-eastern Angola once the land is cleared of landmines. This is the traditional migration route for elephants and, when it is once again open, it should relieve the elephant population pressure on the land in northern Botswana, which is where they tend to congregate, as it is where they feel safe.

It is an immense piece of land and a very ambitious plan, being worked on tirelessly by dedicated people. All five countries have signed an agreement to allow preliminary studies. Such a vast area will have a massive impact on the economies of all five countries, with local people benefiting greatly from job creation.

Map Ives believes he will see this happen in his lifetime. He also dreams of Botswana being linked with Kenya through the parks and wildlife corridors through Zambia, Malawi and Tanzania, and is sure this will happen, though probably not in his lifetime.

The creation of Peace Parks is a bold and grand plan – it has to be in order to work. Is it not possible for mankind to rise to nobility in the 21st century and rescue the last remaining wilderness areas from destruction?

Anton Rupert's inspired idea of Transfrontier Parks is moving on from that early vision at quite a pace. The process went quiet after he died but has moved on again in the last few years. Not all the areas are signed up yet; the majority are, but some are pending and a few are still in the conception phase. However, it is happening.

Map Ives first spoke to me about his dreams and wishes in 2003 and again in 2013, and is thrilled that what was originally called the Four

Country Park has come into being as the Kavango Zambezi Transfrontier Park. This was the most ambitious of all the Peace Parks because of the number of countries involved. Botswana, Zimbabwe, Zambia, Namibia and Angola have signed up to this vast area, which consists of 36 national parks, as well as community conservancies and game management areas. It stretches from Victoria Falls through Chobe and the Okavango Delta, Zambia's Kafue Park to Namibia and down through the area of the Makgadikgadi Pans that is managed by Ralph Bousfield of Uncharted Africa. It is a triumph and we hope that enough operators will go into these areas and create new experiences for discerning travellers. Two of the land blocks were hunting areas and now, as Botswana is banning all hunting, it is imperative that a photographic safari company, or an innovative passionate individual, will develop those areas for tourism, otherwise the cattle will encroach and it will not work.

Another ambitious Peace Park is the Great Limpopo Transfrontier Park, which encompasses the Kruger National Park in South Africa, Gonarezhou National Park and Malilangwe in Zimbabwe, and the Limpopo National Park in Mozambique. This area covers approximately 37 500 square kilometres with plans to extend the area in Mozambique, which would bring the whole to 100 000 square kilometres. I do not think this would have come about without the efforts of Clive Stockil, who has worked tirelessly for decades to improve the lives of the people living alongside wildlife in the Gonarezhou area, and particularly the Save Valley, which borders the park and is the largest private conservancy in Zimbabwe. Clive received the Prince William Award for Conservation in Africa, which was organised by Tusk Trust. This is awarded to distinguished individuals for their outstanding dedication and exceptional contribution over a minimum of 10 years to conservation in Africa. It is considered a lifetime-achievement award. The winner receives a grant towards his or her chosen project.

A corridor between the Kruger Park and Gonarezhou is now in place, although the animals are still nervous to move freely between the parks. A large amount of tribal land is included in these parks, which means that local people have to move themselves and their livestock off their traditional land. The only way this is going to work is for them to see the benefits, which of course means tourism. The goodwill between the governments of South Africa, Zimbabwe and Mozambique for cross-border travel and cooperation has been remarkable. Hunting still exists in Zimbabwe and, until it becomes a popular photographic safari destination, the animals will continue to be wary.

Tourism is much improved in the south-eastern area of Zimbabwe, where the Malilangwe and Gonarezhou national parks are part of the Limpopo Transfrontier project. The benefactor, American businessman Paul Tudor Jones, who bought two very large cattle and cotton farms adjacent to the park, joined them together and put the land back to the wild. This is now the Malilangwe Wildlife Reserve, where the stylish and elegant Pamushana Lodge is situated. Species that had been wiped out, such as rhinos and sable antelopes, have been reintroduced. The security is exceptionally good and to date they have not lost a single rhino. Gonarezhou National Park, thanks to Paul Tudor Jones's funding, is now managed by the Frankfurt Zoo, an organisation with vast experience of African conservation – it has looked after the Serengeti ever since Dr Grzimek, president of the Frankfurt Zoo Society, visited Tanganyika in the 1950s.

All of the national parks in the region are extremely interesting – stretching from the Drakensberg in South Africa and Lesotho, up to Selous in Tanzania. These are exceptional areas and the cooperation between the various governments in endeavouring to link them up is miraculous.

There is no doubt that tourism has contributed hugely to the economies of the sub-Saharan countries that host holiday visitors. Tourism facilities have increased considerably since the turn of the century and, today, conservation is the byword. There are new parks, more lodges, more tourists and certainly many more guides. The quality of guiding has also improved due to an awareness of its importance and the influence of guiding schools such as the Koiyaki Guiding School, established with the help of Ron Beaton in Kenya, and Eco Training, set up by Lex Hes in South Africa. Governments contributed to this initiative and most guides are now licensed to guide. There are many companies that now train professional guides and offer short courses for people who are not part of the tourism industry but are curious and interested to learn a bit more and experience the daily life of a guide.

With the increasing numbers of eager safari visitors, the pressure on the drivers and guides is enormous. There are people who will bribe or promise big tips to see whatever animal they have flown around the world to see – a situation that makes things difficult for the guides. Lions will not necessarily be waiting behind the baobab tree at 7.30 am, as they had been the last time the guide drove that way. Animals can be very elusive. When King George and Queen Elizabeth visited the Kruger National Park in 1947 with their two daughters, every game ranger employed by the park searched for a pride of lions to show the royal visitors. I am told they even used spotter planes, but not one lion could be found.

Photography brings another form of pressure. I have seen an extraordinary amount of very expensive kit brought out on safari. A popular subject is wildebeest river crossings. The migrating wildebeest herds spend their time grazing in the northern Serengeti and the Masai Mara between July and October. The Mara River flows roughly along the border of Kenya and Tanzania, and the animals lured by the thought of greener pastures cross many times. I witnessed this wonderful spectacle quite recently and was horrified by the behaviour of some of the safari vehicle drivers.

The idea should be that the vehicles keep a few hundred metres back from the river, the passengers quietly watching as the animals mass on the far bank and build up the courage to cross. Swimming in fast-flowing water brimming with crocodiles is an extremely stressful manoeuvre for the wildebeest. The minute the first few take the plunge, all the cars rev up and roar down to the riverbank directly in front of the herd – because everyone wants a full-frontal photograph. When I was there, it was late in the season and there were only about seven or eight cars. It was the first time I had seen their tactics. I was told that in August there could be a line of 20 or 30 cars, and these poor animals often find their exit completely blocked by vehicles and get washed down the river, struggling through rocks while desperately searching for another opening.

There is a downside to mass tourism: walkie-talkie radios, a multitude of cars surrounding one sleeping lion and small planes buzzing overhead. But, by and large, everyone does have a good time. And the revenue means the animals will survive; the alternative is the death of wildlife and an increase in volumes of cattle, goats and farming.

It is possible to get away from the madding crowd by searching out specialist guides whose philosophy is just that.

ASIAN GREED AND INTERNATIONAL CRIMINALS

The greatest threat to the precious wild animals is the relentless poaching. The Asian thirst for their body parts has created a worldwide criminal network. Prices for rhino horn, ivory and big-cat bones (lion, leopard and cheetah) have risen to stratospheric proportions. It is almost impossible to control. Because of the gigantic sums of money involved, it is not difficult to lure an employee on the ground to point out where a rhino is. In one moment a man can have enough money to buy a house and feed his family for five years. That is understandably tempting.

Map Ives spoke to me about the rhino problems in Botswana, where he is chairman of the Moremi Game Reserve Management Committee, based in the Okavango Ramsar site, one of the world's premier conservation areas. He is also the environmental officer for Wilderness Safaris, a company that has backed the reintroduction programme. Botswana lost its entire rhino population during the dreadful spate of poaching in the 1970s and after much discussion and planning the country was allowed to import rhinos from South Africa in 2000. Twenty-five white rhinos were released at Mombo, in the Okavango Delta, and they all immediately started to disperse. Two cows walked all the way from Mombo to the

Makgadikgadi, in the Boteti area. Everyone felt they should be returned to Mombo, but Map said:

'I'll tell you what – let's leave them there because, from my reading of historical books, David Livingstone and others encountered rhino in this area. There is lots of grass; the river has started to run again, so let's see what happens. I went to the Khama Rhino Sanctuary and they gave me an old bull that had been found in the 1980s – but he did not do his business, and I thought maybe he had forgotten how. I spoke to Dr Mike Knight from South Africa, who told me the old white rhino bulls are very lazy, so I put in a young bull and, as quick as a monkey, the old boy had mated both females! Those two babies calved in 2011.

'I am very involved in rhino conservation here in Botswana. We have done so well with the white rhino and are lucky to be landlocked, which makes it harder for poachers to come in and out of the country. Our president, Ian Khama, cares enormously about the poaching and rings me up every week to get feedback and to ask what I need. Now, after seven years of negotiations, we are finally getting 20 black rhinos. They are coming from South Africa later this year. We are blessed with a caring, proactive president who is deeply concerned with the safety of all Botswana's animals and takes a keen interest in what is happening with the rhinos.'

Steve Edwards is a renowned Zimbabwean safari guide and owner of Musango Safari Camp, which he set up on the edge of the Kariba Dam in 1990. He has been dedicated to this area all his adult life and for 18 years he was the Matusadona Park warden. He was involved in the introduction of wild rhinos into the park and the reintroduction of young rhinos. I saw these young rhinos while they were being held in a boma prior to their release into the wild. Steve told me the sorry tale of Matusadona's rhinoceroses:

'After we had introduced wild rhino into the park as part of our operation, we had, I think, about 65 rhino in the park. We then started to receive young rhino from Imire Game Park – this was the result of a very successful breeding campaign headed by the Travers family. Many of these young rhino *were held at Tashinga, the headquarters of the Matusadona National Park, and hand-reared before eventually being released back into the wild. Many of those released have since bred with wild rhino and have reared young of their own – a great success story.*

'I ran the national anti-poaching unit under Glen Tatham, the then chief warden of National Parks, specifically fighting the 'rhino wars', where we had considerable success. Unfortunately, the passion we had then within the Department of National Parks has somewhat dwindled within the department's rank and file, but a handful of dedicated men struggle on with no back-up, no equipment, no leaders and certainly no recognition. National Parks failed the rhino and left them to be slaughtered. I am very sad to say that there was nothing that we could do from the outside – many NGOs and conservation groups helped National Parks out with equipment, vehicles, fuel, etc., but without proper leadership and backing there is little that they can do.

'The result is that, in my personal opinion, we have maybe two rhino left in the Matusadona. Tracking rhino was my specialty and I had a track record of over 90%. I don't venture into the park any more but use my own concession area where our animals are protected by us and are relaxed and even recognise our voices!'

South Africa has had a devastating amount of rhinos killed. There is a deep culture of criminal activity there, and even veterinarians have been arrested for poaching. We are still waiting for South Africa's president to speak out against the killings and to come up with a plan to eliminate these criminal activities. The rhino is the one animal that could be saved by farming its horn, which, when cut off, grows back again within 18 months. South Africa has by far the largest number of rhinos in Africa and there is a consortium there that wishes to farm and sell rhino horns at an extremely deflated price, thus hopefully eliminating the black market, but it is a very controversial plan.

The rhino problem is a tragedy that has been played out in reserves and national parks throughout Africa. All countries are desperately trying to save their animals and there are projects everywhere.

There always will be ivory. When elephants die naturally, their tusks do not decompose, but are stockpiled by government agencies. In 1989, the sale of ivory was banned, the elephant population grew and the herds became relaxed. However, in 1997, with pressure from Japan, UN organisation CITES (which seeks to prevent endangered or threatened species of animals and plants being devastated by unregulated international trade) agreed that Zimbabwe, Namibia and Botswana could sell 40 tons of stockpiled ivory. The greed surfaced and the floodgates opened. An elephant must die for people to get the product, and the brutal, merciless ways in which elephants and rhinos are killed are sickening.

The role that safari guides can play is to raise awareness of these issues with their guests. Then, all we can hope for is worldwide pressure on international governments. What began many years ago as a wild and daring adventure has become a serious profession with a deep understanding of its responsibilities. This professionalism and understanding must continue if there is to be a future for safaris and wildlife in Africa.

The Born Free Foundation has laid out a very clear history of the recent plight of the elephant on their website.

ACKNOWLEDGEMENTS

I am indebted to so many people for their help in producing this book and my deepest thanks go to all who encouraged me and believed I could do it. Firstly, I thank my daughter Jessica Hoffman for her sensitive and superb portraits of the 12 guides I originally profiled. I greatly admire her ability to make each of these active men sit still for four hours while she created not only an excellent likeness but also the essence of their personalities. I wish she had been able to do the same for all the other guides I later included.

I am eternally grateful to all the guides who opened up their hearts and put their trust in me relating their life stories. I have done my utmost to do them justice. The original 12 were Ralph Bousfield, Michael Lorentz, Garth Thompson, Benson Siyawareva, Ivan Carter, Robin Pope, Nigel Perks, Ron Beaton, Jackson Saigilu Ole Looseyia, Calvin Cottar and the Schoeman brothers, Bertus and André. Special thanks go to Garth Thompson for getting me started and for being so certain I was capable of writing a book.

My thanks also go to Grant Cumings, Rod Tether and Jo and Robin Pope who all hosted me in Zambia.

Grateful thanks go to Onkgaotse Manga, known as Onx, and Howard Saunders, whom I met early in their careers when they impressed me with their outlook and positive vision for the future and whose progress I have followed with great interest. Thanks too to Super Sande for his incredible knowledge of the Makgadigadi Pans.

I also thank Betty Maitai for talking so candidly to me and for the courage and determination she had to break from tribal customs to become educated and to work alongside Maasai men as a top safari guide.

My thanks to Yvonne Short and Tony Adams who spent hours relating stories of the early days at Londolozi (many unrepeatable), and, of course, to three special guides who were there in their youth and are still great forces in the safari industry today, Mike Myers, Lex Hes and Map Ives. They, too, trusted me with their personal stories.

There are two young men that I recently met whose passion and understanding of the bush and of the animals are extraordinary. I feel honoured to have met Ant Kaschula and John Barclay and thank them both for giving me great faith for the future of good guiding and good safaris, but most of all for their compassion and dedication to the animals and to doing something about their plight.

Mothupi Morutha is no longer with us but I will never forget his enthralling life story told so freely and candidly, and I am sure there are many safari visitors to Khwai Lodge who will remember his fascinating tales round the campfire.

Enormous thanks go to all who have facilitated my visits to Africa – I am indebted to so many of you.

I would also like to thank those who have shared with me some of their own experiences on safari, in particular Jan Astle, Trina McMullen, Fiona Ramsay and Carolyn Elwes. Thanks also go to Louise Cottar for her fascinating insight into working with the United Nations Feeding Scheme in Somalia.

Special thanks go to Christopher Napier who introduced me to Louise Grantham and Bookstorm. To my delight she was in tune with these special characters that I write about and I give her heartfelt thanks for thinking my book would be a good proposition for Bookstorm. Her team is wonderful; Stacey Gouws, Russell Clarke and Nicola van Rooyen have worked tirelessly to produce and market *Legendary Safari Guides*. I also must thank Michael Lorentz for supplying the photographs for the book cover. Thanks go to Francois d'Elbee for the photograph of Grant Cumings and Stephanie Dloniak for the photograph of Howard Saunders.

I have huge gratitude for my family who have been truly supportive, my beloved husband Dick and children Dominic and Olivia who have encouraged me every step of the way.

But it is the guides who are the heroes and I thank them all from the bottom of my heart for the joy they have given me and for opening my mind and eyes while exploring so many remote and beautiful corners of Africa.

WEBSITES
AND CONTACT DETAILS

www.peaceparks.org
www.bornfree.org
www.tusk.org

LEX HES
www.ecotraining.co.za

MIKE MYERS
www.mikemyersphotography.com

MAP IVES
www.wilderness-safaris.com

RALPH BOUSFIELD
www.unchartedafrica.com
www.hickmanandbousfiled.com

SUPER SANDE
info@shackletonandselous.com

JOHN BARCLAY
www.unchartedafrica.com

ONKGAOTSE MANGA (ONX)
Onx.manga@orientexpress.com

MICHAEL LORENTZ
www.passagetoafrica.com
www.safarious.com

GARTH THOMPSON
www.garththompsonsafaris.com

BENSON SIYAWAREVA
www.ngoko.com

ANTHONY KASCHULA
www.gonarezhou-bushcamps.com
www.rawanaandjos.com

ROBIN POPE
www.projectluangwa.org
www.robinpopesafaris.net

ROD TETHER
www.safariadviser.com

GRANT CUMMINGS
www.chiawa.com

NIGEL PERKS
www.nigelperksdiscovery.com

RON BEATON
www.mmconservancy.com

JACKSON SAIGILU OLE LOOSEYIA
www.asiliaafrica.com
www.looseyai.com

BETTY NAYIANDI MAITAI
www.richardscamp.com

CALVIN COTTAR
www.cottars.com

HOWARD SAUNDERS
www.howardsaunders.com

**SHACKLETON AND SELOUS
SOCIETY**
info@shackletonandselous.com

SCHOEMAN BROTHERS
www.skeltoncoastsafaris.com

REFERENCES

Broadley DG & Cock EV. 1975. *Snakes of Zimbabwe.* Longman.

Coates Palgrave, K. 2003. *Palgrave's Trees of Southern Africa.* Struik Publishers.

Heys, H. 1997. *The Leopards of Londolozi.* Londolozi Publishers.

Matthiessen, P & Van Lawick, H. 1982. *Sand Rivers.* Bantam Books.

Moss, C. 1976. *Portraits in the Wild: Animal Behaviour in East Africa.* Hamish Hamilton.

Myers, M, Hoets, P & Woodrow, G. 2004. *Mombo: Okavango's Place of Plenty.* Wilderness Safaris.

Newman, K. 2002. *Newman's Birds of Southern Africa.* Struik Publishers.

Schoeman, A. 2012. *Skeleton Coast.* Protea Boekhuis.

Thompson, G. 2007. *The Guide's Guide to Guiding.* Jacana Media.

Varty, D & Buchanan, M. 2009. *The Full Circle: To Londolozi and Back Again: A Family's Journey.* Penguin Global.

TUSK TRUST

Tusk Trust was founded as a conservation charity in 1990 with the aim of supporting the long-term preservation of Africa's unique natural heritage. The trust recognises that the future of the continent's wildlife depends on the success of combining education and sustainable-development programmes with conservation initiatives that help to underpin nature-based tourism and many livelihoods. Under the Royal Patronage of HRH The Duke of Cambridge, the charity invests significantly into both anti-poaching work and education, including centres such as the Koiyaki Guiding School, which are designed to increase local engagement in wildlife conservation. www.tusk.org

GLOSSARY

Boma	– An outdoor area used for meals and gatherings, often fenced in for protection
Fanagalo	– A pidgin language that developed in South Africa's mines so that workers from different countries and tribes could communicate at a basic level
Ildorobo	– Generic term used for hunter-gatherer groups of Tanzania and Kenya
Koppie	– Small rocky hill
Layoni	– Young uncircumcised Maasai boy
Long-drop loo	– Pit latrine
Mealie-meal	– Ground maize used to make a southern African porridgey staple known as pap
Moran	– Maasai warrior
Shangaan	– Member of the Tsonga people of southern Africa
Shuka	– Toga-like garment worn by Maasai men
Spoor	– Animal tracks
Strandloper	– Literally 'beach walker' – nomadic prehistoric people who lived in coastal areas of the Cape

INDEX

Abu's Camp 8, 17, 98, 101, 102
Adams, Dee 28
Adams, Tony 28
Amboseli 8, 293
And Beyond 34
Astle, Jan 84, 85

Badger, Chris 56,
Bakkes, Chris 299
Barclay, John 86-91
Bates, George 111
Beard, Peter 281-3
Beaton, Charlie 257
Beaton, Gerard 260, 268, 270, 271
Beaton, Ken 246, 247, 248,
Beaton, Pauline 254, 258, 259, 271
Beaton, Rainee 257, 271, 273
Beaton, Ron 42, 245-59, 260, 267, 268, 270, 271, 291, 330
Bell, Colin 47
Berry, Phil 191, 192
Besterlink, Barney 16
Besterlink, PJ 16
Birdlife 115
Bleattler, Daniela 97
Bonham, Richard 178, 180, 192, 196
Botswana 3, 4, 7, 8, 14, 16, 17, 19, 41-9, 51-3, 57-60, 61-120, 152, 154, 167
Bousfield, Jack 52, 53, 69, 70, 74, 75, 76, 77, 79, 86, 277
Bousfield, Nora 68-69
Bousfield, Ralph 17, 64-79, 80, 81, 82, 83, 86, 87, 328

Bumi Hills Safari Lodge 129
Burton, Richard 19

Camp Moremi 45, 73
Camp Okavango 45, 73, 77,
Campbell, Urban 23
Campbell, Wac 22-3
Carr, Norman 6, 191, 192, 201, 202
Carter, Claire 164
Carter, Ivan 11, 13, 14, 15, 158-68, 175
Carter, Sandor 97, 294
Cazenove and Lloyd Safaris vi, 4, 177
Cazenove, Hetti 81
Cazenove, Olivia 17, 18
CCAfrica 33, 34
Chiawa 121, 123, 124
Chibembe Camp 191, 192, 201, 202, 205
Chikwenya Lodge 147
Chinzombo 192
Chizarira National Park 54
Chobe 62, 320, 321, 327, 328
Chobe Chilwero Camp 4
Chobe Game Lodge 29, 47
Chobe National Park 4
Conservation Corporation Africa 33, 34
Coppinger, Carol 184, 202
Coppinger, John 184, 202
Cottar, Bud 276, 277
Cottar, Calvin 276-89
Cottar, Charlie 289
Cottar, Chas 276, 277, 283
Cottar, Danni 284, 289
Cottar, Ella 289
Cottar, Glen 277, 278, 279, 280, 283

Cottar, Jasper 284, 289
Cottar (nee Seaman), Louise 285, 286, 288, 289
Cottar, Pat 278
Cottar's Camp 279, 283, 288
Cottar's Classic Safaris 276
Craig, Ian 324, 325
Craig, Will 255
Cumings, Grant 184, 211-14

Dabbs, John 12, 13
De Rooy, Margaux 199
De Rooy, Ton 199
Desert and Delta Safari Company 45, 115
Dloniak, Steffie (Stephanie) 292, 293
Dorobo Safaris 219, 220, 222
Dove, George 231, 232
Dugmore, David 17, 18, 73, 74, 75, 76
Dugmore, Roger 17, 73, 74, 75, 76

Eagle Island Lodge 115
Earnshaw, Alan 291
East Africa 33, 68, 89, 188, 192, 215-95
EcoTraining 41, 42
Edwards, Steve 332-3
Elephant Back Safaris 97, 98
Endangered Wildlife Trust (EWT) 72, 115, 116
Ethiopia 78, 246, 255
Etosha National Park 298
Evans, Jackie 28

Fabris, Sandro 119
Flatt, Chris 255
Foot, David 16, 79, 196
Formby, Nicola 84
Fothergill Island 147, 148
Fothergill, Rupert 12
Frechette, Ashley 244
Fugitive's Drift 15

Gache Gache 148, 151
Gametrackers 47, 94, 95,
    96, 111, 112, 113
Geertsema, Aadje 231, 232
George, Ashley 168
Gibb, Jim 231
Gibb, Margaret 230, 231,
    232, 233, 241, 242
Gibb's Farm Safaris 220,
    230, 231, 232, 233,
    239, 242
Gilchrist, Melissa 151
Gill, AA 84
Gonarezhou National Park
    127, 169, 170, 172, 175,
    181, 328, 329
Goosen, André 25
Gore-Browne, Stewart 203
Gower, David 30
Graham, Brian 4, 45, 46
Graham, Jan 4

Hancock, Pete 115, 116
Hanssen, Wayne 5
Hartley, David 3, 58, 61
Hartley, Tessa 3
Hartley's Safaris 4, 97
Harvey, Mark 203
Henley, Caro 97
Hes, Lex 24, 25, 30, 35,
    36-42, 44, 56, 59, 257,
    330
Hes, Lynn 41
Hewlett, Neil 167
Hickman, Caroline 79

Hoffman, Jessica vi, 152
Holmes, Katie 96
Hunters Africa 58,
Hurt, Robin 279, 280
Hwange National Park 7,
    78, 123, 127, 143, 151,
    327
Hwange Safari Lodge 127,
    128, 129, 151,160

Imrie, Kate 35
Imrie, Tom 35
Ivan Carter Safaris 165
Ives, Cathy 57, 58, 59
Ives, Map 3, 30, 35, 51-60,
    115, 320, 321, 327, 331,
    332

Jack's Camp 64, 65, 66,
    76, 77, 80, 83, 84, 87,
    89, 172
Jackson, Bryan 202, 203
Jenkins, Cuthbert 187, 188
Jenkins, Rosemary 187, 188
Jones, Paul Tudor 329

Kafue National Park 115,
    122, 188, 207, 327, 328
Kaisoi, Parkipumy 218,
    225, 226, 227
Kalahari Kavango 17, 74,
    75, 76
Kane, Lynsey 213
Kapani Lodge 192, 201,
    202
Kaparo, Francis Ole 325
Kasanka National Park 207
Kaschula, Anthony (Ant)
    169-81, 335
Kenya 8, 19, 42, 67, 81, 90,
    170, 177, 178, 215, 216,
    217, 145, 246, 247, 248,
    249, 251, 253, 254, 255,
    257, 259

Ker and Downey Safaris
    67, 97, 251, 291, 293,
    324, 325
Khama, Ian 332
Khwai River Lodge 106,
    111, 112 113, 115, 117,
    119
Knox, Pam 57
Koiyaki Guiding School
    42, 256-9, 270, 274, 291,
    330, 338
Kruger National Park 6, 8,
    21, 22, 38, 93, 326, 328,
    330
Kruger, Paul 22
Kutundala 203, 204, 206,
    208, 209

Lake Bangweulu 199
Landela Safari Company
    148
Lategan, Anton 41, 42
Leakey, Mary 225, 233, 234
Lindsay, James 81, 83
Lindsay, Lady Amabel 83
Lindsay, Ludovic 81, 82, 83
Lindstrom, Søren 196
Linyanti 45, 46, 60, 152
Little Makalolo 143, 150,
    151, 152, 153
Liuwa Plains 199
Lloyd, Henrietta vi, 4
Lloyd's Camp 7, 115
Looseyia, Damaris 272
Looseyia, Jackson Saigilu
    Ole 257, 260-73, 291
Looseyia, Morris 273
Looseyia, Pauline 273
Looseyia, Selel Ole 261,
    263, 265, 266, 267
Looseyia, Silvia 272
Lorentz, Michael 9, 10, 13,
    47, 92-106, 178, 294, 321

Lower Zambezi National Park 122, 211, 212, 213
Luangwa Safari House 199
Luke, Patricia 178
Luke, Rawana 178, 180

Maggs, Ken 37, 38, 39, 55
Mahale Mountain National Park 235
Maitai, Betty Nayiandi 274-5
Makgadikgadi Pans 16, 64, 75, 86, 328
MalaMala 22, 23, 25, 31
Malilangwe Wildlife Reserve 170, 177, 328, 329
Mana Pools National Park 14, 15, 43, 48, 122, 124, 125, 130, 136, 142, 158, 162, 164, 167, 170, 189, 213
Manga, Onkgaotse (Onx) 113, 114-120
Map Ives Safaris 59
Masai Mara National Reserve 246, 262, 263, 288, 291
Mason, Marian 177, 178
Mathebula, Jack 93, 94
Matthiessen, Peter 192
Matusadona National Park 12, 147, 148, 160, 161, 164, 173, 175, 176, 332, 333
Maude, Glyn 89
McConnell, Charlie 196
McGhee, Kate 102
Meno A Kwena 17, 76
Mnisi, Kimbian 37, 38
Molinari, Filippo 177, 178
Moore, Randall 8, 96, 97, 98

Moremi Game Reserve 3, 58, 73, 74, 87, 90, 106, 107, 109, 115, 331
Morutha, Mothupi 95, 106, 107-13
Mozambique 73, 145, 167, 326, 328, 329
Murchison Falls National Park 217, 247, 293
Musango Safari Camp 332
Mwaleshi Bush Camp 184, 202, 203
Myers, Marian 49, 50
Myers, Johannes 67
Myers, Mike 25, 30, 35, 43-50, 56, 47, 94, 95, 96, 111

Nairobi National Park 245, 246, 247
Namibia 4, 16, 68, 78, 81, 116, 300-14
Natureways 132, 135
Ndutu Safari Lodge 218, 231, 241, 242
Neal, Jessie 45, 73
Ngorongoro Crater 5, 166, 216, 224, 231, 232
Niassa Game Reserve 167
Nicholson, Major Richard Granville 68
Nomadic Encounters 257, 271, 272
Norman Carr Safaris 191, 192,
Luangwa Valley 122, 183, 184, 184, 186, 188, 192, 193, 199, 200, 206, 211
North Luangwa National Park 203
Nsefu 184, 192, 193, 201
Nxai Pan National Park 78
Nxamaseri Lodge 16

Okavango Delta 11, 16, 17, 43, 46, 48, 51, 57, 60, 61, 62, 63, 76, 92, 93, 106, 107, 114, 227, 321, 327, 328, 331
Okavango Explorations 3, 4, 57
Okonjima 5
Ol Donyo Wuas Lodge 178, 192
Ol Seki Lodge 274
Old Mondoro Bush Camp 212
Orient Express Safaris 96
Owens, Mark and Delia 205

Parks (Denton), Fiona 241, 242, 244
Passage to Africa 102, 104
Perks, Jake 242
Perks, Jessica 242
Perks, Nigel 6, 218, 220, 221, 222, 224-244
Perks, Wren 244
Perks, Zinnia 244
Peterson, Thad 219, 220
Phinda 34
Pope (née Holmes), Jo 193-200, 201, 203
Pope, Robin 6, 184, 185-200, 201
Pretorius, Ben 252
Purcell, Roland 196

Queen Elizabeth National Park 247
Quest Africa 57

Raphaely, Catherine 74, 78
Rattray, David 15
Rattray, Mike 23
Rawson, Dan 57
Rawson, Paul 57

Rawson, Penny 57
Rekero Camp 257, 269
Rekero Expeditions 256
Remote Safaris 184
Richard's Camp 274
Robey, Nigel 48
Robin Pope Safaris 203
Rocktail Bay 48
Royal Geographical
    Society vii
Ruaha National Park 235,
    236, 239
Ruckomechi Lodge 130
Rupert, Anton 326, 327
Rushworth, Dave 128
Ruwesi Canoe Trails 162

Sabi Sands 22-38
Sabi Sands Game Reserve
    25, 37, 56
Safari Consultants 132, 135
Safari for Real 42
Safari Guide Company 196
Sakarombe, Nikodemus 43
Sande, Super 79, 80-5
Santawani 94, 95, 106, 108,
    111
Sanyati Lodge 160
Saunders, Howard 290-5
Save the Rhino Trust 116,
    192, 202
Savuti Elephant Camp 115
Savuti Safari Lodge 115
Schoeman (nee Cosburn),
    Amy 305, 307
Schoeman, André 300-14
Schoeman, Bertus 300-14
Schoeman, Helga 304, 309
Schoeman, Henk 304, 312,
    313
Schoeman, Leon 304, 311
Schoeman, Louw 304, 305,
    306, 306, 308, 311, 312,
    313

Schoeman, Marie 304, 307
Schoeman, Maureen 307
Selous Game Reserve 192,
    244
Shaba National Reserve
    269, 284
Shackleton and Selous
Society 106, 294-5
Shearwater Adventures 173
Shirley-Bevan, Mike 196
Short, Pete 26
Short, Yvonne 26, 29, 31,
    32, 33
Siyawareva, Benson 143-57
Siyawareva, Noreen 152,
    153
Siyawareva, Omigo Honest
    153
Skeleton Coast 5, 16, 298,
    301, 303, 305, 307, 308,
    310
Skeleton Coast National
    Park 303, 304, 306, 307,
    308, 312, 313
Skeleton Coast Safaris 5,
    304, 305
Smith, Wilbur 65, 352
Somalia 205, 206
South Africa 4, 15, 21-60,
    67, 68, 87, 102, 111, 187,
    188, 317, 328, 329, 333
South Luangwa National
    Park 191, 195
Stamper, Chris 42
Stevens, John 13, 48, 129,
    162, 196
Stockil, Clive vii, 328
Strydom, Hans 160
Swynnerton, Gerald 68

Tafika Camp 184, 202, 203
Tanda Tula 93, 94

Tanzania 5, 69, 76, 192,
    211, 215, 216, 217, 218,
    219, 220, 222, 224, 229,
    230, 231, 232, 233, 235,
    252, 253, 262, 280, 323
Tatham, Glen 333
Taylor, Elizabeth 19
Tena Tena 186, 193, 194,
    196, 197
Tether, Daniel 206
Tether, Louis 213
Tether, Rod 184, 201-210
Tether, Sasha 206
Thieme, Guz 203, 204, 205,
    206, 208, 209, 210
Thompson, Danny 132
Thompson, David 130,
    131, 132, 140
Thompson, 152, 153
Thompson, Garth 13, 14,
    18, 48, 118, 124-42, 160,
    173, 256
Thompson, Graeme 152
Thompson, Mel 130, 131,
    142
Timbavati Game Reserve
    93
Tinley, Ken 23, 48, 56
Trevor, Simon 149
Tsaro Lodge 3, 58, 59
Tsavo National Park 246
Marshall, Tuffy 246, 248,
    249, 251, 252
Turner, Tina 30
Tusk vii, 325, 328, 338

Uganda 105, 206, 217, 229,
    246, 247, 248, 292, 293,
Ulyate, Robin 254
Uncharted Africa 79, 81,
    82, 86, 88, 328

Van der Reep, Jan 196, 299
Van Lawick, Hugo 192

Van Wyk, Chris 7
Varty, Boyd 23
Varty, Dave 6, 23, 24, 25,
    26, 28, 33, 34, 44, 48,
    55, 56
Varty, John 6, 24, 25, 28,
    30, 33 36, 40, 44, 48, 55,
    56
Varty, Shan (nee Watson)
    25, 33, 34
Voorspuy, Tristan 16
Vundu 162

Water Wilderness 47, 129
Whitcombe, Stephie 97
Whitehead, Peter 67
Wild Zambia Safaris 202
Wilderness Safaris 41, 42,
    47, 49, 50, 51, 57, 59,
    137, 143, 151, 152, 153,
    174, 299, 306, 331
Wilderness Trails 184, 191,
    192, 193, 201
Wildlife Trust 89
Williamson, Troy 174
Wilmot, Lloyd 7, 49
Woods, Janet 254
Woods, Michael 254

Xaxaba Camp 57
Xugana Lodge 3

Zambezi River 18, 121,
    122, 124, 125, 126, 130,
    132, 158, 162, 173, 184,
    187 189, 211, 212, 213,
Zambia 6, 115, 121, 122,
    146, 158, 183, 184, 187-
    200, 201, 202, 205, 207,
    212, 213, 327, 328

Zimbabwe 7, 11, 12, 14,
    21, 53, 55, 63, 78, 93,
    121, 122, 128, 129, 130,
    132, 142, 143, 144, 146,
    148, 151, 152, 153, 162,
    163, 165, 167, 168, 169,
    170, 172, 173, 180, 191,
    206, 323, 327, 328, 329,
    332, 334